CHASING SUCCESS

Praise for *Chasing Success*

This book is the compelling story of one small but significant nonprofit founded to apply research to improve child outcomes in a metropolitan area. It is a story of leadership, innovation, and measurable results. Many lives were changed but the difficulty in maintaining funding and focus underscores the reality that neither government nor philanthropy understands or invests in what is needed to succeed. Einstein said that today's problems will not be solved at the same level as they were created. He was right.

> —David R. Walker, Vice President and Comptroller, Procter & Gamble
>   (retired)

Judy Van Ginkel's thoughtful book, *Chasing Success: The Challenge for Nonprofits*, offers candid and critical insights into the difficulties nonprofit leaders face, from funding, to scaling, to collaboration, to innovation, to assuring equity, and to listening to parent voices. I followed Van Ginkel's leadership of Every Child Succeeds (the case study for this book) and saw first-hand the excellence of every aspect of the program. I examined the compelling data from the Moving Beyond Depression innovation and waited for it to become a normal part of every home visiting program—which sadly it never did. How can programs that are the best in their class not flourish and become models in every state? The book raises important questions about how social services are delivered in this country and demands attention from policymakers and others. If we are serious about supporting parents who are raising the next generation, the challenges illuminated in this book must be addressed.

> —Libby Doggett, PhD, Former Deputy Assistant Secretary
>   for Policy and Education

In short, Every Child Succeeds (ECS) changed the course of early childhood home visiting. Its partners have inspired and supported many, including me, in building regional and national platforms for research to inform evidence-based policy and practice. This book makes it possible for wider audiences to learn from ECS's experience.

> —Anne E. Duggan, ScD, Professor Emerita, Johns Hopkins
>   Bloomberg School of Public Health

Chasing Success is an extremely important contribution to articulating and addressing the meta-issues faced by nonprofits seeking to improve their communities. Congratulations on a substantial contribution to the pragmatic literature on the care and feeding of a community-based nonprofit.

> —Frank W. Putnam, MD, Professor of Clinical Psychiatry at the University
>   of North Carolina and Emeritus Professor of Pediatrics at Cincinnati
>   Children's Hospital

Van Ginkel's *Chasing Success* shares invaluable wisdom from a 20+ year visionary leadership journey with Ohio's Every Child Succeeds. For nonprofit and early childhood system leaders, funders, policymakers, and students, this long-term case study brings a unique perspective to the evolving challenges of leading an exemplary, community-serving successful nonprofit.

    —David W. Willis, MD, FAAP Senior Fellow,
      Center for the Study of Social Policy

Judy paints a vivid and compelling picture of what it takes to lead a successful nonprofit. Her stories and lessons learned would be valuable to any CEO but are especially enlightening for those who lead nonprofits as she describes navigating a myriad of opportunities and challenges in her experiences.

    —Jim Spurlino, CEO of Spurlino Materials and Author of *Business Bullseye*

Van Ginkel astutely identifies challenges many nonprofits face when increasing community impact. She urges us to have courage, know what questions to ask, be part of the solution, and above all, always hold true to our missions. Van Ginkel offers valuable lessons for both new and experienced nonprofit leaders, funders, policymakers, and students.

    —Jennifer Frey, PhD, President and CEO of Every Child Succeeds

Dr. Judith Van Ginkel represents the gold standard when it comes to nonprofit leadership, coalition-building, and sustaining results over time. Her new book, *Chasing Success*, is a captivating exploration of her transformative leadership at Every Child Succeeds in Cincinnati. With a focus on the organization's first two decades, this book unveils the incredible story of growth and impact under Dr. Van Ginkel's guidance.

Every Child Succeeds has been a beacon of support for parents from pregnancy through their child's crucial first one thousand days. Inspired by the wealth of scientific evidence underscoring the significance of early childhood development, the organization emerged in the 1990s to nurture a brighter future for countless families.

Dr. Van Ginkel's narrative is not just about one nonprofit—it's a profound lesson in nonprofit administration. Drawing from her extensive experience, *Chasing Success* offers invaluable insights into founding and nurturing a nonprofit, leveraging research and best practices, adapting to change, and upholding accountability to stakeholders. The book delves into the intricacies of navigating shifting policies and funding dynamics at both the national and regional levels—a perspective seldom explored yet crucial for the success of smaller organizations nationwide.

Key to this journey is the visionary collaboration with former Procter & Gamble CEO John Pepper, whose instrumental role in bringing the organization to Cincinnati laid the foundation for Dr. Van Ginkel's impactful tenure of over two decades. *Chasing Success* is a tribute to her unwavering commitment, and it stands as an essential guide for nonprofit leaders seeking wisdom rooted in evidence-based insights and long-term achievements. I'm so glad she put pen to paper and wrote this book, which can serve as a guidepost for those who seek to fulfill her legacy.

    —Byron McCauley, Founder, McCauley Communications and Co-Author of
      Hope Interrupted: America Lost and Found in Letters with Jennifer Mooney

CHASING SUCCESS

The Challenge for Nonprofits

Judith B. Van Ginkel, PhD

University of CINCINNATI | LIBRARY PUBLISHING SERVICES

About Cincinnati Library Publishing Services (CLIPS)
CLIPS provides professional publishing services for digital and print publications, conference proceedings, journals, affordable textbooks, and open educational resources produced by University of Cincinnati faculty, staff, and organizations with department sponsorship and funding. CLIPS encourages authors to publish in barrier-free open-access formats. CLIPS, an imprint of the University of Cincinnati Press, is committed to publishing rigorous, peer-reviewed, leading scholarship in social justice, community engagement, and Cincinnati/Ohio history.

Judith B. Van Ginkel
Copyright © 2023

Cincinnati, Ohio

University of Cincinnati Press, Langsam Library, 2911 Woodside Drive, Cincinnati, Ohio 45221

ucincinnatipress.uc.edu

ISBN (hardback) 978–1-947603–62-2
ISBN (e-book, PDF) 978–1-947603–63-9
ISBN (e-book, EPUB) 978–1-947603–64-6

Library of Congress Control Number: 2023910355

Cover and Interior Design: Jennifer Flint
Typeset in New Caledonia LT Std
Production Intern: Mars Robinson
Dust Jacket: Author Photograph by Brenda Clark-Conley

Printed in the United States of America
First Printing

In memory: Every Child Succeeds leadership lost
- Anita L. Brentley, PhD
- Catherine Smale Caldemeyer
- Joseph Gibbs MacVeigh
- O'dell Moreno Owens, MD
- Frank P. Smith
- Deborah Lynn Vargo
- Reverend Clarence Wesley Wallace

Acknowledgments

This book emerged from a meeting with my longtime friend and colleague John Pepper, former CEO of Procter & Gamble and community leader. He had been involved with our Every Child Succeeds program since its inception, and his work with socially focused community nonprofits was legendary. He told me, "What we learned through the development of Every Child Succeeds has relevance well beyond our local community and beyond programming for young children. Rather, our work reflects, as a microcosm, the issues and the barriers that most nonprofits face. And, why, when looking with clear eyes and objective vision, too often they fail over time—even though they may have short-term success."

I retired as the pandemic descended and, remembering John's suggestion, began to review notes, develop a chronology, and identify themes that reflected my work with nonprofits over more than 40 years. What began as a history of a small regional nonprofit that met with some success became a treatise on a larger problem. What advice can I offer to leaders working in and/or funding nonprofits so that we can do our work better and serve more people effectively? In short, what have I learned, and what might help someone else?

The work described in this book unfolded with support, guidance, and brilliant insights from many people. Axiomatic as it is, none of us creates alone. The learnings in this book emanate from an extraordinary board and committed staff members at Every Child Succeeds, our partners at Cincinnati Children's, the United

Way of Greater Cincinnati, the Cincinnati-Hamilton County Community Action Agency, our nonprofit colleagues, and our community, both in the business world and in the neighborhoods. Most important, we learned from families—all 28,000 of them—who were and continue to be our best teachers.

Books that have value are imbued not only with answers and prescriptions but also with the right questions. In the first 20 years of Every Child Succeeds, we were surrounded by people who asked the hard questions, held us accountable for achieving our aims, and consistently made our work better.

The quality of this manuscript has been guided from the beginning by my first readers, who volunteered to read a long manuscript numerous times and to be candid about both content and style. John Pepper was invaluable for his keen ability to be insightful and relevant. Tom Boat, Chair of Pediatrics at Cincinnati Children's, brought his clinical expertise and his understanding of collaborative systems. Lee Carter, a remarkable community leader, showed us not only what it takes to be successful but also how to find the resources to make success possible. David R. Walker, retired P&G executive, one of the most thoughtful and pragmatic people I know, always thoroughly answered questions and made you wonder why you had ever considered any other path forward. David insists, "Define the problem you are trying to solve!" Anne Duggan, professor emerita at Johns Hopkins University, who directs the Home Visiting Applied Research Collaborative, is an expert on using research to strengthen services for families. She understood the importance of using resources effectively and asking questions that matter. David Willis, a pediatrician and national leader with a well-deserved reputation for building systems that work, continued to remind me that an effective system is only as good as the ways in which it reflects the needs and goals of the people it serves. Good relationships among people make systems come alive.

I left Kay Johnson for last because without Kay, there would be no book. Nationally recognized for her work in maternal and child health policy, as a researcher, advocate, and consultant, she had been an advisor to ECS for nearly 20 years. She is a friend, colleague, and exacting editor; as well as a relentless voice for reducing the impact of poverty and racism, and increasing access to services for women, children, and their families. She was both a muse and guide for this project. Her encouragement kept me going, while her encyclopedic knowledge of policies and programs ensured that the work was comprehensive.

Always and forever, my family has been essential to my success. My family's role in shaping this story began with parents who believed in me and understood, decades ago, that women could be leaders. My husband, David, has not only been incredibly patient but has also given me the space to grow and the time to succeed. My daughters Jennifer and Leigh, and granddaughters Caroline and Nora, make me proud every day. They are all people who live with kindness, integrity, and a sense of adventure.

Judith Van Ginkel

Contents

Preface

"Why did you write this book?" is always an intriguing question and rarely comes with a simple answer. Writing a book is a difficult undertaking. So, what was it that caused me to sit down at a computer day after day, hour after hour, and write down what happened in my workplace over the last 20 years at Cincinnati Children's—and 20 years before that at the University of Cincinnati and Drake Center—and in the greater Cincinnati community? What did we learn about delivering services that families and communities want? How was learning turned into lessons and guidance for working in the nonprofit world? What was it that made my experiences unique, but at the same time, universal? The answer lies in my belief that by capturing 40 years of experience and developed wisdom, I could help others walking a similar path, people and organizations who choose to address big social issues and are not paralyzed by the enormity of the task. These are people who know that not one of us is successful alone, and that it is through collaborative thinking, deep reflection, and holding ourselves to high standards that we even begin to make the smallest change.

As I retired and began to consider how to spend the time that was left to me, I reflected about what had been important over those working years. Family, friends, and dogs came first and have always been key to who I am. But beyond that, what did I learn in my life of designing and implementing programs for young children? Writing this book began as a way to consider my experience and to be more objective, not only about what I learned, but also—and more important—what I did and whether what I and my colleagues did truly made a difference for children. And, if so, how?

What are the lessons for other nonprofit organizations working to address and remedy large social problems? What is transferable across strategies to provide support to people in early childhood, adolescence, and aging? As I have moved away from the daily operation of leading the Every Child Succeeds (ECS) program in greater Cincinnati (www.everychildsucceeds.org), a nonprofit with an annual budget of close to $8 million, I have been able to see our work from a broader, more realistic perspective, as though someone brought new lighting to reveal unseen new facets. Patterns have emerged that made me think of those dragons that were vanquished and those that were merely prodded. I was able to see more clearly what we did well and where we could have improved. So, this book provides an opportunity to capture those learnings, and make them available to others, as my lifetime-developed wisdom and reflections can perhaps be meaningful for other nonprofit leaders.

I am proud—infinitely and forever—of what we were able to do in the two decades since our founding. We were given significant tools to work with and guidance that was invaluable, but I think that what we did most successfully was to take what we were given and use it well. ECS is a relatively small nonprofit, and a single case study cannot serve as a generalization for all nonprofits. However, I believe that it is a useful empirical reference as an organization that grew responsibly, used resources effectively, and demonstrated value. There is guidance here for existing and new nonprofit organizations working to address social issues, including organizational executives, board members, staff members, students, and consultants, as well as lessons for funders, policy makers, community leaders, and the people who use services delivered by nonprofit organizations.

But with the lessons, there are still questions—complex questions about programs that span generations. What works? What doesn't work? What is really needed? What can we afford? What evolved over time? But what I have kept in mind is this: Over our first 20 years, we served 28,000 families (website of ECS) and at least 56,000 caregivers and young children. Their lives were changed through engagement with us. They received more than 700,000 home visits delivered by a corps of caring, talented, well-trained home visitors. We have evidence to prove that we positively influenced the health and well-being of those people we served. We are often asked about why, if our program is so good, our community metrics have not moved, and my answer is always the same—when you serve only 20% of those who need your service, you cannot significantly change a community metric. But—and this is crucial—the lives of 56,000 mothers and babies were changed. Science tells us that what happens in those first 1,000 days of a child's life has relevance for a lifetime, for two and three generations. I will not apologize for serving only 56,000. Rather, I continue to be proud of what we did, but I ask myself how we might have done more.

I grew up as the daughter of a pediatrician in Charleston, West Virginia (a pediatrician who made house calls—they did that years ago). We seem to be moving back to that model today. When I was a small child, my father often took me with him on those calls. I learned early that being in the house with the family allowed him to make better decisions and recommendations. He was a trusted, valued member of a team for the child and, in time, the siblings and the extended family. He had a way of practicing pediatrics focusing on the parent and the child, but also saw them in the larger environment of the family constellation, the neighborhood, and the stresses upon the entire family that would affect their lifetime trajectory.

Harkening back to what my father learned about the families he served by visiting their homes, the COVID-19 pandemic has brought new insights to many of today's health providers. In May 2020, Jennifer Haythe, MD, a cardiology professor at Columbia University, in a short *Wall Street Journal* editorial (Jennifer Haythe, "House Calls Are Back—Virtually," *Wall Street Journal*,

May, 7, 2020, Eastern Edition), reflected on her experience as a physician during the pandemic. She wrote that though the virtual visits she was making were not ideal for every appointment, they were giving her "insight into the patient's lives that only a house call would provide." And that "COVID-19 has taken much from us, but it has given us back this connection to our patients."

Within the last few years, the concepts of hope and trusted, positive relational experiences have emerged as the best way to engage families—to build on their strengths, to understand that even in the face of trauma, resilience and strength, they can overcome what is negative; and that having even one caring adult giving that positive relational experience can make a difference. Years ago, I worked with a young man who had belonged to a gang in Chicago. He got out. He reported seeing his friends shot on the way to school and his sister afraid to go out of the house. I asked him, "What was it that allowed you to be here today?" His response consisted of two words, "My grandmother." "She cared about me," and he was not going to disappoint her. Intuitive and real. Moreover, many studies point to the importance and value of having that single caring adult in the life of a child, particularly in the early years. Professionals in medicine, psychology, child development, and other fields now embrace the importance of these relationships as foundational to lifelong health and well-being. That has been the work of our nonprofit, and if anything, the work needs to grow. But within this book, I will offer not only our experience, but also ideas we can offer to other nonprofits working to address an array of social needs.

We experienced the stress and challenge that most nonprofits face—to solve a huge, seemingly intractable problem with the lowest budget—and then sustain the initial success. But, fortunately for us and for the families we served, we emerged in the late 1990s into a community that recognized that there was a critical problem to be solved—how to support families in the first three years of a child's life in order to ensure a positive life trajectory. We were given extraordinary support from our business community and our three founding partners, United Way of Greater Cincinnati, the Cincinnati Children's, and the Cincinnati-Hamilton County Community Action Agency (CAA). We were given the latitude we needed to craft our program and deliver it.

Now, 20-plus years later, nationally known and respected, ECS has weathered storms, embraced welcome windfalls, and responded to evolving challenges, but has always held true to its original mission: to ensure that all children can get the best possible start in life. Over the years, science has reinforced and elaborated upon our original basic concept that the first 1,000 days of life are important and foundational to all that follows. Our intervention strategy has been proven to be sound and the prevention focus correct (Shonkoff et al. 2012; Shonkoff et al. 2009). We have celebrated their accomplishments with our families and the hope they bring for the future. So many times, as I met with our families and talked with them about their experiences, I came away humbled yet ever more eager to support them in building upon their strengths, resilience, and opportunities. We walked beside them. Not in front. Not behind. ECS was—and continues to be—as a partner walking together. And, after all, isn't that the magic and the hope for the future?

My personal work reflects decades of senior leadership with more than three dozen nonprofits—as president, board member, volunteer, paid staff, and consultant—on topics ranging from blood banks to health care, to community activism, theater, and fine arts. Issues related to families and early childhood are not appreciably different from those in other focus areas for nonprofits tackling social challenges. Similar challenges face organizations working on the well-being of youth, seniors, or people with disabilities. The systems (and funders) that provide guidelines and expectations for our work heavily influence what happens. Those factors have a profound impact on the potential for success of any nonprofit endeavor. I've contemplated ways to begin to tackle this challenge by holding programs accountable for their expected outcomes—working together to identify those outcomes; determining how the information will be gathered and analyzed; and mindful of what funders expect. One of our board members said it this way, "Find the simplest possible measurement that will tell you what is going on." It needs to be a joint process with decisions made in advance rather than changing the rules after the work has begun. Yet, for programs and organizations of long standing, funding priorities and public perception of the problems change over time, some for the better, and some less so.

In the face of such changes, maintaining focus on the mission and vision of the work is essential and requires steady leadership. In 2007, I wrote to one of our board members to thank him for his guidance, and I ended the letter this way:

> Far too often we forget our roots. We forget the endless meetings, the people who urged us to be better than we thought we could be, the people who saw the future and helped to lead the way. Here in Cincinnati our leaders and our community gave us the support and vigor we needed to go forward each day, and that is what I remember when we are triumphant and when our world grows cold. Thank you for the confidence you placed in us.

ECS stands on solid ground and can say with pride that over the last 20 years, more than 28,000 families made up of 56,000 people were helped. The services improved the developmental trajectory, life course, and opportunities for thousands of children, and their families were changed in a positive way. How we did it is the story I'm going to tell.

Part 1 of this book describes the evolution of ECS as a nonprofit focused on families and young children from 1999 to 2021, as a case study. Understanding that our greater Cincinnati community is but a microcosm of the broader world, we have learned, on a small scale, about the challenges and barriers to scaling programs and the importance of focusing on what works. We have learned much about the challenges and limitations facing small nonprofits who tackle big social issues. Part 2 of this book shares principles of nonprofit management from collaborations, to private and public-sector partnerships, to measurement and financing. The word *focus* is one that you will read repeatedly, because it is at the very center of what happened during my time with ECS and is essential to the principles highlighted in Part 2.

Of course, no one individual represents the full history or life course of an organization. I retired from ECS in January 2021, leaving the organization with an exemplary staff; local and national respect and recognition; and most important, documented positive outcomes for thousands of families. We created a strong institution where none existed before. With new leadership, ECS continues operation, faces new challenges, and plans strategically for the future. As emphasized in this book, changing sociopolitical times call for wisdom, collaborative thinking and execution, account-ability, and even bravery, always keeping the mission in mind and building upon programs that are producing what they promise.

We have a moral imperative to make the home, the village, and the society for that child a safe, stable, and nurturing environment for relationships. The late US Representative Elijah Cummings of Maryland expressed in his words the same understanding of those of us who work with children—we live in the present, but we are committed to their future: "our children are the living messengers we send to a future we will never see. . . . Will we rob them of their destiny? Will we rob them of their dreams? No—we will not do that."

Years ago, I was selected as a winner of the national Purpose Prize, for people over the age of 60 using their accumulated wisdom in their second half of life to make significant social change—to turn life lessons into purposeful projects. Ideas ranged from the ethical treatment of farm animals to food insecurity, to using chil-dren's artwork to decorate corporate offices. They were small and large projects, but each one powerful. And they collectively had an important lesson: Change cannot always be all-encompassing; rather, change can mean working within our own organizations, linking with others where possible, keeping a common goal in mind, and sharing strengths. That may be why I was chosen for this award, as I have held to my mission and vision throughout my career, most notably in my later years. Change in the world can, as Margaret Mead famously said, come from "a small group of thoughtful, committed citizens." (Mead 2005) I hope this book will inspire others to lead, join together, and innovate in ways that foster significant social change, at whatever scale, from a deeply held vision.

CHASING SUCCESS

Part 1

Every Child Succeeds as a Case Study

Chapter 1

The Scientific and Social Context from Whence We Came

This book describes the experiences and lessons of a specific nonprofit, Every Child Succeeds (ECS), dedicated to delivery of evidence-based home visiting to support families during pregnancy and the early years of a child's life. The book uses this as context for understanding the roles and challenges of nonprofit organizations aiming to address social issues. This is a case study of one nonprofit. As traditionally described by Robert K. Yin and others, the case study investigates a contemporary problem within its real-life context (Yin 2014, Yin 2018). Case studies help us understand *how* or *why* by exploring, describing, and explaining what happened. Here the questions are about the opportunities and challenges of nonprofit organizations operating in the role of addressing large, complex social issues. This book relies on the author's direct observation, archival documents, and other information from those who participated in events.

In this case, the issue is related to families with young children and a service approach called *home visiting*. The specifics are explored in Part 1 of this book. In Part 2, lessons that can be generally applied to other nonprofits (e.g., those working to improve life for child, adolescent, and aging populations) are explored in depth.

As with most nonprofit entities striving to address social issues, ECS grew from a particular problem definition, a predefined remedy based on some evidence of impact, and a commitment of public and philanthropic resources. To understand how ECS came about, and the social and scientific context in which it grew, one must go back to the 1980s and 1990s, and see the changes in thinking that influenced our work.

Learning About the Brains of Young Children

Research on brain development expanded in the 1980s, and by the 1990s was virtually exploding and capturing the public's interest. Scientists were able to document, in ways not possible before, that early life experiences have an effect well beyond the early childhood years.

In 1994, the Carnegie Corporation of New York released a sentinel report, *Starting Points: Meeting the Needs of Our Youngest Children*, which described the quiet crisis confronting children from birth to age three (Carnegie Corporation 1994). David Hamburg, MD, a distinguished psychiatrist and longtime president of the Carnegie Corporation, was deeply committed to prevention strategies and the application of research to address social needs. This work underscored the science that pointed to the importance of the first three years of a child's life for subsequent health and development. To accelerate action, in 1996, Carnegie awarded grants totaling more than $3 million to 16 states and cities. The grants were designed to stimulate reform in policies and programs and, simultaneously, to mobilize community action based on recommendations in the report. The *Starting Points* initiative brought messages about the importance of early development to policymakers, including governors, state legislators, and city councils.

The next landmark report came from the National Research Council and was aptly titled *From Neurons to Neighborhoods* (National Research Council, Institute of Medicine 2000). Drawing from the emerging brain research, the report offered important conclusions about the effects of family and community; the influence of politics on programs for children; the costs and benefits of early intervention; and recommendations for action. This report called for health and other early childhood services to be linked, to collaborate at the community level, emphasizing the evidence

in support of change. This National Academy of Sciences committee also issued a series of challenges to decision-makers regarding
issues of racial and ethnic diversity; the quality of early care and
education; the integration of children's cognitive and emotional
development; and the failure of public programs to meet the needs
of families with young children. As described by the report, early
experiences and the environment affect the development of the
brain, and lay the foundation for lifelong health and well-being.
And optimal development depends on nurturing early relationships (US Institute of Medicine and National Research Council
2000, 27–31). The work was widely cited and discussed by other
researchers, professionals, providers, policymakers, and the media,
leading to a shift in public understanding and a groundswell of
support for increased emphasis on early childhood programs.

Ron Kotulak, a Pulitzer Prize-winning science editor at the
Chicago Tribune, wrote a series of articles for the newspaper that
became a book entitled *Inside the Brain: Revolutionary Discoveries
of How the Mind Works*, which detailed for lay audiences what
neuroscience was learning about the importance of early brain
stimulation for children birth-to-three years old and how that
stimulation helped them achieve their maximum potential. Here
is how Kotulak described what happens:

> When it comes to building the human brain, nature
> supplies the construction materials and nurture serves
> as the architect that puts them together. The recent
> discovery that early childhood experiences physically
> shape the infant brain—thereby determining its calcu-
> lating powers and emotional equilibrium—is profoundly
> changing the way we think about the intellectual needs
> of children. (Kotulak 1998, ix)

By the late 1990s, we were visually able to see with scans what
was happening in the brains of our infants and toddlers. Multiple
scientific studies, syntheses of research such as *From Neurons to
Neighborhoods* (National Research Council, Institute of Medicine
2000), and books such as *Inside the Brain* (Kotulak 1998) presented

scientific evidence about what was happening neurologically during the first three years of a child's life. Science firmly indicated that the first three years of life are more important than any three that follow and that optimal development is directly related to changes occurring in the young brain. At the time, we believed the brain had more than 7,000 neural connections being made per second. Today, the Center on the Developing Child at Harvard University, founded and led by Jack B. Shonkoff, MD, reports an estimate of more than one million new neural connections per second (the website for the Center for the Developing Child). These connections become the pathways or neural networks to support the development of cognitive, social, and emotional skills for a lifetime.

In a speech, "Acting on What We Know to Be True" for the National Summit on Quality in Home Visiting in February 2011, John Pepper, Jr., then president and CEO of Procter & Gamble (P&G), explained why his commitment to early child development was so strong. He cited Kotulak's book as one that changed his life. Pepper said:

> It made inescapably real what I had known intuitively: the early years of a child's life are all important. I learned that the support systems, the surrounding environment, the number of words that children hear in their first three years, have an enormous amount to do with the biological development of their brain and their later mental and emotional development.

James Heckman, PhD, Nobel laureate and economist, reinforced the calls for action by letting us know that investing more in proven childhood development, early care, and education programs is the best possible investment for all children—working with the underlying principles that reduction in disparities for children and families is central to success, and that brains are built, not born (Heckman 2012).

Despite many scientific reports and experts describing the urgent need for action, gaining traction for the needs of children ages birth to three has long been a challenge. Children don't vote, and as Bill

Shore stated in his 1999 book *The Cathedral Within* (1999), when he read the Carnegie Corporation report, *Starting Points: Meeting the Needs of Our Youngest Children*, he came to understand that the period from prenatal to age three is demonstrably the most formative. Ironically, it is also the most neglected, because there are no clearly defined institutions, such as preschools, to serve it, nor is there a central national child or family policy to support it. Further, Shore wrote:

> Babies seldom make the news: they do not commit crimes, do drugs or drop out of school. Low-income parents have little economic clout. Children's early experience is in the home—a realm considered private by policymakers and in which they are reluctant to intrude. What the [Carnegie Starting Points] report tries to emphasize is that "researchers have thoroughly documented the importance of the prenatal and postnatal months and the first three years, but a wide gap remains between scientific knowledge and social policy." (Shore 1999, 50)

The Importance of Foundational Early Relationships

Heretofore, we were not aware how much brain stimulation and nurturing parenting mattered for infants and toddlers. Vast and compelling evidence now documents that we cannot begin too early to nurture brain development and early relationships (Willis et al. 2022; Willis et al. 2020; Bethell et al. 2019; National Academies of Sciences, Engineering, and Medicine 2019; Centers for Disease Control and Prevention 2018; National Academies of Sciences, Engineering, and Medicine 2016; Center for the Developing Child 2007). What we had not fully understood was that brain development and early relationships in those first months and years of life was foundational to nearly all child development, as well as an influence on lifelong health and well-being. By carefully listening to the field and research around us, ECS increasingly came to focus itself on the importance of early relationships. Here are some examples of learnings that shaped ECS.

Describing these foundational early relationships for non-professional readers, Kotulak tells us:

> It is the most fantastic and provocative discovery to come out of the world's neuroscience laboratories. An infant's brain thrives on feedback from its environment. The early relationships are of fundamental importance. It wires itself into a thinking and emotional organ from the things it experiences—the sounds, sights, touches, smells, and tastes that come its way, and the important give-and-take interaction with others. (Kotulak 1998, ix)

The Center on the Developing Child at Harvard University synthesized the scientific evidence this way:

> Early childhood is a time of great promise and rapid change, when the architecture of the developing brain is most open to the influence of relationships and experiences. Yet, at the same time, significant disadvantages in the life circumstances of young children can undermine their development, limit their future economic and social mobility, and thus threaten the vitality, productivity, and sustainability of an entire country. A remarkable expansion of new knowledge about brain development in the early years of life, linked to advances in the behavioral and social sciences, is now giving us deeper insights into how early experiences are built into our bodies, with lasting impacts on learning, behavior, and both physical and mental health. These insights can be used to fuel new ideas that capitalize on the promise of the early years and lead to breakthrough solutions to some of the most complex challenges facing parents, communities, and nations. (Center for the Developing Child 2016, 4)

The importance of these relationships was further articulated by the Center on the Developing Child at Harvard, which concluded that:

> No matter what form of hardship or threat may have
> been experienced, the single most common research
> finding is that children who end up doing well have
> had at least one stable and responsive relationship with
> a parent, caregiver, or other adult. These relationships
> provide the support, scaffolding and protection . . . that
> enable them to respond to adversity and thrive. (Center
> for the Developing Child 2016, 14)

In 2015, the prestigious *Journal of the American Medical Association* carried an editorial supporting a focus on the first 1,000 days of life as the path to creating lasting change for children, "Because the brain is the organ from which all cognition and emotion originates, early human brain development represents that foundation of our civilization. Accordingly, there is perhaps nothing more important that a society must do than foster and protect the brain development of our children (Luby 2015, 810)." The American Academy of Pediatrics' Early Brain Child Development Initiative elevated the importance of the first 1,000 days and the critical importance of early relationships (Garner et al. 2017; Garner et al. 2012; and the website of the American Academy of Pediatrics).

In 2021, the American Academy of Pediatrics reinforced these messages in an important new statement that placed increased emphasis on the importance of focusing on safe, stable, and nurturing relationships that buffer adversity and build resilience. In this updated organizational policy statement, Andrew Garner, MD, and a group of AAP pediatric leaders in early childhood development called for a paradigm shift in thinking about services, research, and advocacy emphasizing the promotion and protection of early relationships between parents and young children. They also called for increased efforts to link families to community-based support such as that provided by home visiting programs. The statement emphasizes that:

> To move forward (to proactively build healthy, resilient
> children), the pediatric community must embrace the
> concept of relational health. Relational health refers to

> the ability to form and maintain safe, stable, and nurturing relationships (SSNRs), as these are potent antidotes for childhood adversity and toxic stress responses. . . . These findings highlight the need for multigenerational approaches that support parents and adults as they, in turn, provide the SSNRs that all children need to flourish. (American Academy of Pediatrics et al. 2021, 6)

Other scientists and thought leaders, including Christina Bethell, PhD, MPH, MBA, at Johns Hopkins University (Bethell et al. 2019) and Robert Sege, MD, at Tufts University (Sege and Harper Browne 2017) have advanced understanding of the role of positive childhood experiences (PCEs) in protecting against toxic stress and the impact of adverse childhood experiences. Adverse childhood experiences (ACEs) endanger health and development, yet early relationships and positive experiences can offset the risks. This emerging body of science helps us to understand how PCEs can promote optimal health and well-being. It also offers new reasons to support parents in their efforts to foster early relationships and positive experiences through programs such as home visiting.

And in a more intimate way, Robin Karr-Morse and Meredith S. Wiley in their seminal 1997 book *Ghosts from the Nursery: Tracing the Roots of Violence* built on a theme first raised in a landmark 1975 paper by esteemed professor of child psychiatry Selma Fraiberg. Karr-Morse and Wiley maintain that in every nursery, there are ghosts from the past haunting many parents, as relational and intergenerational factors, including historical trauma, which may affect their experiences with their infants. They created a remarkable word picture of this phenomena and the newborn brain, writing:

> While she is still wet from the womb, as she breathes her first breath, cries her first cry, feels her first gusts of cool air, her brain is building itself at a rate never to be repeated. She already knows the sound of her mother's voice and turns to it. She gazes at her mother's face with great concentration. Synapses in her tiny brain are sprouting in response to each sensation. The most

> powerful computer in the world has been waiting for these moments of light and smell, and touch, and sound, and taste—the carpenters of the human brain.
>
> She will turn toward her mother's voice to keep it coming. She knows her mother's smell and her father's voice if he has been close to her mother in the last two months. She may already recognize . . . a familiar nursery rhyme, or song, or concerto. Her limbs may move spontaneously toward her mother's voice in a dance that mirrors the rhythms of the words. Within a few weeks, her own sounds will replicate those rhythms. She can imitate facial expressions. She can follow a bright object moving slowly across her field of vision. She sees the world in color and contrasts. She is fully equipped . . . to learn, to connect. Everything is new. And every system is poised to take information—for the first and perhaps the most incisive impressions of a lifetime. (Karr-Morse and Wiley 2013, 94)

In his role as leader of the Early Relational Health Hub at the Center for the Study of Social Policy, David Willis, MD, emphasizes that foundational early relationships shape the well-being of both the child and the parent/caregiver.

> The two-way nature of early relationships affects two-generational health and well-being in the moment and long term. Decades of research from the fields of child development, infant mental health, and neurodevelopment has established the centrality of relationships between caregivers and very young children for optimal health, development, and social-emotional well-being. When we focus on and support these foundational early relationships, children and their caregivers thrive—now and for a lifetime (Personal communication).

The Importance of Community Context

ECS was built upon what was known in the 1990s and adapted as further knowledge emerged, using neuroscience and expert opinion to guide the development of our program. We took action in response to the science about brain development and evidence in support of home visiting as an effective intervention in the period from prenatal to age three. What we did was to create a voluntary home visiting program focused on brain development and early relationships for prenatal to age three, especially for those families facing health, economic, and other social risks.

Along with strong community leadership, ECS had a cadre of personally committed, professional home visitors—heroines all—to partner with families who were willing to accept a frequent and regular schedule of visits, beginning prenatally and continuing until the child reached three years of age. The work of the home visitors was guided by a carefully crafted curriculum allowing parent and child to learn together. They helped parents understand that talking to the baby mattered—really mattered—and that holding the baby and being emotionally present was more important than any high-tech device or complicated activity. Science let us know that it was the relationship that grew between the infant and the parent that grounded brain development to support the child for a lifetime. Lived experience told us all families want the best for their babies. Our program was grounded in efforts to promote these relationships with the coaching and support of a trained, empathic home visitor.

The real-life need for a program devoted to moms and their at-risk infants and young children was made clear to me early in the development of ECS. I received a visit from the co-directors of the Perinatal Institute at Cincinnati Children's, James Greenberg, MD, and Jeffrey Whitsett, MD. The message they delivered and the poignant concern they expressed was this: "We can do an outstanding job clinically with infants in the hospital, but what happens when they go home? Is there adequate food? Support for breastfeeding? A safe place to sleep? A parent who has the skills and resources to support optimal development?" These were important questions, indeed admonitions, from two fine physician scientists as they asked for coordination and a continuum of care for their youngest patients and their parents.

What we learned was that the larger social and community context left too many parents without the resources they needed to provide safe, stable, and nurturing environments. The environment, and what is now known as the social determinants of health, were crucially important to the safe, stable, and nurturing relationships between parents and young children. Parents often experienced stressors related to racism, poverty, community disinvestment, and fragmented services. How unstable is the family's economic situation? Are they about to be evicted? Are the home and neighborhood safe? Is the child or parent the victim of violent behavior? Does it occur around them? Is there enough to eat? Is there enough money to pay rent and keep the utilities on? Is there a safe and nurturing childcare arrangement when parents have to go to work? Understanding of these community characteristics has been growing (Acevedo-Garcia et al. 2020; Sandel et al. 2016; Acevedo-Garcia et al. 2014; Tandon et al. 2007; Schorr 1997).

Local data indicated that too many families lacked the resources to provide a safe, stable, and nurturing environment. Hamilton County, Ohio, where ECS and Cincinnati Children's are located, was then ranked among the bottom (worst) 10% of counties across the nation for infant mortality rates. Cincinnati child poverty rates are among the highest for cities across the country for Black, White, and Hispanic children. Tensions related to racial disparities in poverty, infant mortality, and other factors have been high at various points, and community leaders have sought remedies. A Child Opportunity Map from Brandeis University shown on the next page illustrates the fact that many census tracts in greater Cincinnati have low Child Opportunity Index scores, particularly for Black children (note the Avondale neighborhood highlighted in red in the center of the map is the location of Cincinnati Children's and some of the ECS's intensive community engagement initiatives, as well as the site of ongoing disparities and occasional civil unrest). Certainly, recognition of the situation for Black children in greater Cincinnati was one important reason that civic leaders and social activists supported the development of ECS.

Source: diversitydatakids.org 2023. Waltham, MA: Institute for Child, Youth and Family Policy, Heller School for Social Policy and Management, Brandeis University.

We learned a lot from our journey with ECS, while the larger research community continued to inform us, and expand our understandings. The Center for Community Resilience, led by Wendy Ellis, DrPH, MPH, at George Washington University, has articulated the Pair of ACEs Tree which depicts the interconnectedness of adverse community environments—the soil in which some children's lives are rooted—and adverse childhood experiences. Factors such as poverty, discrimination, lack of economic opportunity, inadequate housing, and community violence can contribute to—and are the socioeconomic roots of—many adverse experiences in childhood. The Pair of ACEs Tree model encourages thinking and action beyond addressing individual family-level challenges, toward enriching the community context and opportunity (Ellis and Dietz 2017).

The importance of community context, the "village" that raises children, has been widely discussed. Too often, for too many children, geography becomes destiny, with lack of opportunity in the village and community context in which they grow and develop. What the child experiences and learns there will guide and shape the remainder of life. A poem, "Celebrating Childhood," by Adonis (2006), translated from the Arabic by Khaled Mattawa and printed in *The New Yorker* magazine included the following line: "Your childhood is a village. You will never cross its boundaries no matter how far you go."

In April 2000, at a workshop for the American Society of Newspaper Editors, David Lawrence, Jr., formerly publisher of the *Miami Herald*, president of the Early Childhood Initiative Foundation in Florida, and self-described as a "recovering journalist" said this:

> A community and a country of the greatest wisdom and common sense and decency would strive to make the basics available to every child. Surely all children—rich and poor, and in-between—deserve the same start in life. And if moral grounds do not furnish a great enough imperative—though they should—surely it is to a community's advantage for all children to get off to a good start in school and life. (Lawrence 2000)

Science to Action through Home Visiting

Grounding in science and evidence-based practices is considered important in today's world for nonprofit organizational missions and work, particularly those tackling large social issues with public funding. On the surface, the concept of turning science into action seemed straightforward and yet, determining how to translate knowledge into programs can be complex. In the vernacular of Cincinnati Children's, the challenge for ECS was: How could we move from emerging research findings to a strategy that would turn the science into actions to help children receive the optimal start in life that they deserve?

Because science was telling us that the first 1,000 days of a child's life are more important for development than any that follow, our community came together. While knowledge has expanded dramatically since the late 1990s, when ECS was launched, we applied what was known then. The evidence was clear that children exposed to safe, stable, nurturing environments early in life make more synaptic connections in the brain and that the more of these connections are made, the greater the positive impact for all domains of child development—cognitive, physical, and emotional-relational. In other words, waiting until kindergarten or even pre-kindergarten to begin educating and nurturing the brain was far too late. When earlier brain stimulation and learning has been deficient, essential time has been lost. Thus, the concepts that became embedded in our work were: a focus on the prenatal period to age three, brain development, early relationships, nurturing parenting, safe environments, and prevention.

Acknowledging the importance of early brain development, the Ohio Business Roundtable emphasized that the case for investing in young children had clearly been made:

> The time for methodological research and development has passed. The brain-development research has proven that early pre-natal and postnatal experiences and exposures influence long-term outcomes—and that experiences during the early years influence how well or

poorly the brain's architecture matures and functions. Put simply, infants, toddlers and preschoolers who use their newly formed brain connections keep them. Those who do not exercise these connections lose them. Furthermore, research provides powerful evidence of the benefits of quality early-learning experiences—that early interventions matter in children's health, social-emotional and cognitive development—and in children's academic achievement from preschool to postsecondary education. (Ohio Business Roundtable 2017, 21)

On a parallel track, researchers were conducting studies to examine how the home visiting services approach from the early 1900s could be modernized, with professionals visiting families to provide support, connect them to resources, and help them fulfill their life goals. The published results of the first-rate studies from David Olds, PhD, and his colleagues who founded the Nurse-Family Partnership™ (NFP) model showed strong positive and long-term impact on an array of family issues, such as optimal use of health care, improved parent-child relationships, and family economic self-sufficiency (Olds et al. 1988; Olds and Kitzman 1990; Olds et al. 1997; Olds et al. 2019). Other models such as Healthy Families America (HFA) and Parents As Teachers (PAT) also had published positive results from their home visiting evaluation studies (National Home Visiting Resource Center 2021; Ammerman et al. 2021; Goyal et al. 2020; Green et al. 2020; Finello et al. 2016; Minkovitz et al. 2016; Goyal et al. 2014; Goyal et al. 2013; Avellar and Supplee 2013). Researchers such as Anne Duggan, ScD, at Johns Hopkins University, helped to advance a larger body of research about the effectiveness and characteristics of home visiting (Duggan 2022; Duggan et al. 2013; Duggan et al. 2007; Duggan et al. 2004). Notably, the NFP studies were done in randomized trial studies, where many external factors were controlled. The HFA and PAT models were more likely to be launched by state health departments and evaluated in real-world contexts. Results of implementation in some states showed mixed but generally positive results. In response to this growing body of research, states and communities began to use these evidence-based home visiting models and similar programs with the promise of improving maternal, young child, and family outcomes. By 1999, 37 states were operating 49 state-based home visiting programs. The most frequent reasons for launching these efforts were to improve parenting skills, enhance child development, and prevent child abuse (Johnson 2001).

The logical question was: Science is clearly telling us what to do, but how are we going to put into practice what we know? Pepper argued that we must overcome the inequality by creating high-quality early childhood programs, beginning as early as possible, to ensure that all children get the best possible start. There are, Pepper told us, no magic bullets, but there are programs that make a difference. He captured the essence of the path ahead—use science to guide program development and funding, to build upon what works, and to ground collaboration and cooperation. And, as he says quite often, "Never give up." Focusing in, Pepper said:

> Let me say it plainly. We need to act on what we know to be true. What is missing is the exchange that takes research findings to practice. What is missing are the organization structures bringing together all of the interested parties who can provide the informed and sustained advocacy needed for continued learning and the required funding. ("Acting on What We Know to Be True" for the National Summit on Quality in Home Visiting, February 2011)

When the time came for the United Way, Cincinnati Children's, and the Cincinnati-Hamilton County Community Action Agency (CAA) to agree on a program strategy to ensure all children had the best possible start, two evidence-based home visiting models (NFP and HFA) were initially chosen as the pathway. Over time, we were able to use what we drew from research and evaluation to enhance our original program offerings. ECS grew into a robust regional Cincinnati initiative with home visiting services provided through a network of contracted community-based agencies. However, none of this would have been possible if the community leaders had not accepted the challenge to act upon the science and to commit themselves to changing opportunities for children and families.

Lessons

For nonprofit organizations charged with addressing large, complex social problems, many opportunities and obstacles exist. Building on the best evidence may be in some ways the easiest step. Overcoming the challenges that solo nonprofits face may be the toughest. The conundrum we all live with—resources are finite, needs are infinite—is reality for nonprofit organizations designed to address social problems. How then can we do the best job with what we are given, and in the situations we find ourselves? Knowing that simply looking at the size of the problem can lead to paralysis, yet maintaining one's vision, is important. In a pragmatic approach, one must start with something that is manageable; stay focused; be creative and determined; do what our quality improvement friends call "small tests of change;" and create a strong case for support for a solution that has the potential to expand and grow.

Pepper's challenge was—and continues to be—real and immediate. An infinite number of worthy causes and effective responses to social problems exist. How do we as a society address those issues in the best possible way, using resources most effectively and documenting that what we are doing produces the results we seek? How can nonprofits be better supported in fulfilling their mission, their social-change assignment? Our society must confront the uncomfortable truth that there are, at a minimum, dual expectations for nonprofits—high-quality program delivery and outcomes, but with the lowest budgets and often-ambiguous funding incentives.

In 2011, as part of a national address to people involved in the home visiting field, P&G's Pepper asked himself, "Having been involved in this effort now for 15 years, what have I learned?" His answers continue to inform ECS's work and have value for other community nonprofits.

1.   I have learned that this is a hard, difficult undertaking. Yet, as hard as it is, we can never give up on the objective of doing what it takes to support the development of not just some children but all children who need this support.

2.   I have learned that early childhood is one area where we do need more money to get the job done, and we need to make better choices on how we allocate funds.

3.   I have learned that the only way to succeed is through public/private partnerships.

4.   I have learned that quality standards can and must be improved . . . establishing transparent, minimal quality standards for these programs based on research and a high level of accountability is essential to delivering better-quality outcomes, ones that deserve funding.

5.   I have learned that continual learning and innovation are just as vital here in the nonprofit world as in business.

6.   I have learned that while effective programs are essential, in the end, like everything else, it all gets down to people.

Chapter 2

Community Leadership
and the Creation of ECS

Based on what we learned about the science and our community context, we opened the doors to a new Southwest Ohio/Northern Kentucky program called ECS in March 1999. Our hope was to connect with first-time moms who were most often poor, unmarried, young, victims or witnesses of violence, living in disinvested communities, and having had inadequate health care before and during pregnancy.

The foundation for ECS was laid by private-sector and public-sector community leaders who showed the courage and compassion to step forward and contribute their time, talent, and resources. They had the clout and the influence to engage others, and to issue a call to action. They built upon the knowledge that what happened to our children from birth to three not only had the potential to give them an optimal start but also to affect their lives for years to come. They believed that every child deserves access to opportunities that better their lives.

Our board and community leaders helped us develop a program based on the best available science and evidence, then held us accountable for continuing on that path to achieve results. Critically, we kept a focus on foundational, early relationships between parents and their young children. We ensured that home visitors had the training and tools to support parents' efforts to provide safe, stable, and nurturing homes. We used community leaders and volunteers to make the larger context more supportive for families. We followed the research and harnessed new tools to ensure our communities and families had the best support.

How It Began

The most accurate answer to "How was ECS created?" is that we were able to rely on relationships with people in our community who understood the compelling and well-documented need to focus on early brain development in young children. They were people with the kind of influence that inspired change and knew how to make it happen. Our relationships ranged from the business world to nonprofits, from funders to policy makers, and from families to the community.

Let's begin with the role of John Pepper, whom I have often called the grandfather of ECS. In 1996, he approached our regional United Way board, including John C. Haller, regional president of PNC Bank, and Richard Aft, president of the United Way, then known as the United Way and Community Chest. Pepper, an ardent United Way volunteer and donor, suggested to board members that they consider asking the United Way to lead an initiative to ensure that children from birth to three, especially infants in high-risk and low-resourced situations, had the opportunity to get the best possible start in life. He stressed the effort would benefit not only the children and their families but the entire community.

The clear and compelling evidence led Pepper to ask community leaders, business leaders, and funders these provocative questions: "What is it about this opportunity that you don't understand? Why are programs so balkanized? Why is funding skewed in the wrong direction? Why are seemingly like-minded people unable to advocate effectively for causes both authentic and documented? Why doesn't policy and funding follow science?" Pepper, as the CEO of Proctor & Gamble (P&G) with headquarters in Southwest Ohio, had the clout to challenge community leaders and funders to create new programming that would concentrate on our youngest children. This programming would put into practice what science was telling us, that the foundation of a successful society is built in early childhood and that all our children and their families deserve the best possible start in life.

Pepper found fertile ground at United Way. A Blue Ribbon Task Force was formed, a community steering committee was assembled, community partners including Cincinnati Children's and the Community Action Agency were enlisted, a business plan was written, and, after working for 18 intensive months, ECS was born.

Blue Ribbon Task Force on Focus

By 1996, efforts to expand early childhood programming were underway across the country in response to new guidance about brain development in young children and the Carnegie Starting Points Initiative (Carnegie Corporation of New York 1994). Beyond those receiving direct support from the initiative, state leaders, including those in Ohio, were making new commitments and investments to advance early childhood programs and systems. In parallel, Cincinnati-area leaders were responding in unique ways.

In August of 1996, Haller guided formation of a United Way Blue Ribbon Task Force on Focus. The group was charged with doing three things: 1) identify all other community organizations that would be part of a system or a continuum of services for young children; 2) discover what data were available in the community to support creation of an inclusive, comprehensive early childhood database; and 3) highlight the gaps in the system. The task-force work was summarized in a set of conclusions and recommendations that became a report delivered to the United Way board. The task force distilled input from across the community and determined that the birth-to-three population was the most underserved and was thus the best area to focus on.

Basically, the task force affirmed that the needs of the children in our service area were acute. No system was in place to address those needs, services were largely uncoordinated, and no one was in charge. David R. Walker, formerly vice president and comptroller at P&G and later president of the ECS board, speaking for the task force, built upon an adage from W. Edward Deming and advanced by P&G. Walker characterized it this way: "It has been said that every system is perfectly designed to produce the results it achieves. Our current approach to children's services produces unacceptable results. The Task Force sees no evidence that is changing."

Outcome measurements were sporadic and unclear, leadership was inconsistent or missing, and, although the United Way was just one part of the collaboration, it had key leadership and relationship strengths. The task force recommended that the United Way make children an area of special focus, insisting upon collaboration among partners, including governments, parents, schools, hospitals, churches, agencies, and communities.

Importantly, in its comment about focus, the task force recognized that concentrating on the needs of children involved many players and issues. They acknowledged that not everything could be addressed in the short term, nor would the broader and consequential societal issues, primarily poverty, be adequately addressed. However, the report continued, "Our choice is to start with a core focus on children and to use the ongoing breadth of United Way and other providers to address those broader issues."

Following investigation of research and practice locally and nationally, evidence-based home visiting was chosen as the first strategy to address the challenge of giving all children the opportunity for the best-possible start in life. Home visiting studies from a number of researchers told us that many pregnant women and families with young children could benefit from a regular schedule of home visits, sound curriculum to support parents, ways to measure progress, and respect for the family itself. Studies suggested we could use home visiting to support and foster foundational early relationships between young children and their caregivers. The home visitor, of course, was key to success.

While evidence-based home visiting seemed like a programmatic solution, the issue of service fragmentation and lack of an early childhood system remained of concern. The task force report emphatically recommended that the United Way board assume a stronger leadership role to address gaps in services for children and to improve coordination among existing programs created to serve them. They acknowledged that the leadership role would be neither comfortable nor easy. There were challenges and risks involved in making a concentrated, major new programmatic investment. However, the task force argued, unless there was improvement in service delivery and coordination, the current disjointed system would continue to produce the same inadequate results. To achieve better results, a more aggressive role was mandatory. David R. Walker provided additional guidance, highlighting the major issues:

1. **United Way must be willing to make a major multi-year commitment of time and resources,** including a full-time person at the vice-president level, a share of other staff, and funds for the research effort. Walker estimated that cost to be about 1% of the United Way budget during the startup year. Over the next years, United Way would have to raise significant money because, as one task member said, "If we are serious about making a breakthrough intervention in children's services, it would be a mistake to assume that we can get significantly different results without a significant investment."

2. **Finding solutions for fundamental systemic problems focused on early childhood and challenged families presents a conundrum no one has ever really solved.** Solutions are complex and risk of failure is high. Having modest goals is essential. The community—from parents to grassroots activists to government agencies—will want more rapid change and progress than it is possible to produce. Educating the community about the size and fundamental nature of the issues is key.

3. **The outcomes of the task force were more than another United Way initiative and should be a separate entity, not an in-house operation of the United Way.** Creating an independent 501(c)(3) nonprofit was the way to structure this new community organization. The United Way board would

approve this idea, and ECS was set up in this way, with its own board and independent structure.

4. **We must have a compelling business case and plan; and must enroll the key leaders.** Asking business and individual donors for additional resources and volunteer time is crucial, because we are planning an initiative both bold and expensive.

5. **Collaboration among community partners (governments, schools, unions, agencies, health-care facilities) must be attended to early and often.** It is crucial for success, yet in many cases, this work will be seen as threatening to existing programs and current spending patterns. Collaboration is possible and absolutely essential for success, but it will take major effort to work through these issues both privately and publicly.

6. **When one area is chosen as a "focus," the question always arises regarding what else will be diminished as one area is lifted up. This must be sensitively managed so as not to create a zero-sum game!** For an organization like United Way, this is especially sensitive with substantial relationships with 140 agencies and boards, all representing real needs in our community. Those issues must be addressed given that resources are finite while needs are infinite.

The task force recommended that the United Way concentrate on supporting programming for children from the prenatal period to age 18, and financially support the work that would be required to create and implement the programs. They were aware that large-scale social-service programs could not be sustained on the shoulders of philanthropy alone and that public-sector advocacy would be required to obtain the essential public-sector portion of the money. They acknowledged, however, that the private money raised by organizations like the United Way was essential to pay for research activities and administrative tasks typically not covered in public-sector budgets. We saw this as inspired understanding. We were aware as we began to plan and then implement ECS that virtually the only funds that we had for administrative and research/ evaluation activities would come from the United Way and other philanthropic donors. The public monies we were able to secure would only pay for the home visits themselves. As the program grew, this gap widened, even though we were sometimes able to use grant funds when we successfully competed for those monies.

At this point, we had what I call a prosaic problem. We needed a name that was memorable, action-oriented, and reflective of our work. We needed to stop referring to what we were working on as the "Task Force on Focus Report." We needed to make it real for us and for those we wanted to enlist to support us. So far, nothing had fit. And our marketing and public relations advisors had not come up with anything that met our needs. One day, David R. Walker, the "numbers guy," unexpectedly said three words out loud—Every Child Succeeds—and we knew immediately that they were right. They reflected our focus, were action oriented, and were memorable.

We had given voice to those words as a team, but it was Walker who provided the headline. Critics have said, "You know that every child won't succeed, so why are you saying that they will?" We had to answer that. We—and our families—were aspirational. We knew that families who came to us would do well. Internally, we have speculated that the name should have been Every Mom Succeeds, because if moms don't thrive, children's opportunities are diminished. This is a legitimate and relevant position. But as of this writing, the name has not changed, even though many offers were made over the years.

With the name came acknowledgement that ECS was more than just a vague idea. The mandate from the task force was to develop a program to turn its ideas into action, and that became our challenge.

That role was delegated to a newly created steering committee charged to gather information, evaluate best strategies across the country, ensure that the effectiveness of the strategies was grounded in good data, and guarantee that what was being proposed clearly reflected what our community wanted for its children. Additionally, the task force called for the steering committee to outline a best-practice continuum of service over the lives of the children so that gaps in the system would be visible. The goal, of course, was to work toward designing a continuum of services for young children in our community so that they would be healthy and would live with caring families in a community that sees their welfare as a priority. Recognizing the difficulties and accepting the challenge, the United Way board voted to commit the resources that would be required for the steering committee to begin its assignment to bring ECS to life.

Blue Ribbon Task Force Phase One Report

The Phase One Report, as presented to the United Way board in October 1997, emphasized taking on a larger leadership role in children's services, committing a larger share of United Way resources toward the needs of children. A statement adopted four months later in January 1998 by the ECS steering committee (which included future board members and other community leaders who would guide this work over the coming years), reflected the task-force recommendations, stating:

> Based on our research, we recommend adopting a comprehensive, collaborative program to strengthen families and address the needs of children beginning with the prenatal period and extending to age three. We believe that the foundation upon which this program should be built is a comprehensive home visitation program. After extensive research and analyzing programs across the country, we have selected evidence-based home visiting as an approach that has documented results in enhancing development and reducing maltreatment of very young children. We believe that it can be feasibly and effectively implemented over the nine-county Cincinnati United Way region. (Every Child Succeeds Steering Committee, January 1998)

John Haller emphasized that the Phase One Report encouraged the United Way to take a major leadership role for program deployment and implementation; and that programming rely not only on new science related to brain development during infancy, but also adoption of an evidence-based home visiting approach that research showed could save infant lives and reduce cases of child abuse. The task force leaders emphasized an enduring truth—the key to success of a program is in good execution. Program success is always tied to effective implementation, not only design. Plans come alive through good leadership, teamwork, and conscientious attention to detail.

The Phase One Report delineated best practices throughout the country and the more than two-dozen Southwest Ohio and Northern Kentucky community focus-group sessions that were held to better understand what the communities themselves viewed as high priorities for their children. Close to 400 community residents attended, representing families, business, faith, human services, health, and neighborhood organizations. Together, the task force and the focus groups determined which program strategies had the best evidence of success and which ones most closely aligned with community interest.

It is instructive to look at what we identified as the key opportunity areas to present to the community groups because, taken together, the 14 discrete but closely interwoven factors shown below are the ones that influence the growth and development of our children; underscore the problem; and substantiate the need for a network of services. Home visiting was not then, and is not now, an end in itself, but rather, it should be part of a system or a set of interlocking services relatively easy for families to navigate and driven by what users of the services let us know that they need.

Not one of the following opportunity areas stands in isolation—trying to choose among them or to create a priority list becomes a Hobson's choice, because each area is important, and there is not one right answer. We worked with the community representatives to condense the 14 opportunity areas into four. What happened over the next years—and not unexpectedly—is that programming emerged around all 14, but unfortunately, rarely in a coordinated way. The 14 opportunity areas are:

1. Transform schools to be responsive community resources.
2. Strengthen community cohesiveness and ability to better support families.
3. Provide family support and parenting information to all parents of young children.
4. Develop community resource and recreation centers.
5. Provide health education that promotes positive outcomes.
6. Increase access to affordable quality childcare and early childhood education.
7. Increase access to health care for working poor families.
8. Ensure that children and youth have opportunities to interact with adults.
9. Promote health and development of children from prenatal to three years.
10. Enhance children's access to healthy, nutritious meals.
11. Strengthen support of teen parents and their children.
12. Connect families to neighborhood assets and people.
13. Promote safe environments for children.
14. Increase economic resources available to families.

Community Leaders Advance the Case for Action

When John Pepper went to the United Way with his challenge to create programming for children birth-to-three years of age, he had some unexpected help from *The Cincinnati Enquirer*. On February 1, 1998, under the banner front-page headline, "Despite Efforts, Children's Plight Virtually Unchanged," the newspaper printed its "Everybody's Four-Year Report Card" as evidence of the plight of children in our community. While there is nothing that establishes a direct relationship between the *Enquirer* article and approval by the United Way board to support new programming for young children, the timing was propitious. The piece seemed to alert the community to the poor condition of our children, particularly those of color, and recognition that existing programs were not sufficient. Perhaps—and this is more intuition than provable fact—the piece set the stage for what the United Way was able to initiate with urging from Pepper, Haller, and others. Unfortunately, the report card was not continued, and the effort to create a periodic assessment to provide community-wide visible accountability, transparency, and sustainability for programs serving children foundered.

By the end of 1998, we were able to make the case that investing in prevention in early childhood can produce quantifiable results. We also had created an organization to deliver home visiting services to families facing higher economic and social risks. Our public messaging included six key points:

1. Optimal child development begins with a healthy birth.
2. Birth to three is the most active period of brain development.
3. Toxic stress in early childhood has disruptive impacts.
4. Parental support mediates the deleterious effects of poverty.
5. Maternal depression impacts child development.
6. Investment in early childhood yields a strong return.

This messaging, along with its strong advocates, were compelling, and engaged our local funding community. The United Way board was persuaded, and the organization initially committed $750,000 in 1999, with consideration for up to $3 million from the 1999 community campaign to create an evidence-based program. It would be focused on our youngest children and their families with the understanding—and I use that word most deliberately here—that the foundation for what comes later for these children would be built in the first three years of their lives, the first 1,000 days.

Michael Fisher, then president and CEO of Cincinnati Children's and formerly CEO of the Cincinnati USA Regional Chamber of Commerce, was closely involved in that initial campaign. He pledged and successfully increased the number of Tocqueville Society members, people who donated $10,000 to the

United Way, from 100 to 200. This raised an additional $1 million for ECS. Four years later, he and his wife, Suzette, co-chaired the entire United Way campaign. He remembers that on the very first day the campaign was launched, Michael and Suzette went on a home visit to better understand the challenges our moms were facing. They sat on the floor, talked with the mom, and watched how the home visitor, the mom, and the baby learned together. He said they developed a clearer understanding of why raising money to support the first 1,000 days of life mattered. This strategy of having funders and leaders experience firsthand the family experience in ECS proved invaluable again and again.

It was into this environment that what became the ECS program was born, with its passionate leaders who witnessed the families we served and who also made a vigorous commitment to being data driven, evidence based, and quality focused. From the beginning, we combined community leaders and families in this endeavor.

For more than 20 years, that commitment from the United Way and our other two founding partners, Cincinnati Children's and the Cincinnati-Hamilton County Community Action Agency, was unwavering. Local leaders, funders, staff, families, and the community understood that if the foundation is not properly laid for children in the earliest days and hours of life, amelioration later is more expensive and less effective. Most important, it denies children their right to an optimal start. Prevention is a good investment.

Writing the Business Plan

I was selected to chair the steering committee to write the business plan. I would serve with our P&G-loaned business executive, Frank P. Smith, assigned by Pepper to work with us for one year. Margaret Clark, the United Way director of women's and children's services, rounded out the leadership team for the work going forward.

Smith was an outstanding choice. He brought strong management skills, a sense of humor, and a focus on brevity and action. He was tall and lanky, with a Tennessee drawl. He had a sign above his desk that I have replicated numerous times. It read:

The six phases of a project:

1. Enthusiasm
2. Disillusionment
3. Panic and hysteria
4. Hunt for the guilty
5. Punishment for the innocent
6. Reward for the uninvolved

It was Smith, with an entire career in the for-profit world, who truly set the stage for our ECS business orientation. We were able, in the early and formative months, to put solid systems in place, and adopt effective principles for execution that guided the work.

Margaret Clark came to ECS from an 11-year career at United Way. She had a background as director of a Montessori program, a firm understanding of what communities needed, and a solid grasp of how to enlist their help. She had many long-standing relationships in the community, and she was trusted, insightful, and collaborative.

The ultimate decision to focus on evidence-based home visiting was recommended because home visiting was seen as the most promising strategy to create a comprehensive approach for our challenged families and their young children. By offering a dedicated professional home visitor to a family, the services could be tailored to the needs of the individual family while embracing what else was available in the community. The professional home visitor could follow our established curriculum, identify specific needs of the family, and determine—to the extent possible—what would work best for them. This kind of individualized and focused work, now often termed precision home visiting, allows the frequency and type of services to be linked more closely with the family by identifying their personal needs and goals.

What the Phase One Report called for—engaging the community, using best practices, and following the sound business principles and entrepreneurial actions described throughout this book—is exactly what happened over the first 20 years as the ECS program was deployed across our community's nine counties in Southwest Ohio and Northern Kentucky.

Ironically, the evidence-based home visiting strategy was meant to be the first of the opportunity areas to be addressed. The leaders hoped that other programming would emerge to focus on the rest of the 14 opportunity areas, and move to more unified, connected services for early childhood. ECS has evolved over 20 years into an outstanding example of a collaborative, blending the interests and the work of the founding partners, board, provider agencies, home visitors, and staff. However, with a few limited exceptions, the continuum of services that were envisioned has not materialized. But, as we will explore further, there are glimmers of hope, changes are occurring in the community, and there is reason for optimism.

Enlisting the Founding Partners

A crucial step in launching ECS was to elicit support and participation from the three partners that the steering committee identified as essential to success: the United Way of Greater Cincinnati, Cincinnati Children's, and the CAA. Together, these three organizations were understood to be credible leaders—committed to tracking and measuring results with the means to develop and expand successful strategies, and support growth with the requisite public policy network. All three had significant respect in the community and were beginning to work more actively at the neighborhood level.

Precision Home Visiting

The home visiting field uses many programs and models, each with different strategies, goals, and target populations. For example, some begin during pregnancy with more emphasis on health, and others might be designed to serve families whose children have been identified as having special health or mental-health needs. Initially, most home visiting models took a one-size-fits-all approach for a specific population—offering the same content, sequence, and duration of services. Research suggests home visiting might be better tailored to family needs and goals.

ECS began to think about what works best for whom in 2006 and accelerated this focus in the years since, including changes in ways to engage, interview, screen, and address mental health. As part of the national Home Visiting Applied Research Collaborative (HARC), ECS leaders have done studies on their own and joined with others to understand how to better serve families and make greater gains in improving outcomes. A federal Home Visiting Research and Development Platform launched in 2022 will support this and related work.

Precision home visiting, a term originated by Lauren H. Supplee and Anne Duggan, is an approach that differentiates what works, for whom, and in what contexts to achieve specific outcomes. It uses innovative research to identify what aspects of home visiting work, for which families, and in what contexts. It focuses on the specific needs of each family, allowing improved individual outcomes and use of scarce community resources.

It is related to concepts such as precision medicine and precision public health. Within medicine, there has been a push toward customizing treatments so that patients receive the care and interventions most likely to be effective in light of their biological and other characteristics. Precision public health similarly customizes interventions for various communities and populations. Precision home visiting, as a public health intervention, considers not only the individual but also the families' social and community context.

United Way of Greater Cincinnati

Through the Blue Ribbon Task Force on Focus and the steering committee, the United Way can certainly be credited with generating the strong proposal for change and, over the months, highlighting the concept of more cooperative thinking, improved transparency, and focus on effectiveness. They had agreed, at the board level, that the recommendation from the task force described a courageous path forward that was sorely needed.

United Way brought access to business contributions through their annual fundraising campaign and a sizable commitment of private-sector dollars. The organization was in fact the original ECS private-sector funding partner and, over the last 20 years, continued that commitment. However, and this is an important point, the United Way financial support was not guaranteed. With more than 100 other grantees and partners, the potential for large and sustained financial commitment to one organization was unprecedented. What was allocated each year was based on the success of the annual fundraising campaign, the availability of funds, and the priorities established by the United Way board.

It was with United Way dollars, other grants, and private-sector contributions that ECS was been able to 1) provide the match required to draw down additional public dollars, leveraging both sources of funding; 2) buttress the research/measurement component that has led to more than $14 million in grants over ECS's two decades; and 3) allow the development of program enhancements including the maternal-depression treatment program; home-visit planning guides; community engagement; and improved parenting and early literacy activities. The United Way monies have not grown exponentially, although the amounts have been stable and sizable. With United Way support, ECS maintained an enviable private and public-sector funding mix (typically 60/40)—subject to the results of the annual United Way funding campaign and vagaries in the availability and stress upon public-sector budgets.

What was especially consequential was that United Way policies and funding continued to emphasize the significance of programs targeting the first 1,000 days of life and the recognition that what happens in those early hours and days lays the foundation for so much that follows. However, there is no legal requirement for the United Way to continue to fund ECS, or indeed any of United Way's approximately 135 affiliated agencies. The level of funding and other funding decisions are made by the United Way board, typically on an annual basis.

Cincinnati Children's

Next was Cincinnati Children's, which was then and continues to be one of the premier children's hospitals in the world. When we gained support from Cincinnati Children's, we received, by affiliation, the imprimatur of quality medical care and good science—and as I have often said, credibility before we had earned it. It is easy to say that now, because over the years, we earned our name, but in the beginning, none of us was sure we could do what we promised. We said, and firmly believed, that we would deliver, but it was the prominence of Cincinnati Children's; the well-deserved acknowledgment of the quality of their operation; their fine science and emphasis on outcomes, professionalism, and belief in the value of community health that allowed us to flourish as more than just another aspiring nonprofit.

But one could logically ask, "How did this happen?" Cincinnati Children's is frequently approached by individuals and groups who know what we knew about the value of recognition from them. Having the Cincinnati Children's stamp of approval was part of our success.

How did we get it? The first and most-influential contact was made by John Haller and Richard Aft, who scheduled an appointment in spring 1997 with James M. Anderson, then president of Cincinnati Children's, and Lee Ault Carter, president of the board of Cincinnati Children's and later an ECS Steering Committee member.

Both Haller and Aft, representing the United Way, were able to provide compelling documentation regarding the effectiveness that evidence-based home visiting had demonstrated over nearly 20 years of pilot studies and trials—most notably by David Olds, who founded the Nurse-Family Partnership and did seminal work in the home visiting field. In many ways, all of us in home visiting today stand on his shoulders. What Haller and Aft were proposing was to rigorously deliver an evidence-based home visiting program in greater Cincinnati derived largely from the Olds research.

Both Anderson and Carter had been affiliated with Cincinnati Children's for decades, and they had been active United Way volunteers and funders. They frequently articulated their belief that a hospital needs to be there when a child is sick or injured, but a hospital also has a commitment to community health, in other words, to keep children out of the hospital. So when Haller and Aft met with Anderson and Carter at Cincinnati Children's to propose a partnership to address the needs of moms and their young children, the response was enthusiastic and positive, but not without stipulations. Anderson and Carter emphasized two conditions—service delivery must be of the highest quality, and strong evaluation must be in place. Before any final decision was made about Children's backing ECS, hospital leaders needed to be assured that what Haller and Aft were proposing was sound. Anderson and Carter also needed to confer with Thomas F. Boat, MD, chair of the department of pediatrics at the University of Cincinnati Medical Center and chair of the Cincinnati Children's Research Foundation. Boat, nationally recognized for his clinical and policy expertise, and active in the prestigious National Academies of Sciences, Engineering, and Medicine, would be key to the decision.

When consulted, Boat recommended that Cincinnati Children's join, but with a caveat. He reiterated that the program be supported with strong research and evaluation to monitor program operation and to uncover information about the effectiveness of home visiting as a strategy for improving outcomes for families. Not unexpectedly, it was Boat's advice that allowed the embryonic ECS to favorably lobby the United Way to provide funds so that Frank W. Putnam, MD, and Robert T. Ammerman, PhD, two outstanding scientists, could be brought to Cincinnati to join the ECS staff to create the requisite research and measurement infrastructure; to collect and analyze data; and to guide research and evaluation activities. This would provide the bedrock ECS needed and would be the bedrock over the next 20 years. It has been fundamental to our evolution as a strong organization that can document its outcomes, its operation, and its effectiveness.

In October 1999, Putnam and I were asked to present to the Cincinnati Children's board about the progress of the ECS initiative. They always look for accountability, and we were positioned to respond. I presented the program itself—the intrinsic value of our prevention model, our 1,200 stakeholders (organizations and individuals engaged in our work), and the business plan that was our roadmap—while Putnam explained that our research was designed to be what our P&G friends called actionable. The Cincinnati Children's board was pleased and gave us a green light. What we proposed was bold. We needed smart, insightful, demanding partners. Cincinnati Children's was right there with us.

The plan was built upon decades of research regarding the effectiveness of home visiting for changing the outcomes of mothers, children, and families. It turned the science into action. ECS would not just provide an evidence-based home visiting model, we would demonstrate its effectiveness for families and communities in greater Cincinnati.

Cincinnati-Hamilton County Community Action Agency (CAA)

The third significant organization approached for partnership was the CAA, which had deep roots in the community and was viewed by residents as an essential advocate for its interests. Thus, CAA acceptance of the proposal for investment in home visiting would signal wider community connection. CAA was led by Gwen Robinson, an emphatic and eloquent spokesperson whose participation was essential for success. CAA reflected the ECS commitment to community engagement and to inclusion, equity, and diversity. Their involvement was germane to gaining acceptance in the community that would translate into referrals for the program, enthusiasm, and legitimacy for what our home visiting strategy could do for families. Robinson understood and, along with her CAA commitment to partnership, became an ECS provider, offering the wealth of services and contacts from CAA to ECS families. CAA provided training, amplified our work community-wide, and brought the voice of the community to all our deliberations.

But there is another CAA story that needs to be told, because it validates what a community-focused agency in partnership with a prestigious health institution and known funder can bring to an enterprise such as the one that we were proposing. The story emphasizes the potential for change when community leaders concentrate resources and pull together.

What became a highlight in our history began in 2004 when I read an article by Paul Tough in *The New York Times Magazine* (June 20, 2004, Section 6, Page 44). Tough focused on Geoffrey Canada and his amazing transformational work with the 24-block Harlem Children's Zone in New York City, viewed as a national model for place-based innovation. Canada himself was recognized as a model for all of us, having raised considerable private dollars and, with Mayor Michael Bloomberg, identified a circumscribed area in Harlem where challenged families and their children could have access to a variety of services that provided what a child needed for an optimal start, beginning with The Baby College and continuing with parenting workshops, preschool, charter schools, and child-oriented health programs.

Anderson invited me to speak to a small group of African American leaders from the Avondale neighborhood that is home to Cincinnati Children's. Anderson met with these leaders on a regular basis and wanted them to hear about the opportunities for their families with ECS. I used the astonishing Harlem Children's Zone as an example of what was possible.

The logical question from the group was, "Why not here?" That set us on a course that became highly rewarding. Robinson was my partner in this enterprise, and together we met with Reverend Clarence Wallace, head of the Carmel Presbyterian Church on Reading Road in Avondale. Wallace became one of our best advocates, making his church available as a central location, enlisting his church members as volunteers, engaging other members of the clergy, and welcoming Geoffrey Canada to Carmel when he came to launch our Avondale program. That was a memorable day. Canada is a compelling speaker with much success to report. The church was filled with community leaders eager to ensure that our work in Avondale would be successful. Under the leadership of

Carter and Thomas G. Cody, then a senior executive at Federated Department Stores, we raised an additional $1 million to enhance services for Avondale families.

Anita Brentley, our tireless and creative ECS outreach coordinator, brilliantly led the staff work. It was an exciting and fruitful endeavor as we engaged over 85% of eligible community moms during our three-year involvement. Other outcomes were important and substantial: program retention improved, moms accepted more visits, prenatal enrollment increased, and wait times for the initial home visit decreased. We all learned what could be achieved with greater focus on equity, authentic community engagement that provided enthusiasm, and a sincere belief in what is possible when people work together. Our community leaders—Reverend Wallace and Gwen Robinson—were partners who ensured our success. Brentley was the heart and soul of this effort, bringing critical community connections and knowledge of families to our staff team.

ECS Community Board of Trustees

We carefully selected board members to bring the capacity and skills that we needed to augment paid staff. Our board was never ceremonial. Rather, its members worked through our committee structure or as individuals to offer the guidance that we needed. We sought board members who had a demonstrated interest in our work.

When queried, one potential board member told us that she wanted to create her own legacy, rather than to be part of ours. We appreciated her candor and chose someone else, because we needed to be able to look to our board for ideas about how best to navigate the crowded, competitive public arenas in the birth-to-three category; clearly identify our unique contributions; look for new sources of support; and improve awareness about ECS in the community. We wanted board members who reflected the Pepper call for "one team, one dream."

Unlike some boards, we did not require a financial contribution from board members. Rather, we asked them to lend us their experience and their time—in law, public policy, marketing, accounting, program operation, and science—to assist in decision-making. And we have always been mindful of the value of having a board that represents an array of perspectives and expertise, knowledgeable people willing to offer opinions and engage in dialogue.

Legal Structure

With three strong partnerships secured, we turned to creating the legal structure that was needed to go forward. We applied for and received designation as a 501(c)(3) nonprofit organization, with three founders: United Way, Cincinnati Children's, and CAA. We employed legal counsel skilled in the creation of nonprofits to write our ECS Inc. Code of Regulations that specified how we would operate; how board members and officers would be chosen; and what the role of the three founding partners would be. We executed a contract with Cincinnati Children's to be the managing partner of the three. Our administrative staff and later a few nurse-home visitors would be employees of Cincinnati Children's.

We issued a community-wide request for proposals (RFP) asking agencies interested in being part of our new initiative to respond. We chose 14 of the 18 proposals submitted and executed contracts with them to employ the ECS home visitors but to operate under the direction of ECS, through the terms of our contractual agreement. We considered hiring all the home visitors ourselves but rejected the concept for two reasons. First, we wanted to maintain maximum neighborhood involvement. Second, we believed that having administrative responsibilities at the agency or Cincinnati Children's level, rather than housed in a community-based organization, reduced duplication in the system. We have occasionally made small changes to our Code of Regulations, contracts with the provider agencies, and with Cincinnati Children's, but we operate basically as we did in March 1999 when we opened our doors to families.

Opening Our Doors

By October 1998, we were ready to turn planning and policy into action. We had a business plan, a legal structure, a funding partner with access to business contributions, and a sizable commitment of private-sector dollars. We had a science partner with world-class measurement, research, and evaluation experience and a community partner in contact with people who needed and wanted our services.

We had a compelling name and a logo that made our mission visual—a mother with her arms raised, a baby, and stars. The logo employed purple, teal, and gold.

Cincinnati Children's had identified an Oklahoma woman who had the credentials for leadership to be president of the new organization. She visited with us twice in Cincinnati, but late in the process informed us that she had a family emergency and would not be able to come. What to do? We were ready to begin but did not have a senior executive. During a short but important conversation with Boat, he and I discussed next steps. With only a few seconds of forethought, I bluntly asked, "Why not me?" He seemed surprised but apparently saw me as a reasonable option, as I had chaired the steering committee; been involved with Cincinnati Children's and children's issues for many years; and had a history of advocacy and project management. Boat agreed that Cincinnati Children's could hire me to be the president of ECS. If he were asked today, I think and hope that he would see it as a good decision.

We had an ambitious list of critical tasks that needed to be completed to begin enrolling families. That list of our 10 broad focus areas became our work plan to ensure that we were on target for a program launch by March 1999. We were singularly concentrated on these assignments:

1. Contract development with more than a dozen organizations, including the states of Ohio and Kentucky
2. Evaluation protocols for program operation and outcomes

3. Funding and fiscal management for internal operations, budgets, legal, and IRS requirements
4. Marketing to create community awareness, and enroll moms
5. Identification to develop and delineate roles and assignments
6. Provider council (now lead agency) formation to begin engagement and collaboration
7. Staff hiring, determining which services would be provided by partners, and where consultants were needed
8. Structure to inventory referral sources, set up proper training, determine best program elements, neighborhood and agency assignments
9. RFPs for agencies to discover which ones wanted to operate the Nurse-Family Partnership and the Healthy Families America models
10. Outcome assessments and information systems to describe primary and secondary outcomes; and the computer hardware, software, personnel, and facilities for home-visit coordination and training

Cincinnati Children's gave us office space and access to accounting, budgeting, marketing, legal, and business-development services. We were initially housed in a clinical lab that was waiting for the arrival of a prominent scientist. Our first secretary stayed only two weeks, because she was concerned about the visible shower systems along the halls of the research building that would mitigate any potential contamination event in one of the labs.

We soon moved from the lab to a shared space with Putnam and the Mayerson Center for Safe and Healthy Children, an identification and treatment center for victims of child abuse. Putnam and I saw our ECS prevention approach and the Mayerson identification and treatment program as synergistic.

But when space became available in a new but small building several blocks away, still on the Cincinnati Children's campus, we moved again. The new location, only two blocks from the main hospital, proved to be ideal for us, because our families, home visitors, board, and community partners who met with us frequently found that coming to the smaller, more-accessible building offered convenient parking, accessibility for strollers, and a real footprint in the community of Avondale.

So we got to work—Putnam, Ammerman, Clark, and I—to launch the new venture. Clark and I shared a desk with a tape down the center to keep our papers separated.

Organizationally, we implemented the work plan that we completed in January 1999. Committee assignments included marketing, contracts, budgets, hospital screening, public relations, data collection and assessment, program audits, and, critically, we announced our new carefully chosen board engaged to lead the new 501(c)(3).

As president of ECS, my commitments included fundraising, government relations, marketing, scientific advisement, research, and managing evaluations. Clark, as director of operations, was not only responsible for program implementation but also writing grants and preparing reports—more than 50 of them each year. She had help, of course, from our business director and measurement team, but she was the one who compiled the information and delivered it to the funder or the state or the federal government in a timely manner.

As we set out to promote ECS to the community, we explained it this way: ECS is a regional, voluntary program to help first-time parents in their most important job; to ensure an optimal start for their children. We identified our three founding partners, service area, and outcomes we expected to achieve: reduced child abuse and neglect, improved pregnancy outcomes, reduced infant mortality, and enhanced family functioning. We explained what services and supports ECS would provide for an eligible family, how to enroll, and how the program would work, beginning with referral, agency assignment, family contact, and length of service. We promised transparency.

We received outstanding media coverage based on what we intuited to be acknowledgment for the critical need for our service and confidence that our organization could accomplish what we promised to do. We could not afford expensive media buys, so we relied upon personal media contacts. In those days in greater Cincinnati, most media organizations had health care reporters. Part of our work was encouraging reporters to let people know that ECS was open for business, and we were eager to enroll high-risk pregnant women and new moms who met the qualifications in our service area.

We had to dispel fears that our home visitors were there to remove babies to child protective services or to judge a lifestyle. Repeatedly, we emphasized that we were there to offer professional guidance and to help moms be the best moms they could be in order to give their children an optimal start. And, in truth, this is where the magic of home visiting occurs—where a strong, supportive relationship between a mom and her home visitor creates just the right environment for the baby. People frequently asked about fathers and where they fit. We encouraged two-person parenting when possible. With about 14% of our families, dads were eager and enthusiastic. We celebrated one parent, two parents, and extended families; however the family defined itself and whatever worked to ensure that the little ones got what they needed.

Within the first few months, we received 1,700 referrals—and they just kept coming. In 1999, we enrolled 799 families during the first 10 months we were operational. For comparison, the number of new families enrolled in 2020 was 1,870. Balancing program growth with program quality has been a key concern for everything from training modules for home visitors, to contact with referral sources, to data collection and analysis, and financial planning.

One of the ECS provider agencies, Beech Acres Parenting Center, coordinated our training for home visitors and supervisors, using what was offered by the state and home visiting models but augmenting that with modules for learning that we deemed important. We kept track of training hours for each individual home visitor and required 90 hours of training in year one. Moreover, we urged the agencies to select managers who could motivate their home visitors to work as a team, to communicate well, and to think strategically and tactically.

ECS Provider Agencies

The three founding partners, steering committee members, and our working team recognized that what we were proposing was bold, and there could be repercussions from other community organizations feeling vulnerable as a new, large initiative was forming. Some organizations might see us as competition. We were especially careful when we issued the community-wide RFP for agency participation, and we made sure that our public presentation—and, over time, our implementation—was inclusive, clear, and honest. Trust was and is a key element for success. Having communities engaged and being able to build with them to deliver new services while weaving in their understanding of their community narratives were fundamental. We not only needed community support but also provider agencies eager to deliver evidence-based home visiting to families in their neighborhoods. Our goal was to enhance the existing relationships among the community agencies and their families, not to supplant them.

When 18 agencies responded to our RFP, and we selected 14 from across the region for contract negotiations, we knew that we had crossed the first of many implementation hurdles. In February 1999, Aft thanked Pepper for making ECS possible and reported that "the set-up time for this multi-agency effort is going much more quickly than projects typically go in our community."

From the corporate perspective, Pepper responded by urging us to create a timeline for enrollment and to establish a means for getting an early measurement of results. He added that, "I continue to believe that this is the single most important and promising initiative that I have seen to make a 'big difference' for at-risk youth and their families. I am delighted to see the progress being made, but I would push . . . push . . . push."

When we later discussed our sign-up process with the agencies, a few told us that they were initially afraid of losing their identity when they joined, because they thought that with our large medical-center partner, the involvement of smaller organizations would be minimized—that they would become invisible. They also expressed concern about ECS reporting requirements and the data-collection component. Resistance to our data-collection requirements was strong. The agencies viewed data collection as time taken from families and even perhaps an unnecessary, burdensome part of the visit. But they had agreed, with their contracts, to provide data using a variety of forms and inventories assembled by our research staff. Slowly, the home visitors began to see the value in the work and, to their credit, became in many cases our biggest advocates.

Later, after ECS had been operational for some months, we had gratifying news. Rather than finding the data collection onerous and time-consuming, the home visitors were pleased to have more information about their families so that they could serve them better, and they reported feeling more competent.

In the beginning, and before we were able to use the eECS data-collection platform we developed with the University of Cincinnati, everything was done manually. Home visitors and agencies completed their forms and delivered them to our office. An employee remembers walking to our UC data office through the tunnels at Cincinnati Children's to deliver the paper data forms. She called it "sneaker mail."

The relationship between our ECS administrative group, provider agencies, and Cincinnati Children's proved beneficial in several substantial ways. Most notably, we had opportunities for enhanced training in motivational interviewing, quality improvement, early childhood development, literacy, and maternal-depression treatment. We were bolstered by the credibility that came through affiliation with a major medical and research center. We learned how to integrate quality improvement (QI) strategies into our daily work, and importantly, to do our work better. Home visitors reported that moms frequently expressed confidence in ECS, because it was part of Cincinnati Children's. They joined ECS, and stayed with us. We were continually reminded that a central organization must add value to engage community-based organizations in such an arrangement.

We prepared a contract manual for provider agencies to accompany their ECS provider agreement. The contract manual was written to detail how the complex ECS program would operate to achieve high-quality care across all provider agencies and would ensure that our evaluation instruments would be used consistently. There were two audiences for the manual: 1) current providers and staff, so that they would have a single source for guidelines and philosophical approaches; and 2) those new to the program who needed an introduction.

To me, the preparation of this manual was emblematic of how we endeavored to be inclusive and thoughtful as we fostered this new alliance with strong community-based organizations. We needed to engender successful relationships based on good contracts and trust. Everything we were doing was new, from the people to the processes, and if we were going to achieve the outcomes we promised, and serve the families as we intended, consistency, transparency, and reliability had to be part of our daily work. We were careful all along to maintain the unique identity of each agency while emphasizing the unifying principle that ECS brings to the enterprise.

Administrative Structure

We described our rather-complicated structure as centralized management but decentralized service delivery. This model was reflected in our monthly meetings for all the agencies. To me, the meetings exemplified a well-executed collaborative. Administered by Clark, ECS senior program director, these monthly meetings were held faithfully for more than 20 years. Information was shared transparently; ideas and problems discussed openly; offers for collaboration were frequent. Not once during those 20-plus years was there a serious argument; rather, disagreements were addressed and solutions found.

On occasion, we brought in experts to help us, such as Kay Johnson of Johnson Group Consulting for the national scope and improved understanding of funding opportunities, and the firm of Deloitte Touche for management guidance. Interns from Yale University, University of Michigan Ross School of Business, and the University of Cincinnati Institute for Health Policy and Health Services Research helped with the eECS data platform, our public opinion surveys, and strategic community guidance; and used graduate-student projects to address specific questions.

An example is graduate student Alex Lee's 2010 report to determine whether ECS mothers were making the necessary medical appointments for their babies during the first week of life (*Are Mothers Establishing Medical Home Visiting During the First Weeks of Life?*). Unexpectedly, the research provided a crucial piece of information that influenced how we communicated with moms going forward. When queried about why the number of physician appointments were low, moms told him they often would hang up before making appointments, because they were on hold too long and didn't want to use their valuable phone minutes. This applied to more than just communication with medical offices; it applied to all the communication home visitors had with families.

We also used public relations and marketing consultants, groups such as the Cincinnati Children's Innovation Ventures group to help us better understand our ethnography and to conduct program evaluation. In addition, we had fundraising consultants, most notably Ignite Philanthropy in Cincinnati, a group familiar both with our work and our community.

A note here about nonprofit administration. As small and midsize nonprofits endeavor to keep their operating costs as low as possible, people frequently are not hired to fill organizational needs—fundraising, business development, marketing, government relations, research, evaluation infrastructure, and grant writing. In turn, one of two things happens. Either people within the organization take on additional responsibilities, adding new work to already busy schedules; or people are hired as freelancers, temporary workers, or consultants. Too often, the temporary worker comes to the work with inadequate knowledge of the organization, or the work is assigned internally to a staff member who may or may not be skilled in that area.

ECS itself is an effective collaborative and a good example of how a group of different organizations can commit to a common purpose, and work together. The elements are good leadership, focus, transparency, proper incentives, and productive communication. Any of the ECS agency partners could have delivered a home visiting program independently, but ECS added significant value, and together we were stronger. We paid careful attention and kept good records for everything from training modules for home visitors, to contacts with referral sources, to data collection and analysis, to home visitor performance, to financial planning. The operating strategy and the tools were introduced to ECS early in the development process, largely by our business partners.

Essentially, we always kept a Pepper admonition in mind: "Do not hold meetings where nothing happens, and nothing gets done." I submit that for our dedicated staff, our volunteers, and community leaders, their willingness to engage with us and to stay with us was buttressed by knowing that we would not waste their time, and we would focus.

Trust Matters

Underlying all of this, of course, is trust—trust that leadership will do what is promised, trust that the agencies will be consulted and considered in all decision-making, trust that each agency, indeed each staff member and each family, will be treated with respect.

As part of our due diligence, representatives from the United Way, Cincinnati Children's, and Beech Acres, our training partner, met in July 1997 with Karen Bankston, RN, professor emerita at the University of Cincinnati College of Nursing, to seek guidance regarding how to best establish a collaborative that would deliver on its promises to: 1) acknowledge tension between and among agencies, and address issues as quickly as possible; 2) put aside institutional egos; and 3) respect all parties. Following Bankston's guidance, that is what we did. I cannot say that every day and every meeting was smooth, but I can say without hesitation that ECS was effective and supportive. It wasn't as if we didn't have problems to face. Rather, the difference has been in the way we faced them—beginning with looking at reality.

Whether it was a concern from one provider agency or many, one home visitor or the entire cohort, one state or two, funding or training, we have always sought to surface issues, and look at them squarely. We have never ignored the truth—often at our own expense. We supported our work force. It has not been easy. It required a bit of bravery, solid ground for evidence, and a willingness to speak truth to power.

Several years ago, we approached a nearly fatal stress point when our provider agencies were anxious about the amount of their reimbursement from us and if ECS as an entity was viable. They told us they were barely breaking even financially. We understood that they weren't being paid enough, yet we did not have additional public or private money to distribute. They questioned whether the benefits from their ECS affiliation justified staying in the collaborative and whether they couldn't do just as well on their own. We had several contentious meetings and numerous side conversations with agencies threatening to leave ECS and work on their own.

Rescue came in the form of a new leader of our largest provider agency. After his first meeting, John Banchy, CEO of The Children's Home of Cincinnati (now Best Point Education & Behavioral Health), wrote a short note to me saying, in effect, that we were stronger together than apart and that he was willing, bravely as someone new to the group, to take that stance, and ask others to join him. He elaborated on the benefits of our common operation and successes and, through conversation, slowly drew others to his point of view. Elements such as data collection and QI, shared training opportunities, and other centralized support were of value to the provider agencies. The words we had often used were more effective with this audience when they heard them from another provider and director. He came to the nonprofit world from the private sector, and he recognized reality when he saw it.

As I reflect on my decades of experience with ECS, one of the comments that has made me feel most proud came from a provider-agency manager who told me she was so pleased to work with ECS, because she knew that we would always "have their back and stand up for them as needs arose." That certainly was my plan, though on execution, it was not always easy. Having your colleagues' back is, to my mind, what leadership is all about.

Lessons

This is what we learned in terms of home visiting, specifically:

1. Home visiting is an effective, two-generation service for families in our community. We built upon the research done in other places and adapted the work to fit what local families wanted and needed. At ECS, we were fortunate to have a strong research-and-evaluation component for our work (for more about the ECS approach to measurement and research, see Chapter 7), but we always knew that our primary purpose was to ensure that children have the best possible start in life, and one of the best ways to do that is to provide coaching and support for their parents. Aiming to serve very young children alone, without addressing the needs of the family overall, is not as effective during the period from prenatal to age three.

2. Early relationships matter. Research tells us that early relationships between parents and infants are a foundation for lifelong health and well-being. Home visiting services can help to reduce the stresses—poverty, racism, community

violence, mental health conditions, inadequate housing, and so forth—that inhibit these foundational relationships, and help parents provide safe, stable, and nurturing environments.

3. Home-visitor skills and competence are key. Whether a nurse, social worker, or early childhood specialist, a home visitor needs training and skills in how to build trust, support families, and serve in a culturally responsive and respectful manner. As the COVID-19 pandemic unfolded, the role of the home visitor, which had always been important, became a lifeline. They became trusted friends, links to a larger group with similar interests and needs. Our families embraced the concept, joined the program in record numbers, and accepted many more visits during the pandemic years.

4. Community connections and social support are critical to the service design. The parents that participated in our voluntary home visiting services were typically young, poor, and socially isolated. Home visitors offered coaching and support in the home, as well as ways to link to other services and social supports. Whether the parent gained the benefit of a mom's group, nutrition services, job training, or other services, the resource-and-referral aspect of home visiting was as important as what happened within the visits.

5. Home visiting programs must give greater attention to what works best for whom. Among all families having babies, many could benefit from a few visits, and an estimated one-quarter have risks or needs that could be addressed through intensive evidence-based home visiting models such as that provided by ECS. Overall, at least 10% have more extensive needs calling for interventions to address risks such as serious mental health conditions, substance use, family violence, or homelessness. For example, Moving Beyond Depression™ sought to augment home visiting. One size does not fit all.

As important as *what* ECS did is *how* we did it. We were fortunate to have outstanding mentors and willing community partners joining with us from a variety of backgrounds (e.g., business, religion, human services, and health sectors). Many of these people are quoted in this book, but, on the day he retired, James Anderson—for 12 years CEO of Cincinnati Children's and a lawyer and successful businessman—presented what for me should be the guiding principles for ECS and other mission-driven nonprofits:

- Be the very best that we can be.
- Don't get caught in the details. Consider the long term. Are we doing the right thing?
- Count on your workers and your associates.
- Be optimistic and see ambiguity as opportunity.
- Be credible and brave.
- Do what matters.
- Be stronger under fire.
- Like and respect people.
- Be what you are.

For other nonprofits, the lessons from the ECS startup, administrative design, funding structure, and strategic partnerships are as follows:

1. Keep mission and people top of mind. Amplify the reason to believe. Nonprofits should be mission-driven organizations, striving to take action to advance their goals.
2. Clearly define the problem to be solved, as well as killer issues to help the organization keep focus during times when they are lean or flush with resources. Knowing where you are aiming and what barriers you are likely to encounter is critical.
3. Emphasize the positive, using strength-based approaches. Aim to fix problems and community challenges rather than focusing on fixing people.
4. Listen to the voice of the people. Focus on equity, transparency, and accountability. Engage in codesign, including those who receive the services, when determining which services should be delivered and how that will happen.

5. Use good communication at all levels to support the work. Give reliable feedback internally to board and staff, and externally to community stakeholders. Launch educational, marketing, and public relations campaigns that generate demand for service rather than telling people what they need.

6. Work toward community consensus and collaboration. Engage community and business leadership for expertise and support—strategic, comprehensive, systemic.

7. Create a board that is not merely ceremonial, manage it effectively, and take advantage of the strengths that its members bring to you. Encourage their questions, discussion, and input on solutions.

8. Know that the quality of implementation determines ultimate success. Deliver on your promises. Identify the most compelling measures that will, in the next one-to-two years, validate you are achieving the results you promised, or if not, why not. Agree on measures, outcomes, and expectations—and then hold everyone accountable.

Chapter 3

Design and Essence of ECS

ECS became a nationally recognized voluntary home visiting program designed to support optimal physical, social, and emotional development for mothers, infants, and toddlers who face elevated economic and social risks. Operating regionally in Southwest Ohio and Northern Kentucky, the program uses a two-generational approach focused on parental support and education, resulting in children living in safe, stable, and nurturing environments and families moving toward independence and economic self-sufficiency. The work has been guided by the ECS mission, vision, and values since our doors opened in March 1999 and continues today.

The Essence of ECS

Officially, the carefully prepared mission, vision, and values statements describe ECS, but to understand us better, one needs more context than what is reflected in those words alone. Who are we really? A sound investment? A program with results? How are we different from other good programs? Hearing from people who receive the service and those who provide it to families is how to truly understand what we are.

In 2004, to celebrate our fifth anniversary, we held a large community luncheon celebrating those who parent children. We sought community nominations and selected families to honor, who had been nominated by the community for special recognition. Among them were one family with three children affected by autism spectrum disorder and another in which the mother was an ECS graduate, a teen mom who, with the help and encouragement of her home visitor, graduated from high school with honors, lived independently, and had a job at Walmart. She was described by her home visitor as a "terrific parent to an energetic, smart and thriving two-year old son."

The luncheon keynote was delivered by then-Ohio Governor Robert Taft. A video was presented by human rights activist and writer Kerry Kennedy. The 600-person capacity audience over-flowed the room. The message was: "Parenting matters. Really matters! What ECS is doing is valuable and is working." We were propelled by our belief that everyone wants to be a good parent and that positive reinforcement and celebration leads to stronger families and children.

ECS was founded on the premise that babies need to feel loved and protected. Families need to be listened to, understood, and respected. Fostering social connectedness helps. Early rela-tionships affect people throughout their lives. Mothers with high self-esteem and self-agency are better able to parent and achieve their goals.

We assumed: Parents are the child's first and most important teachers, and everyone wants to be a good parent. By volunteer-ing to join ECS, mothers, fathers, and children would develop the tools needed for success. We could create a model that would work here and in other communities.

We promised: Our families and our community that we would make a difference—and we delivered.

We ended most of our communications with the words, "With your help and ours, every child succeeds." Inspired by our families and the promise we made to them, we highlighted nine key words as themes in all our presentations: evidence-based, focused, collab-orative, regional, public-private, power-of-prevention, business-oriented, accountable, and outcomes-driven.

Guiding Mission, Vision, and Values

Mission

Every Child Succeeds provides an optimal start for children by promoting positive parenting and heathy child development prenatally and during the first 1,000 days of life.

Vision

Every Child Succeeds will support and strengthen families so all children reach full potential. Every Child Succeeds will be the national leader in developing quality programs, conducting high impact research, and effectively meeting the needs of children and families.

Values

We believe:
- All children deserve an optimal start.
- All parents want to be good parents.
- What we do and how we do it matters.

Guiding Principles

ECS is a voluntary prevention program based on these principles:

1. Enroll mothers prenatally or during the first few months after birth.
2. Reach mothers early in the parenting experience.
3. Promote a strong and close bond between parent and child.
4. Provide services in the home.
5. Work with other community partners.
6. Engage communities and reflect the community narrative, listen to the community, and respond to community needs.
7. Respect and reflect cultural differences.
8. Generate new strategies and promote innovation through research.
9. Use public-private partnership for more flexible, stable long-term funding.
10. Apply business principles for more efficient/effective program operations.

This was how we described ourselves both internally and externally. ECS moms, home visitors, and community partners saw how we added value in the broader landscape of programs for at-risk pregnant women and young children in greater Cincinnati.

What happened when a family was engaged with ECS was reflected most compellingly by a young boy who had graduated from ECS and was in grammar school. He nervously brought home a letter from his teacher for his mother. The teacher wrote to compliment his work—his response to his mother was: "Of course I am doing well in school because, after all, you allowed me to be an ECS child."

For families, ECS provided support and resources and helped them to overcome barriers to success. By connecting with a trusted, experienced home visitor, families can be the best they can be and fulfill life goals for parents and children.

Avondale moms wrote their own mission statement, saying, "Starting prenatally, we want healthy, happy babies. We want to become resourceful and instill goals and values in our children's lives that will carry them into adulthood."

The board believed that the ECS program produced results. Its strength lies in the families who join and thereby create a better start for their children. These are families who face challenges that most of us will never know.

Looking Back on ECS Design and Implementation

The positive impact we had on thousands of lives, improving the well-being of women, children, and families, was largely due to rigorous implementation of effective home visiting practices, supported by following a carefully crafted business model that included quality improvement activities, performance monitoring, research and evaluation, community connections and a public-private funding mix. We've learned that this is a common recipe for long-term success in nonprofit organizations.

What Moms Tell Home Visitors

- "You are the only person in my life who has consistently been there for me no matter what. You kept visiting me even when it was hard."
- "Thank you for not giving up on me."
- "My home visitor made sure I knew what I needed to know to help my son, protect my son . . . she helped me with development skills for myself and my child. I learned how to be a wonderful mother . . . I had a goal for breastfeeding, and my home visitor supported that goal for the whole nine months I breast-fed."
- "I would recommend this program to all new moms. It's not just the wealth of knowledge they provide to you about how to be a parent, but they supply you with resources if you ever need anything. They're there to be your friend and make you feel comfortable. It's just a great experience for everyone."
- "They're not like a Band-Aid; they're life changing."
- "My favorite part about the home visit is setting goals."
- "The program is a head start to get children prepared for preschool."

How Home Visitors Characterize This Work

- "One of the lessons that I taught my young mothers when their babies were about nine months old was attachment. During this lesson I asked the mothers to weave two colored strips of paper together and tell me about some of the great times they had with their babies, along with some of the challenging times. After a warm and lively discussion, I asked them to untangle the two strips of paper. I pointed out that the strips were forever changed, having been creased. The two strips of paper represented the mother and her infant; they make impressions on one another and are forever changed. I have been forever changed by the relationships I experienced as a nurse home visitor for Every Child Succeeds."
- "I have several moms who text me every night so that the baby can say good night to me!"
- "I am usually recognized by my Every Child Succeeds logo wear when I am walking through the neighborhood. I feel safe as I am sure our public health nurses felt years ago when they visited patients in relatively unsafe areas but were wearing their Red Cross badges. Our purple bags and Every Child Succeeds clothes clearly identify us. And people are comfortable approaching me to tell me how much they appreciate the program."

Although ECS was not unique in its ability to coordinate multiple stakeholders, operate several models of home visiting, deliver high-quality service, and verify outcomes, we were in many ways first among equals, and we were lauded for our operational strength and our ability to generate a return on investment for funders. RAND Corporation research shows that well-designed early childhood interventions generate a return for society of $2–4 per dollar invested (Cannon 2018; Kilburn et al. 2008; Karoly et al. 2005; Karoly et al. 1998).

The ECS governance and management structure had an unusual but effective framework that included three of Cincinnati's most influential organizations as founding partners: Cincinnati Children's, United Way, and CAA. Cincinnati Children's was the managing partner. Provider contracts were executed with established Ohio and Northern Kentucky community organizations that hired the home visitors and provided the direct service. Provider activity was centralized through the contracts to assure consistent high quality and effective implementation and data collection. The agencies, selected through a request for proposal process, were those that had firm and respected footprints in their communities. I termed our structure "centralized management and decentralized service delivery." Home visitors were hired and services delivered through contracts with nine provider agencies in seven counties across Northern Kentucky and Southwest Ohio—agencies with firm and respected community footprints. The contracts assured consistent high quality and effective implementation. These nongovernmental community-based agencies were grounded in their communities, drew from the local workforce, and served the neighborhoods that surrounded them.

Since 1999, ECS has served approximately 28,000 high-risk families (56,000 parents and children). We made more than 700,000 home visits, meeting approximately 20% of the need for the service among people in our region who qualified under our program criteria—single, low-income, younger than 18, and/or with inadequate (late) or no prenatal care. Many had a history of trauma. According to the 2020 ECS annual report, 45% of the families served were African American/Black, 32% were White, 13% were Hispanic/Latinx, and 10% were of other or unidentified race/ethnicity. The majority of those served were families of color, facing the challenges of structural racism in their daily lives (*Every Child Succeeds Report to the Community*, 2020).

Unmet Need and Use of Home Visiting

This book notes that ECS met 20% of the population need. For home visiting, it is common to estimate unmet need based on five priority criteria—those families who have an infant, low-income, single parents, teen parents, and less than a high school diploma. The federal Maternal, Infant, and Early Childhood Home Visiting program has a similar list of criteria. The *National Home Visiting Yearbook* using similar criteria estimates that about half of families met one of the five criteria, and 19% met two or more priority criteria (*National Home Visiting Yearbook*, 2021).

Research suggests these may be overestimates of the share of the population of families who will voluntarily participate in home visiting programs over a period of years, from prenatal to age three. In other words, one can estimate who is eligible and then comes the question of who will voluntarily enroll in a program and continue participating for years.

ECS researchers are among those who have studied this challenge. They found that among first-time mothers eligible for home visiting in ECS, one-third were referred and 19% were enrolled.

For program implementation and at both the high and low ends of the continuum, the level of family needs affects both enrollment and continued participation. Approximately 40–60% of families leave home visiting within a year.

Researchers need to explore what is happening within ECS that may be different from other home visiting programs and whether there are lessons that could be adopted more universally. Factors may include trust of the services, cultural bias in programs, and/or safety of the community (Condon et al. 2021; Morris et al. 2021; Sabo et al. 2021; Williams et al. 2021; Zephyrin 2021; Barton et al. 2020; Perrin et al. 2020; Scott et al. 2019; Nygren et al. 2018).

The positive ECS experience with community engagement and involvement, especially in the Avondale community, comes to mind as one potentially transferable learning. Improved community engagement was a key to enrolling Avondale moms who could best use and wanted to continue home visiting services.

An evidence-based curriculum tailored for each family was delivered by approximately 80 professional, well-trained home visitors who met with the family two-to-four times per month. We went beyond the basics of the evidence-based home visiting models being delivered by contracting agencies. The expanded ECS home visitor-friendly curricula included elements of the Ohio Help Me Grow program, which is funded by the federal Maternal, Infant and Early Childhood Home Visiting (MIECHV) program and state general funds. The Kentucky Health Access Nurturing Development Services (HANDS) home visiting program was funded through Medicaid and tobacco-settlement proceeds. ECS delivered five federally approved evidence-based models: Healthy Families America (HFA), Nurse-Family Partnership (NFP), Safe Care (Silovisky et al. 2022), Early Head Start (Chazan-Cohen et al. 2019; Jones Harden et al. 2012; Love et al. 2002), and Kentucky HANDS (Williams et al. 2017). The Parents As Teachers (PAT) model was used as part of the curriculum only (Drotar et al. 2009; Wagner and Spiker 2001). ECS also relied upon service improvement and augmentation initiatives, age-focused family success priorities, and program enhancements that included but were not limited to evidence-based treatment for maternal depression, children's executive function, early literacy, smoking cessation, and home safety.

Data from each visit were collected and became part of the Maternal and Child Health Data Hub at Cincinnati Children's. Outcomes and performance metrics were documented and used to continually improve the program and to support robust research and evaluation activity.

The annual program budget ranged from $7–9 million annually. Close to 60% of ECS funding came from public sources and 40% was secured privately. The annual cost per family per year was approximately $3,500.

We understood and advocated for home visiting as only one part of a continuum of services for mothers and babies. We saw home visiting as a tactic toward a larger goal for the child and the family.

Home visiting, we believed, was not an end in itself. Home visitors helped families achieve their goals both through direct support and referrals to other services (e.g., nutrition, housing, mental health, education, and employment). Again, community context matters.

Cookies Never Hurt

Early on in the development and implementation of ECS, as we were thinking about how to generate more referrals from pediatric offices, I asked my husband, a busy pediatrician, what would capture his attention at the end of a long and typically stressful day. He had a one-word answer: "cookies." So we went to work. One of our provider agencies, The Children's Home, had made wonderful chocolate chip cookies for events (actually they were the best chocolate chip cookies I have ever eaten and I never learned their secret recipe). The agency was willing to sell the cookies to us for a reasonable price. We found small cookie boxes that looked like houses, put on an ECS sticker, and filled the boxes with two dozen of The Children's Home chocolate chip cookies. We hand-delivered the cookies to pediatric practices to ensure that they stayed fresh and that we had a chance to interact with people in the office. Referrals from pediatric providers to home visiting and goodwill both went up. Eventually, we provided cookies to anyone who had helped us either with referrals or something else related to helping families. It was, without doubt, our most successful marketing initiative. And, happily, as we filled the little box houses, there were always cookies left over for us too.

Volunteers Added Value

For years, we operated a warehouse where nearly 1,500 Parent Aid bags were assembled each month. Most items were donated items for baby and mother. The bags always included an age-appropriate book for the child. Home visitors delivered one bag each month for each family. The home visitor, with her special bag,

was welcomed with enthusiasm. Our home visitors let us know that
even the babies began to recognize the gift bags, lighting up when
they saw them or even reaching for their new books as soon as the
visitor got in the door.

Often the books we provided were the only books in the home,
and there was a well-stocked home library by the end of year three.
Moms were glad to have something for themselves too—a little
makeup, body lotion, special soaps.

Our diverse cadre of volunteers was drawn from the community, especially the faith-based organizations, our board members,
friends of ECS, and our colleagues. More than 50 volunteers
managed the warehouse, putting in many hours of work to find
the items for the bags, assemble the bags, and deliver them to the
agencies. We had funds to employ one paid volunteer coordinator.
Eventually, we could not afford the warehouse rent and the coordinator salary and this popular, worthy project ended.

Family retention is always an issue in a long-term, intensive
program like ECS. Committing oneself and one's family for weekly
and/or monthly visits for a three-year period can be daunting. The
program must have value to the family. Mothers told us that the
monthly bags we provided were valuable to them. They viewed
the bags as special gifts, and we endeavored to present them that
way. Along with the age-appropriate book for the child, we made
sure that the bags themselves had items of high quality, were well
designed and useful for the mothers themselves. We made them
as appealing as possible. Special bags came on certain occasions:
birthdays, celebrations, holidays, any time that we could help these
women feel valued and proud of what they were doing for themselves and their children. We wanted to celebrate their successes.

While the Parent Aid Bag program was operational, we distributed 130,000 bags and nearly 100,000 books. We gratefully
accepted over 15,000 volunteer hours and presented workshops
for at least 150 corporate events where, under the guidance of our
volunteer coordinator, the employees made things to include in
the bags: woven blankets, handmade toys, and small assemblies of

items so that the mother and child could make toys together from easily accessible items in the home, such as paper-towel tubes, plastic bottles with lids, magazines, yarn.

Our commitment to early literacy and recognizing the importance of having books in the home led two of our key longtime volunteers and board members, Mary Ellen Cody and Digi Schueler, to create the Bringing Books to Babes fundraising campaign to ensure that even when the families could no longer receive the bags, at least they would have the books. Over 10 years, these two caring and effective volunteers raised more than $400,000 to ensure that all ECS families would receive an age-appropriate book each month.

In the early years, we had birthday events sponsored by P&G at the Cincinnati Zoo, learning opportunities at the Underground Railroad Freedom Center and annual Mother's Day parties—large, raucous, warm events with hundreds of moms, babies, and friends—creating stroller gridlock. We had gifts for moms and events that awarded prizes. The days at the Cincinnati Museum Center were especially memorable, as each family received an annual pass for free repeat visits to the Children's Museum.

When I asked Angie Coyle, my administrative assistant at that time, what she remembered most about her years with ECS, this is how she described one Mother's Day at Cincinnati Children's: "The place was standing room only. We were over capacity and cramped but when I looked out and saw the mothers and the babies in that auditorium that day, it made me very proud that I was part of the ECS family. I knew then that ECS was a unique and special program." We had over 500 families in attendance that day. And the next year the event at the Cincinnati Museum Center was even bigger and better, with 800 mothers and babies.

Lessons

I asked our staff to let me know how they would describe ECS. Our referral coordinator, Theresa Popelar, powerfully spoke for all of us when she described how she saw the heart of the program, the magic of this work. Beyond our specific mission, her words reflect what so many nonprofit organizations hope to have: more people reached with meaningful and effective services, more basic needs met, more healing of trauma, dedicated staff and volunteers, partnerships with families, and more people with positive outcomes and lifelong success:

> The countless numbers of babies and children who are meeting their developmental milestones, bonded and securely attached to their parents, showing up at school ready to learn, immunized, with not only their basic needs met but whose houses now have books and toys, who know they have the work of play to attend to, as well as school graduation and meaningful work ahead.
>
> The countless numbers of moms and dads who were brave enough to let a home visitor into their homes, develop a connection, trust all the paperwork, and learn the importance of playing on the floor with their kids, showing up to be a primary caregiver to their child, talking more to their babies, healing their own past hurts, drawing other parents in, and journeying toward self-sufficiency.
>
> The countless hours of time ECS staff have spent fundraising, reporting, data mining, screening parents on the phone, brainstorming in meetings, advocating in the community, and trying to keep the program alive.
>
> The countless hours supervisors and managers have spent supporting home visitors by listening reflectively, caring about their people, attending meetings, balancing resources, and dishing out chocolate.
>
> The countless hours home visitors have spent driving in their cars, completing forms and inventories, processing stories, reading to and holding babies, gathering supplies, preparing activities, creatively solving problems and nourishing relationships so families have hope and feel a little more resilient and empowered.

Part 2

Insights to Guide Action for Nonprofits

In Part 1, I chronicled from the inside how the idea for ECS came about and developed into a significant local organization. Since I was there from the beginning, I was able to describe how the idea for ECS evolved and how conversations and work from the Blue Ribbon Task Force, the United Way of Greater Cincinnati, Cincinnati Children's, and the Community Action Agency led to its implementation. From the science about the activity in the brains of young children and the recognition of the importance of foundational early relationships, we were able to use science to drive our action plan. Further I explained the importance of guidance from the Board of Trustees; the creation of the legal and administrative structures; the growth of and interaction with policymakers at the local, state, and federal levels; and the value of the contributions of our countless volunteers, our communities, and our families.

What happened in greater Cincinnati at ECS does not offer a panacea for any nonprofit. Rather our experience offers a way to think about how to structure the work and how, most emphatically, to ask the right questions to make the best decisions.

In Part 2, my lens shifts to combine perspective, experience, and retrospection with nonprofit leadership principles that I wish I had had when we launched ECS, an example of a program that began with outstanding strength—financial resources, community involvement, family engagement, and evidence-based program tools. Yet even with a strong and compelling mission to ensure that all children have a good and optimal start in life and an amazing set of resources, our growth and scale were truncated by the same barriers that face nearly all small to midsize nonprofits relying on public and philanthropic funding—sustainability, scale, competition, and politics.

Being aware of the challenges and creating effective strategies to address them is what I hope you will take from this book. I want you to be aware of questions to ask, the realistic expectations for success, the courage needed to demand accountability. In short to be able to ground your work on a firm foundation to succeed, to know that lives were changed in a most positive way because of your work or your financial support or your insistence on high quality service, quantified outcomes, a return on investment.

Chapter 4

Evolution and Relevance

The story this book tells starts with a group of dedicated community leaders, in various roles, who were able to translate scientific findings into an exemplary program designed to make a significant impact in a community area of need. In this case, the lifetime trajectory for children and families was significantly improved for those served. Like other organizations, we came face-to-face with the challenges that limit the opportunity for so many nonprofits to grow and have wide-scale impact. It is one example, one case story. Our first 20 years of experience generated a set of lessons much larger than the ECS example, lessons that can be applied to countless other programs around the country.

Our story illustrates many of the common limitations nonprofit entities face when tackling the larger social issues they are designed to address. ECS was launched with strong community support and funding. For us, the beginning was a halcyon time—adequate funding, media support, community consensus, and nearly laudatory praise. We began with privilege, and we executed well for over two decades. Yet the dual challenges of inadequate funding for nonprofits and the absence of a community system approach for fostering early childhood development meant that 20 years later we still were meeting only 20% of the estimated need for our service, even though we had robust evidence that our strategy led to consequential positive results for families and a return on investment for funders. This scenario can be applied to countless other organizations. This chapter discusses our evolution and draws lessons for other nonprofits.

The Limits of Solo Nonprofit Success

There are literally hundreds of thousands of nonprofits operating in the United States today, and their efficacy ranges from poor to outstanding. Many millions of dollars are spent annually for good works, to address larger social issues and health and human services challenges. Our experience in Southwest Ohio and Northern Kentucky offers an opportunity to learn from our successes and our failures. What did we do right? And what was not so good? Where are the big looming barriers that we have barely dented? What does the future look like? How does one stay two-to-three steps ahead? The leadership principles discussed here can be applied to many nonprofits, both in and outside of health and human services. Just having a strategic plan isn't the answer, because as the world unfolds at accelerated speed, a strategic plan that seemed reasonable six months ago may be useless now.

We learned important lessons about the challenges faced by nonprofits and the challenges inherent in the way that nonprofits are funded, validated, supported, and ultimately sustained—or not. We learned lessons about what it meant to move a model service from scientific study into the real world with community and resource limitations.

Therein lies a story with suggestions for next steps, fraught as they may be with political implications large and small. Restructuring systems and weaving in the social infrastructure takes courage and stamina. But research is increasingly telling us that we are not making the kind of progress that would be possible from clear structural changes—improved funding models, greater concentration on the shifts in community context and larger ecological impacts on child and family development, focused and transparent accountability along with better coordinated work and a wider commitment to reducing the impact of racism and poverty.

What we were not able to do, to the extent that it was needed, was to help to create or be part of a large-scale early childhood system focused on a continuum of services for infants and young children—a transparent system funding programs that work, taking advantage of the strength of collective impact and collective advocacy. No doubt other nonprofits have had equal frustration in trying to create a continuum of services for youth, for people with disabilities, for isolated senior citizens, and so on.

While federal, state, and local investments have been made in early childhood comprehensive systems, they reach only a handful of communities. Even for existing efforts the fiscal and operational incentives are too small, and the programmatic, professional, and organizational barriers remain too high. The result may be multiple care coordinators for the same family and/or resistance by families to having public or nonprofit agencies approaching them again and again without really responding to their concrete needs. Despite the vision of early childhood systems being advanced by many over the past 10–20 years, we continue to fail to take advantage of our collective strengths and to engage enough families in the design of systems. New federal investments in children and families are being made in 2021 and 2022, including a new round of grants for state and community action to advance early childhood systems (e.g., Health Care Resources and Services Administration funding opportunities for Transforming Pediatrics for Early Childhood; Early Childhood Developmental Health Systems—Evidence to Impact; Early Childhood Comprehensive Systems; and Early Childhood Development for Health Centers). Perhaps we are learning incrementally, but still not making the needed financial investments to bring equality and opportunity to neighborhoods, communities, and the local systems that surround so many families with young children. Yet we remain hopeful for continued progress from our learnings.

Be Creative, but Hold True to the Mission

Our mission has been our mantra, and our willingness to adopt new or different strategies for going forward has always included resistance to saying no and persistence in looking for more creative ways to solve a problem. We have looked for ways to help families achieve the best outcomes. We have been challenged on many occasions to change our approach, but we have been able to hold true to our mission and do our best to deliver on our promises.

ECS Lite

As the program grew to serve just over 20% of mothers eligible for the service, we began to receive political and public pressure to loosen eligibility requirements, reduce numbers of recommended visits, and lower caseload sizes so that more families could be enrolled. The rationale was that we could then broaden our reach and move from 20% enrollment to something higher. At the ECS board and staff level, resistance to shift from our core mission was strong. We did not believe that what was called "ECS Lite" was true to what we promised. We had committed ourselves to achieving specified outcomes with our enrolled families. We did not want to provide minimal service, hoping that there might be some effect. We sought maximum effect.

We held to the principle that we would not make changes just to save money; rather, we would make changes based on evidence to save and improve lives. Taking a chance that less service for more families might lead to the same result was not a gamble we were willing to take. Our private-sector colleagues endorsed our position, reminding us that "investment in a life-changing intervention seems as wise a bet as any one of us can make."

Eventually, we rejected the idea of "ECS Lite," but we experienced considerable pressure to modify our program, and offer a sequence of visits that we did not believe would be as effective. Not only would that change mean moving away from validated programming, but also, we did not have the research to tell us how our visit schedule could or should be changed without potentially altering the outcomes for families. Further—and this touches upon the importance of supporting what is working—we were being asked to move away from a strategy that had demonstrated effectiveness. Not to build upon something that was working, but rather to change it, with no evidence that the new plan would produce results. As one of our colleagues poetically described it, if you put sawdust in the horse's feed to make it stretch farther, over time it will kill the horse.

What Works Best for Whom

We didn't know then, and it remains unknown, precisely how many home visits should be recommended for families to achieve positive outcomes. We had few guidelines to determine in advance which families were going to require more visits and which fewer. More research is needed to provide information to inform a visit schedule as well as to assess with greater precision the impacts of the experience as calibrated by family capacities, family needs, the key elements of the home visitor–family relationship and realistic expectations. This is an example of a missed opportunity and one that has emerged not only for ECS but also for home visiting as a discipline, so that visit schedules and the experience of the visits could be better focused, understood, and delivered with individual families and correlated with realistic expectations. At ECS, this line of thinking was termed, "What works best for whom?" In subsequent years, it has come to be called precision home visiting and is now one of the emerging topics for home visiting researchers across the nation.

The ECS data file of 700,000 home visits could help to tell the story. Because we created trusted relationships with families and the community, families were emphatic in telling us about what they were willing to do and what they needed. Our statistics for duration of program participation are revealing: 53% of the families were out of the program by the end of the first year, and by the end of the third year, only 25% of the families were left. On average, mothers remained in the program for 18 months, compared to an expected 36 months. Initially, we saw these numbers as evidence of failure; however, as we continued to analyze quantitative and qualitative data regarding what was going on, we realized that, in many cases, rather than evidence of failure by us or by the family, leaving the program early may reflect family success: the mother declaring that she was ready to move forward, to be more independent and confident, as we encouraged our moms to become. This is an indication of the need for home visiting programs to shift from a mindset of "retention" toward a focus on "successful transitions." We needed data to understand when departure from the program was a success and when it might indicate we had failed to meet a family's needs. Family, program, and community factors all affect home visiting enrollment and participation (Goyal et al. 2016; Goyal et al. 2014).

Meeting 20% of the Need

We have been criticized for meeting only 20% of the need for our service among eligible families—young, unmarried, poor, or with late or no prenatal care. We have been chided for not being able to improve community, population-level outcomes. Our response is that 20% (56,000 people) is considerably better than zero. Moreover, we don't know the precise proportion of families who will volunteer to participate in home visiting and for whom ECS is what works. The important message is this: If funders and policymakers were willing to build upon programs that either have demonstrated that they work or have good evidence that they can work, delivering outcomes and using funds wisely, the community metrics and the numbers of enrolled families would show progress. Growth without the money to pay for it is impossible. Scaling what works requires greater investments.

Only First-Time Moms

Another challenge came when we were asked to broaden our eligibility from women pregnant for the first time to women who had a prior pregnancy or a child. This initiative had a different outcome.

From day one, our ECS board emphasized that ECS services should be provided only to first-time mothers. Prior research suggested that home visiting services were most effective with women experiencing pregnancy and childbirth for the first time. This was the particular emphasis for models such as the Nurse-Family Partnership, which ECS had used. When we began, the first line of our eligibility criteria was: first-time moms only. We understood that women who had had prior pregnancies or children also could benefit from home visiting support, perhaps even more than the first-time group, and we were aware that communities and governments were lobbying for a more expansive definition of eligible mothers. The Ohio Department of Health let us know that it was willing to fund services for both groups of moms. We resisted at first but realized that this was an opportunity to do more for more women. So, with the funding commitment, we acquiesced. We began training our home visitors for this new population. We worked with our provider agencies to put the proper accounting and billing procedures in place, and we revised information shared with our referral sources. It was the right thing to do.

So, after years of saying "only first time," we opened eligibility. Within a few months, our operational processes were in place and, although it wasn't our choice to change, ultimately, we pivoted and were flexible. Over time, we realized how various models can meet the needs of those other than first-time mothers. This speaks again to the importance of understanding what works best for whom.

ECS as an Example

The evolution of ECS in Cincinnati illustrates what is possible with the proper elements in place for launch, execution, and sustainability. We really had it all—engaging mission, money, leadership, business and nonprofit support, a critical need for a service, a willing community, and a reason to believe in the potential of evidence-based service models. In many important ways we did succeed. The lives of more than 56,000 ECS mothers and babies were changed, and that is a significant accomplishment. Philosophers and poets tell us that an act of creation must be its own reward. But it is also important to be aware of the tension that is inherent in deploying and sustaining nonprofits. The tension is related to desire for program development, while being stymied by limited resources for program growth. Too often, nonprofits are forced into reliance on money from philanthropic sources, while simultaneously lobbying for money in the vagaries of the public-sector marketplace. Often efforts to develop other sources of independent income are not successful, meaning that opportunities to grow are totally dependent on what the organization is able to garner each year from the two primary funding sources, knowing that both are at best episodic. For 20 years, this model worked for ECS—not to allow the growth we had hoped for but to sustain our program and to allow us to serve a substantial number of people. However, there is no assurance that funding will continue and/ or continue at the same level. The availability of both public and private-sector funding for nonprofit agencies that deliver family services varies from one governmental budget or agency to the next, from one foundation priority strategy to the next. Political changes both large and small often have unforeseeable effects, including the expectations of stakeholders and the development of unsteady relationships with key organizations.

Lessons

Our evolution led to many lessons. Along the way, we did our best each day and we refined our work program to reflect what we were learning and what our families needed. Each nonprofit working to solve larger social issues has a similar and parallel need to focus on those they serve, the mission, being part of a community-wide solution, being accountable through measurement, and delivery of services that make a difference.

1.   Listen and respond to the needs of your community. In our case that meant focusing on families—at least two generations.

Whether your organization serves children or older adults; a multi-generational perspective helps guide the work. Stable and safe home environments and neighborhoods are essential. Listening and responding to the voices of those you will support and their community of support—for ECS, community needs and family voices—is key.

2.   Remember, the mission matters. ECS built partnerships and strategies to ensure connection to prevention and clinical services in primary care, medical homes. Other nonprofits will need to build partnerships in alignment with their mission.

3.   Be part of the solution. For example, home visiting is part of the solution for strengthening families, not the total solution. Because community service systems are complex, assisting families in navigating and connecting to available services is as important as direct supports. Most nonprofit organizations can structure operations in ways that help families navigate and overcome systemic barriers. Some nonprofit organizations can help to change systems in order to remove such barriers.

4.   Emphasize measurement. Inclusion of quality improvement, performance data, and research activities allowed ECS to learn and adapt as we moved forward. Use data for change, to drive performance, and to advance equity. Be accountable.

5.   Invest in programs and services that have demonstrated effectiveness. This anchors sound policy and program decisions. Diluting investments reduces effectiveness and the potential to achieve results. Nonprofits cannot do more with less.

Chapter 5

Collaboration Is Difficult
but Crucial to Success

Community Leadership and Connections Ground Success

Not surprisingly, as ECS made a place for itself in the community, we faced challenges and skepticism, but we had strong support too. We made some good decisions. We focused. We relied heavily on our colleagues in the private sector, especially in the early years when our path forward was less clear. We listened to the admonition "fail early, fail fast." We chose partners and funders who shared our belief in holding true to our mission and making decisions with evidence. We assembled a diverse board that was more than ceremonial and who, with their connections in the community, could help to generate public acceptance—not to mention resources when we needed them.

It was a boost when *The Wall Street Journal* featured ECS as a front-page story in June 2006. Our attention to research, our engagement with community, and our families' results made this a compelling story at a time when home visiting was moving up on the national policy agenda. In addition, *The Wall Street Journal* and others were interested in how we had incorporated a business approach to implementation of a social service. In June 2006, I explained that our board brought us the kinds of minds we could not afford to buy, bringing immeasurable assistance that extended well beyond dollars alone.

At several junctures, our corporate volunteers were surprised at the paucity of data that was available to us to make decisions. They understood, as did we, that we would never have the complete information that we needed for the business plan but that we had to go forward with what we knew at the time. We had confidence in the need for the service and the geography we would serve. We had an administrative structure outlined and founding partners identified, we had funding commitments, and we had found two national home visiting models to follow for the initial program delivery. We still had to identify which outcomes we would specifically focus on, how we would contact moms and enroll them in the program, and how and where we would collect data.

I remember a seminal meeting that we held with a dozen corporate community leaders to discuss the possible road forward for ECS. After two hours of presentations by our program and evaluation/research staff, one corporate senior executive said emphatically that if he waited until he had all the answers that he needed to make a decision, he would be out of business. The message: don't be afraid to try and don't be afraid to fail. But if you fail, understand why something happened so that you can use what you learned to get better. Unless you can discern the why, you cannot replicate and/or improve. We have used our quality improvement strategies to answer those "why" questions.

Fundamental to all our planning was awareness and sensitivity to our community. If we did not present a program that responded to needs and worked with local leadership, we would never be able to deliver what we promised to the community and to the families. Our primary goal was to improve the lot of children and to ensure that all children were able to have the best possible start. So while we assembled the right structure, with many of the right players, it was the families who mattered most. That belief guided our decision-making, including the focus on quality and verified outcomes. We asked for trust, and we delivered trust in return. We infused our family relationships with respect, equity, and hope. With a little guidance from us and incredible work from our families, we all succeeded. We know now that what happens in childhood affects an entire life for one generation and beyond. The families deserve the credit because they not only did the hardest work, but they also knew what they wanted for their children, and they were willing to take a chance with us.

I strongly believe that there were two basic factors that were essential to our success: the inclusion of private-sector thinking into our deliberations and incorporating the voice of the community into our decision making. There were lessons for all of us as we struggled to assemble the right program with the right leadership and right commitment. Together, we created responsible and accountable systems to address opportunities and problems. Our community helped us identify the best paths to follow, let us know what was working, and told us candidly how what we were presenting was being received. Understanding of community and family perspective is essential, beyond data and research about model effectiveness. On both sides, we kept in mind what Dr. Bankston of the University of Cincinnati told us years before, "Trust must be the common denominator." For over two decades, we have worked to establish and maintain that trust by delivering on our promises and ensuring that every child had a realistic chance to succeed.

> Include private-sector thinking in your deliberations and incorporate the voice of the community into your decision making.

Striving for a System: Not Just a Program

Working collaboratively, in a coordinated manner, community nonprofits can improve efficiency and effectiveness, reduce gaps among service systems, and get results. Going back to the Starting Points Initiative, many experts have called repeatedly for better integration of early childhood systems. In recent years, federal, state, and local governments, along with philanthropic partners, have invested in early childhood systems development. An early childhood system brings together health, early care and education, child welfare, home visiting and other human services, and family support programs—along with community leaders, families, and other formal and informal partners—to work collaboratively to achieve agreed-upon goals for thriving children and families.

Since 2003, the federal Maternal and Child Health Bureau, Health Resources and Services Administration of the US Department of Health and Human Services (MCHB-HRSA-HHS), has funded three distinct cycles of an Early Childhood Comprehensive Systems (ECCS) program initiative (the website for the Health Resources & Services Administration, Maternal & Child Health, "Early Childhood Systems Programming"). The first functioned through small grants to states (Johnson and Theberge 2007; Johnson and Knitzer 2006; Halfon et al. 2004) and the second through a collaborative innovation and improvement network (National Institute for Children's Health Quality n.d.). The latest iteration (for 2021–2026) seeks to build integrated maternal and early childhood systems of care that are equitable, sustainable, comprehensive, and inclusive of the health system. This new grant cycle seeks to promote early developmental health and family well-being and increase family-centered access to care and engagement of the prenatal to age three population. The grants released in 2021 reflected a decade of incremental learning. At the same time, an entire generation of children has grown up without comprehensive, coordinated, and equitable service systems.

Some communities offer examples of success in organizing their services into systems. These include efforts like the Bridgeport (Connecticut) Baby Bundle Initiative (Gruendel, 2020), All:Ready in Greater Portland (Health Share of Oregon, All:Ready), and California's First5 Alameda County, First5 Orange County, and First5 LA (First5 California). All have created notable successes in broad early childhood systems development. Sustained resources, effective leadership, collaboration, and community engagement are helping these efforts succeed. At the same time, in Cincinnati and communities across the country, early childhood systems efforts have had variable and mostly limited traction.

In 2015, Neal Halfon, MD, director of the UCLA Center for Healthier Children, Families, and Communities, issued a paper, "The Networks We Need for Early Childhood" (Halfon 2015). Based on ideas that emerged in the early 2000s concerning federal and state funding for early childhood systems development and reflecting on lessons learned in the prior decade, Halfon told us:

> A focus on simply creating more programs is out of step with what we know about how to best support child development. The next surge of efforts must bring together partners from across the community, including those sectors not traditionally focused on children's development. This forward-thinking approach will promote new and innovative collaboration with a shared goal of improving the first five years of children's lives as the most crucial foundation to optimizing their overall development.
>
> By involving education, health, housing, criminal justice, parks and recreation and other sectors in developing a holistic early childhood agenda, communities can help families with young children overcome the many common challenges to more optimal development.
>
> The stakes could not be higher, not just for our children but also for our communities. By addressing such risk factors as poor health conditions and toxic stress that inhibit children's development, we can better leverage the earliest most critical years. This approach not only reduces disparities based on income but gives all children in the community the opportunities they need to become healthy and productive members of their communities in the future. (Personal communication)

Where and How ECS Had Success in Collaboration

Our experience with ECS in greater Cincinnati includes the stories, the decisions, the barriers, and the successes. Collaboration and competition played a role in what happened and are both inescapable in the community context. They will coexist within the overall field of the nonprofit, with shared communication and understanding of the problem one is trying to address. Obviously, there are various solutions to try, strategies to deploy, and programs to carry out. Coming up with the best combinations of those may lead more quickly to an effective response.

Collaboration—especially over time—is difficult. A board member explained it this way when we were working to effect cooperation among local home visiting services. "It is tough and delicate work, trying to decide how to best collaborate and it gets more difficult as more people are at the table in the early stages. Our intent is to be neither secretive nor to exclude anybody but merely to be successful in getting relationships built in this area. We need to walk in these efforts before we try to run."

Without a structure in place that offers incentives to initiate and then sustain a complex collaborative effort, attention and resources fade away. This means coming together to solve a common problem, each person or each organization typically giving up something to achieve a solution. Too often, modifications are made for short periods, but unless there is a compelling—and rewarded—reason to work together, interest wanes. The basic question is: Under what circumstances can cooperative thinking be animated and sustained?

Within ECS, we had the incentives—our provider agencies had a financial interest in joining with us, we had political strength, we had identified solutions for addressing a well-documented problem, and we enjoyed both private-sector and nonprofit-sector leadership. And probably, of utmost importance, we valued our partners and our stakeholders, causing us to work each day to bring value to them. Together we had agreed on the problem that we wanted to solve: How to ensure that every child has an optimal start in life beginning with the prenatal period and continuing until age three.

For over two decades, we sustained a healthy collaborative within ECS itself, delivering a highly effective service. Admittedly, we worked better together because we had a contractual relationship between our ECS administrative group and our provider agencies. We needed each other, and together we endorsed our "reason to believe." We each had something to gain and from the ECS perspective, without our community providers, as a home visiting program we could never do our best work.

We had long recognized that ECS is just one program with limited scope and influence. Building a system among a larger constellation of programs locally, statewide, or nationally must come from organizations with a bigger agenda and broader platform. ECS can be the example, the team member, but not the leader. ECS is part of a solution, but it can only be that—a part. What families and children need is a system that operates collaboratively, incentivizing cooperation, co-developed with families, using an evidence-based continuum of services beginning in the prenatal period and continuing until the child enters school.

An example of where there is a gap in the system is that ECS services end when the child is three, meaning that there can be as many as three years between leaving ECS and entering school. This is time that should not be lost but rather time that provides an opportunity for a bridge to the next point along the continuum, the next new opportunity. We termed this initiative, Ready for Pre-K. Partners needed to be enlisted, including community organizations and parents who could tell us what would really work and not simply what we might write down in a plan. Issues included transportation and cost and perhaps even creation of centers where the gap could be closed.

Barriers to an Effective Early Childhood System in Cincinnati

What happened in greater Cincinnati relative to ECS and other programs that either directly provide services to young children and their families or have the potential to be part of a continuum of early childhood services tells a revealing story. After the conscientious and comprehensive work from 1996 to 1999, led by the United Way, Cincinnati Children's, and CAA to write a case statement and create an implementation plan for what was to be the first of multiple programs focused on creating an early childhood continuum, within a few years, multiple new early childhood programs emerged. They included programs addressing early care and education, infant mortality reduction, and literacy. But the link among these initiatives was tenuous, and because there was not an accepted forum for shared decision-making in place, programming became fragmented and competitive. Had there been an accountable body to amplify the value, build on programs that were working, and provide the incentives for cooperative work, the path forward would have been clearer and resources could have been used more effectively.

The problems are not limited to our community. National experts caution that existing policy and funding frameworks encourage balkanization of programs. Funding is typically not available for the systemic efforts needed to support program integration and/or collaboration. Data from various programs are siloed or not shared at all. To add further complication, the largest amount of public money is expended on older children rather than the youngest age groups, where the impact is stronger and the return on investment higher. To underscore the issue: the Carnegie Starting Points Initiative declared: "The period from prenatal to age three is demonstrably the most formative. Ironically, it is also the most neglected because there are no clearly defined institutions, such as preschools, to serve it (Carnegie Corporation of New York 1994, 5)." Heckman provided the economic argument for funding effective early interventions (Heckman 2012). Carnegie referenced the absence of advocacy/policy support that leads to change and noted that we are still arguing about policy and funding decisions, establishing new programs, and nearly ignoring what we have learned.

As of this writing, in our community, a unifying forum had not emerged, despite the efforts of many. The original United Way "umbrella concept" of ECS as a coordinator and not just a provider of home visiting services did not take shape.

There are, of course, legitimate reasons. Agencies are consumed with just getting their daily work done with little time left over for new work; funding policies tend to create silos as monies are available only for specific services and not for coordinated administration and innovation; there is not a common forum for considering how to create a community strategy to address community issues and to evaluate the effectiveness of various programs, supporting those that produce results and collaborate constructively. Our community has many programs of value, led by people eager to do good work and serve their constituencies, and they have made a difference, but often they have singular missions. The problems they address are real and their work extraordinary but not in alignment with true collaboration. What is absent is recognition of the strength that comes when programs work jointly to solve common problems, serving more families and expending resources more productively.

Building on her decades of thinking and writing about social policy, particularly her landmark book, *Within Our Reach* (1988), Lisbeth Schorr recently wrote:

> A critical examination of past efforts to strengthen our social institutions suggests that they have been largely unsuccessful because our goals, our vision, and our investments have been far too modest. We have been trying to fix isolated pieces of the disparity problem with circumscribed, disjointed and underfunded remedies, which have contributed only marginally to better outcomes. (Schorr, 2022)

Over the years, the situation became even more competitive rather than less so, more confusing and often less trusted by families, less effective, and less efficient. Too often administrative tasks that could be combined were not, services such as care coordination were duplicated, marketing money was spent to promote one program over another instead of educating the community about what children needed and how those services could be delivered. Families reported to us that instead of having one person coming to serve them, there might be several essentially doing the same job or similar jobs. In 2019, we identified 15 local programs or organizations focused on the ages birth to three (excluding those like housing, transportation, nutrition, and safety, which were germane to the well-being of the family but not considered strictly programs in the birth-to-three sphere). For our use, we created a matrix to highlight the mission of these programs, the challenges and the opportunities, and we distinctly saw the overlap. But ECS did not have the influence or the political power even to encourage effective collaboration. Efforts along those lines were seen as intrusive or threatening.

Thus, new programs were planned without building upon community experience and taking advantage of research. Existing work was either invisible or ignored, while money was spent to launch yet another new initiative. A prime example was the deployment of multiple and expensive demographic and ethnographic studies, repeated over and over again, going back to the same people to ask the same questions. Most often the exercise just reaffirmed what was known, but the new work was commissioned because a governmental or philanthropic funding source asked for a new assessment of needs and risks. Rarely did such requests include questions about existing community strengths or existing successful programs. Had there been a forum for collaborative thinking, there would have been an opportunity to use what had been learned and/or to build upon previous work. Expenses could have been minimized, and more importantly, collaboration and systems development would likely have led to more sustainable programs and better results for families.

Periodically, in most communities, a person or an organization gives voice to the need to work together, schedules a few meetings, creates community enthusiasm, perhaps spends community dollars, and makes pronouncements for improvement. But nothing really happens except that a lot of money is spent and, tragically, the community is disappointed. What are the barriers? Politics at all levels, absence of funding to do the collaborative work, organizations feeling threatened, unequal ability to evaluate success and collect clean data, leadership with insufficient influence to cause organizations to come together. All of these contribute. Until there is community consensus around recognition of the value of forming and supporting a coordinating group, one with families in shared power roles, and long-term committed funding to allow the work to happen, the situation will no doubt fail to improve.

With relatively dysfunctional guardrails in place and no influential organization stepping forward to lead change, the loosely configured system will continue. But if the community and/or the community leaders seek something better, how can improvement occur?

On a small scale, ECS offered a good example of collaboration success in the early childhood space in greater Cincinnati—an exemplary organization, doing many things right, collaborating within our structure and with our partners, agencies, and a few other organizations outside of our immediate range. And, although there continues to be room for improvement, we worked within an environment where collaboration was valued, and we learned what was required for success.

Emerging Directions at the National Level

On the national level, more is happening. The Early Childhood Working Group that started back in the 1990s continues to convene dozens of national leaders and organizations to advance the vision for early childhood systems. Their efforts are intended to keep focus on the need for early childhood systems and to encourage funders to think *systems,* not just programs and projects. Start Early (formerly The Ounce of Prevention) continues to grow and support early childhood services and systems nationwide, including early care and education, home visiting and others. With federal funding, the Association for Maternal and Child Health Programs (AMCHP) retained David Willis, MD, and Kay Johnson to study the relationship between home visiting and early childhood systems programming (Willis and Johnson 2020). They created a "Roadmap for Improved Collaboration" to encourage national, state, and local cooperative work (Corona et al 2020).

Also, with federal funding, the National Institute for Children's Health Quality (NICHQ) convened a network of state and community initiatives that are designed to use early childhood systems development to yield a 25% increase in age-appropriate developmental skills among three-year-olds in their communities (NICHQ, n.d.). This NICHQ effort concluded with a call for stronger, more comprehensive early childhood systems that include:

1. Funding to coordinate state and community-level supports.
2. Leveraging two-generational approaches.
3. Using intentional design to address system gaps.
4. Putting families first.
5. Maintaining adequate data.
6. Focusing on equity.

Like early childhood systems, every small, locally based program is part of the solution that can be viewed at a national level. NICHQ reports, not surprisingly, that states and local communities with coordinated systems were better able to respond to the coronavirus pandemic crisis. They are using this outcome as evidence for the need for building broader systems of care.

In an "Insights" paper, "Strengthening Early Childhood Systems: Lessons from the Pandemic and a Call to Action," NICHQ early childhood comprehensive systems project director Loraine Swanson, MPH, says,

> Let this be a call to action for all of us—early care and education programs, schools, communities, businesses, health and social service providers, public and private agencies, philanthropy, community and faith-based providers and policy makers—to come together as system builders. It's time to re-challenge ourselves to move out of our respected silos and bring our limited resources together to better examine gaps and build a truly responsive early child system. When we do this—when we come together as system builders, we can make changes necessary to assure the health and well-being of our nation's youngest residents now and in the future. (NICHQ, n.d.)

It is important to mention, as well, that since the early 1930s, the prestigious member organization of pediatricians, the American Academy of Pediatrics (AAP), has served an important unifying and collaborative role for advancing the health and well-being of children and youth. AAP updates and disseminates valuable guidelines for early childhood immunizations, well-baby visits, safety protocols, parental interaction, early care and education, and school readiness. The August 2021 release of a new AAP policy statement "Preventing Childhood Toxic Stress: Partnering with Families and Communities to Promote Relational Health (American Academy of Pediatrics et al. 2021)," specifically emphasizes the importance of linking the community, including home visiting and other supports for families with the medical home, in efforts to build out a public health approach to advance relational health. In addition, the articulation of the high performing medical home, by Kay Johnson and others, includes intentional efforts to create team-based care models that are intentionally linked to home visiting and the community (Johnson and Bruner, 2018).

Moreover, although most of what home visiting does is outside of the clinical setting, when we take a focus on population health and community engagement for future child health care, the relationships among the physicians, home visitors, the community, and families offer the best opportunity to generate a tiered team-based community approach. Many expert papers and recommendations have noted the overlap in goals and the complementary nature of activities between home visiting programs and pediatric primary care. ECS work at Cincinnati Children's with pediatric primary care providers speaks to the importance of the interaction. Bringing the community into the mix is essential, yet carefully developing an innovative process, given the historical struggles with failed collaborations, will be required to be successful. The four leadership sectors including families, home visitors, child health, and community must chart a new course with shared vision, collaboration, and humility. The weight of the findings of AAP provide needed leverage to make change occur in coordinated ways. Some communities will respond favorably to this while others will continue with the siloed overlapping approach. Nonprofit leaders who can navigate these waters and stay on top of the research, news, and funding availability for broader systems can feed this information back to state and local leaders and inspire community change.

Such efforts must lead the co-design with families and other community stakeholders–the people with lived experiences in disinvested communities for whom the services are designed. Decades of experience, particularly since the 1960s Great Society and War on Poverty programs, demonstrate that the most enduring and successful efforts engage community stakeholders and clients as partners in the design and management of the programs. Two notable examples are federally funded community health centers and Head Start sites. In 1965, the founders of Head Start understood that parents are essential partners and that parents should help decide how Head Start services can most benefit their family and other families in the community. As a result, Head Start programs instituted a policy council that serves as a formal mechanism for engaging parent leadership. Federal regulations call for parents of children currently enrolled in the Head Start site to be proportionately represented on the policy council. The same is true for the community health center movement and federally qualified health centers, which have requirements for community policy councils made up of 50% community members. Leaning on the learnings of community leadership for system building for the prenatal to age three population seems to be a new opportunity, too.

As we talk about cooperation and collaboration, there is a case to be made for independence, but there is a stronger case for working together. Competition should not live where working together is the better option.

Some years ago, I had occasion to meet with Paula Bennett, who at the time was a New Zealand member of Parliament and minister of Social Development, Employment, Disabilities and Youth Affairs. She later served as a deputy prime minister and held portfolios in services for women and state services, among other roles. Having had experience as a young single parent with Māori heritage, Bennett had a strong interest in early childhood issues and family support. Her role in government, social investment, and social services reforms included efforts to build early childhood systems and supports—including home visiting programs—that worked for families. Under the leadership of this extraordinary woman, the New Zealand early childhood effort achieved success through collaboration. They enrolled all children. They had data for who needed what, and they endorsed better ways of operating that could be shared. Bennett was a big personality, enthusiastic and articulate about these issues in particular. She was proud of New Zealand's moms, and she had the courage and charisma to encourage policy makers and moms to follow her lead. Her obvious joy was contagious, and the benefits for families remarkable. There is a lot we can learn from this example of vision and leadership!

Public and Private Leadership Driving Local Change

I have often thought that a wise initial step would be to engage a well-regarded national organization—independent, neutral, out of town—to guide needed change. Under the influence of a group with an excellent understanding of the subject matter and with endorsement by community leaders, the process could move forward without the baggage and parochialism naturally resident with local groups. Such an activity would require the blessing of our community fathers and mothers who possess the influence necessary to make big decisions and assure compliance and sustainability. The potential benefits of a stronger system of service systems are inescapable in terms of increasing numbers of families served, strategies that produce measurable, validated results, and allocation of scarce resources. At the same time, it seems likely that no national organization or consultant would have all the best or right answers for our community.

As with most endeavors, good leadership makes the difference between success and failure. Delivering social services is no exception. Leadership, in the finest sense of the word, brings with it a vision, a commitment to accountability, and the bravery to make hard choices. Outstanding leadership does not come with a title, rather it comes with an ability to execute a plan that not only asks the question, "What is the problem you are trying to solve?" but follows with the essential questions: "How are you planning to solve it? How will you know when you are making progress?"

Most nonprofits operate with an independent board structure. Effective leadership requires integrating the strength of a committed and knowledgeable board with strong nonprofit administration and accountabilities.

Focus and sustainability are required as efforts to concentrate on one problem dissipate over time as other issues or causes rise to the top of the public agenda. Focus on early childhood requires a special kind of patience because the promised outcomes may not be seen quickly. We must wait months, sometimes years for the child to grow and demonstrate what we promised. I remember meeting with elected, sometimes appointed, public figures to explain the importance of support for children birth-to-three years of age and being told that what we promised was outside of their tenure in public office. They wanted results that would help them get elected, not in three years or five but in one or two. This could be considered a reasonable consideration for them but not compatible with creating and sustaining a system of services for our youngest children.

> Effective leadership requires integrating the strength of a committed and knowledgeable board with strong nonprofit administration and accountabilities.

ECS board member David R. Walker put it this way: "Organizations don't change until they hurt, and the amount that they change is proportional to the amount that they hurt."

So, for those of us who work in social service and especially those of us who work with young children, we just keep trying. We produce results that are compelling. We tell our stories over and over. We build upon small changes, as in the 20% example of families ECS can serve. We can lament that we aren't seeing 40% or 50%, or we can be proud of the work that we have done for families and for the community. ECS stands as a worthy and replicable example of what is possible. It's not the complete answer to the community challenge but a step forward, maybe more than a baby step.

In 2021, as we entered another decade, changes were visible in greater Cincinnati. The City Council formed and planned to fund and staff an Office of Children and Families to serve as an "administrative hub for tackling the most prominent issues that impact our children and the families that support them." They cite their three primary functions: use data more accurately to address issues, pinpoint interventions, and execute problem solving measures."

The County Commissioner's Association of Ohio was bringing individuals from a variety of disciplines together to consider early childhood issues as a group. At the start of his administration, Ohio Governor Mike DeWine created a Cabinet level position for children's initiatives to improve coordination among the many state programs. The Ohio Legislative Children's Caucus was focused on the issues of early childhood.

Groundwork Ohio and the Bethesda Inc. bi3 initiative in greater Cincinnati began working cooperatively on advocacy and public awareness for early childhood. The United Way and local leadership contracted with a skilled, neutral third-party consultant to provide guidance for better community coordination.

The Ohio Department of Health is now requiring central data collection and central referrals for their Help Me Grow home visiting program. Both are effective strategies for centralizing decision making and program operation.

The commitment to collaboration was further highlighted for me early in the development of ECS when board member Carter and I traveled to Cleveland, Ohio, to meet with the early childhood advocates in their community. Together, the Cleveland/Cuyahoga County group sat around a large conference table: public-sector directors, foundation chairs, senior program officers, volunteer leaders, philanthropists, elected officials and families—all searching for the solution to their children's dilemma. They outlined the problems and examined possible solutions. I wish that I could say now that they have a perfectly integrated set of services for children. What I can say is that they made progress and are better aligned than many other communities and they were talking with each other. Through their Invest in Children initiative that includes everything from a variety of home visiting services to mental health and early literacy programs, they successfully raised awareness about the importance of addressing the needs of children early and helping families not only access services but also understand the importance of quality services in the early years.

Over the last few years, groups such as Ready Nation, a national-business membership organization whose 1,500 executives support improving the workforce through effective public investments in children and youth, the Ohio Business Roundtable, Ohio governor Michael DeWine and Department of Health have taken notice and identified a focus on early childhood as basic to their public platforms and funding decisions (website of Mike DeWine, September 30, 2022). For example, on the administrative side, the Ohio Department of Health is encouraging better coordination among the programs within the state home visiting program, Help Me Grow. A giant step forward because, by requiring and monitoring the provision of data from programs throughout Ohio, the state will know what is happening with all children in Ohio home visiting programs not just those in one program or another and they will be able to better coordinate their initiatives, target their strategies, and base program expectations on real time data.

Moreover, in 2017, former State Senator Shannon Jones revitalized an existing organization called Groundwork Ohio to bring together like-minded organizations interested in improving the lot of children in the state—to "lay a strong foundation." Jones was recently term limited after serving 10 years in the Ohio General Assembly (two years as a representative and eight as a senator), where she focused her legislative work on the needs of young children and their parents. When she moved to the private sector, she identified Groundwork as the vehicle to become "a research and advocacy organization that champions high-quality learning and healthy development strategies from the pre-natal period to age five." Jones' leadership made Groundwork Ohio the outstanding Ohio "go-to" group to advocate for children. Through their newly launched Center for Family Voices and their continued coordination of children's advocacy, lobbying and public education, and with a grant from the Pritzker Children's Initiative and one from Cincinnati based Bethesda Inc. bi3, they have support for their statewide work to advance early childhood programming.

In Columbus, Ohio, Celebrate One, through its infant-mortality-reduction initiative, created a simple-to-use phone network that quickly links pregnant women needing prenatal care with clinics and private physicians. Supported by more than a dozen organizations, ranging from the Ohio Department of Health to the Franklin County Board of County Commissioners and the Columbus Urban League, Celebrate One began implementing the recommendations of the Greater Columbus Infant Mortality Task Force. This is an excellent example of an effective collaborative endeavor.

Collaboration Opportunities within ECS

What follows are examples of collaboration opportunities that ECS either identified or that had been presented to us by other groups. Some worked; some didn't. Leadership was key. Sometimes we were in alignment with a prospective partner and collaboration served interests on both sides of the table. But not surprisingly, at other times there was a moose on the table that could not be dislodged. Collaboration is not always the answer, but it should always be among the options.

Collaborations that worked well included those with Cincinnati Children's, CAA, and United Way; the Ohio Department of Health; and the Kentucky Health Cabinet. Others with promise didn't materialize.

ECS has been able to demonstrate that collaboration is possible. It currently operates with seven provider agencies, three founding partners, and numerous other funders and stakeholders. ECS has maintained an effective collaborative for more than 20 years with centralized management and contracted agencies. We had core elements for the organization from the beginning: a clear mission, a common data system, an agreement to deliver the program with fidelity, an incentive structure that offered more to the provider agencies than they could have produced on their own, and access to increased resources.

Basically, what we offered was a way to deliver our services to families more efficiently and effectively based on a reason to believe in our mission and a reason to believe in what ECS could provide to the agencies and families who joined with us.

Collaborating across community organizations was more complex, because control and leadership were often diffuse, and the problems to be solved could differ from one group to another. We struggled from the day we opened our doors to gain traction for the needs of children birth to three. We found ourselves competing with school systems, childcare centers, and individuals who believed that early care is best left to parents. Some of these organizations or individuals did not view what happens in the first 1,000 days of life as their priority. Yet, as those of us who work on early childhood have aimed to demonstrate why the first three years of life for a child are foundational for everything that follows, movement is accelerating to support the birth-to-three work and to create the links that are required for sustainable community solutions.

Through its newly launched Center for Family Voices and continued coordination of children's advocacy, lobbying, and public education, Groundwork Ohio received a large grant from the Pritzker Children's Initiative and another grant from Cincinnati-based Bethesda Inc. bi3 to support statewide work advancing early childhood programming. Groundwork Ohio and Bethesda Inc. bi3 collaborated on an innovative maternal and child health-transformation center to improve systems to better serve Ohio's pregnant moms and young children. That is the good news, but historically there are three examples where we failed to forge collaborative relationships—Medicaid managed care, a regionalization proposal for the Ohio Department of Health, and P&G Pampers.

Managed Care Organization Partnership

The first of these instances was with a large managed care organization (MCO) contracting with Medicaid in Ohio. We approached the MCO to explore ways to use Medicaid financing to sustain and enhance home visiting services. While Medicaid funding cannot be blended with federal funding through the Maternal, Infant and Early Childhood Home Visiting (MIECHV) program, Medicaid could, we believed, be one of the several sources of funding for home visiting. Our proposal was to create and deploy a pilot project to demonstrate how home visiting programs could cooperate most effectively to serve at-risk families and help them achieve important positive birth, child development, and parenting outcomes.

Interest was high among MCO leadership. Multiple meetings were held to demonstrate value, with information exchanged about services, data, size and length of the pilot, its policies and definition of operational concepts. But when it was finally time to determine what the pay structure would be, the MCO offered $64 for a home visit that cost $178. The proposed payment could not substitute for our private-sector dollars and supplement what the Ohio Help Me Grow was paying us for the visit. Moreover, the state of Ohio had not given permission for this dual funding approach. We pursued the relationship with the MCO probably longer than we should have, because we knew that the pilot project offered the opportunity to test how the Ohio Help Me Grow program could be delivered within a Medicaid managed-care environment, providing controlled, data-driven, and thoughtful strategies to measure outcomes and identify best practices.

Ultimately, after two years' work to determine how to collaborate with an MCO to test a new funding and service-delivery structure,

the project had to be abandoned. Our efforts at private-sector collaboration had failed, not due to lack of goodwill and diligence on
the part of the two parties but due to siloed funding and lack of
flexibility in state policy and finance structures.

Regionalizing Ohio Help Me Grow

The second effort also involved the State of Ohio and its
Department of Health. This time it was a proposal to restruc-
ture the state home visiting Help Me Grow (which includes the
federal MIECHV) program for improved organization and service
delivery. In February 2011, we wrote to the Ohio Department of
Health suggesting a new regional administrative structure for Help
Me Grow that would mirror what ECS had been using for more
than a decade. We cited our proven track record for delivering
program outcomes, supporting our work with an enviable public/
private funding mix, using a business model in a social service
world, reducing program operating costs, and enlisting community
cooperation.

We recommended using ECS as a prototype for restructuring
Help Me Grow. Basically, the idea was that rather than having
administrative structures in 88 counties with the attendant redun-
dant expense, the counties could be consolidated into six regions
defined by the existing and effective six perinatal regions. We
offered eight reasons for supporting the new structure:

1. Reduced administrative cost and duplication of effort
2. Improved collaboration and coordination for scarce resources,
    program delivery, evaluation, communication, training, and
    education
3. Opportunity to augment public dollars with private dollars
    and/or earned income to bring in additional funding
4. Increased private-sector involvement
5. Benefit of economies of scale
6. Balanced resources for urban and rural settings
7. Accelerated return on investment

8.   Better use of resources to serve more at-risk families and thereby improve outcomes for families and the state

There was some conversation about the proposal and a few meetings, but once again, this movement toward a more collaborative structure was not implemented and barely considered. As a result, most home visiting program grantees in Ohio are small operations without organizational efficiencies, economies of scale, the capacity to deliver multiple models, ability to enlist private-sector dollars to augment public monies, or enough resources to reach more families in underserved and rural areas.

P&G Pampers

A third effort occurred from 2012 to 2013 with the private-sector P&G Pampers and New Chapter vitamins. You can imagine our delight when we began to have conversations with a Pampers marketing team about the opportunities to essentially co-brand our ECS home visiting service with Pampers. We envisioned millions of boxes of Pampers diapers with ECS logos, nationwide acknowledgement of our effectiveness, the link with P&G Pampers quality, and a chance to disseminate our new early literacy curriculum not only for our ECS families but for any family with children in the birth-to-three-year-old age group.

We recognized that stress was ubiquitous in most families with infants and young children, and that the issues we addressed with our programming crossed socioeconomic lines. For example, our Let's Talk Baby interactive online early literacy curriculum we knew would be useful not only for our enrolled families but for other families which often had two working parents, limited time with their young children, and an interest in having ready-made/tested digital tools to enhance cognitive development. P&G acknowledged our proven success, saying:

> Empirical research shows that a nurturing and stimulating environment during the first 3 years of life is critical to brain growth, cognitive development and social/

> behavioral skills. ECS is a prevention program based on this research and provides services and support to at-risk first-time mothers to optimize their children's development from prenatal through the first 3 years of life. (Internal communication)

We envisioned a partnership where Let's Talk Baby could be digitized and delivered through the Pampers Village. I thought of it as Pampers University. We saw collateral activities for families using Pampers to collect points for gifts. Pampers saw Let's Talk Baby and ancillary activities as a strategy to expand its interaction with moms, attract new moms, and improve the lives of other moms they were not reaching.

In the P&G vernacular, we were going to be able to "bring the concept to life." Ultimately, the plans did not materialize largely because ECS, as a regional program, did not have national-brand recognition.

This collaborative effort didn't work out, not for lack of leadership or shared vision. It was rejected as a business decision and, for ECS, an organization founded on a business model, the decision was one that we understood even though we were disappointed.

Collaboration through Initiatives

Cincinnati Children's

Our collaborative relationship with Cincinnati Children's had several facets beginning with our cooperative research agenda, continuing with our involvement with pediatric primary care, our joint Start Strong project in the Avondale community of Cincinnati, our contribution to medical resident training, and our exploration of linking the field of home visiting with children's hospitals across the country. Further, Cincinnati Children's included us as part of its quality brand, along with the expectation that we would perform to meet the high standards of the academic medical center. We felt the pressure and, at the same time, welcomed the challenge, knowing that we were committed to delivering on the promises we had made. Although important work remained to be done, for more than two decades we had demonstrated that the hospital's contract with us was well made.

As Cincinnati Children's has expanded its community footprint, holding to the belief that the hospital is essential for children who are sick or injured but that the hospital also has an important role in community health, ECS has had a place within the medical center's community continuum. While we brought our own public and private money to the table, Cincinnati Children's provided a fertile place for us to grow and the goods and services to help to fund our infrastructure.

For all of the first 20 years, Cincinnati Children's had an essential role in defining and executing our research agenda as we were forming as an organization. It was clear from the beginning that if Cincinnati Children's was to be a partner, robust research and evaluation must be an integral part of our work. This stipulation allowed us to hire research staff, work with the University of Cincinnati to build our eECS data collection platform, submit joint funding applications with scientists from Cincinnati Children's, and host the Maternal and Infant Data Hub. The Data Hub consisted of over 20 years of comprehensive records and yet-to-be uncovered material from nearly 700,000 home visits for 28,000 at-risk families. The ECS data file has the potential to become a highly valuable learning resource; it is focused on some of the following learning-agenda items. It was clear that in addition to finding additional money to serve more families, we also needed to formulate and answer essential questions about service delivery and outcomes, including:

- How can we enroll pregnant women earlier?
- How can we retain families in the program longer?
- How can we effect better transitions to programs for three-to-five-year-olds?
- How do we determine which families need which levels of service?
- What home visiting interventions work best for each family?

- How should/could funding structures change?
- Should funding mechanisms based on pay for performance be considered?

Through our Cincinnati Children's research-and-development staff and our scientific advisory committee, answers to these questions were explored. Without access to our partners at Cincinnati Children's, this level of exploration would have been difficult if not impossible.

Linking Home Visiting with Pediatric Primary Care

One area where I feel we missed an opportunity to learn and to improve the way home visiting was delivered was linkages between ECS and pediatric primary care (i.e., practices and clinics staffed by pediatricians, family physicians, nurse practitioners, and others who deliver primary care to children) in our community. This care was most often affiliated with Cincinnati Children's, where most of the pediatricians in our area were trained. There is a growing national movement to, as Kay Johnson told us, reinforce the role of pediatric primary care as the "hub" where 90% of infants and toddlers are served (compared to about half who are seen in organized child-care centers and 2% to 3% by home visiting). A partnership between home visiting and the medical home has the potential to advance healthy development from birth to age three and to connect to the community. A few studies show the potential impact, and organizations such as the American Academy of Pediatrics have made the case with recommendations for collaboration and partnerships (American Academy of Pediatrics et al. 2017; Garner 2013; Paradis et al. 2013; Toomey et al. 2013; Tschudy et al. 2013; American Psychological Association et al. 2013).

Within ECS, we had an active medical home committee. We executed pilot work at several pediatric primary care sites using care consent forms to allow information to be shared, and we had credibility based upon decades of work with Cincinnati Children's. In the end, the primary care linkage effort limped along for a while, but the barriers of the Epic medical records system, which barely included us; the large number of staff members who were already too busy at many pediatric primary care sites; and the paperwork we requested doomed the effort. Despite a proposal based on pilot efforts, a strong relationship with Cincinnati Children's, and national recommendations, ECS attempts to secure funding from philanthropy for a large and focused pilot study failed. Some health foundations maintained they didn't fund home visiting projects and those foundations funding home visiting said that they didn't fund health projects. Such funding would have provided support for practice redesign, demonstration of proof of concept, and startup of a more systematic approach to collaboration and integration of home visiting and pediatric primary care.

Joint efforts between primary care and home visiting are still a good idea but would necessitate a system change and financial investment to seriously implement such efforts. To date, no major philanthropic or public investments have been made. Shifts in thinking about the role of pediatric primary care may eventually support this type of change. Similar issues arise for nonprofits with other types of missions (e.g., aging, adolescents, housing) when they attempt a paradigm shift in the status quo for delivery of services focused on optimal child development, early relationships, and collaborations with families and communities. Within this new paradigm, embedding or linking home visiting makes even more sense.

Collaboration between Home Visiting and Other Children's Hospitals

Realizing that our relationship with Cincinnati Children's had the potential to show other home visiting programs and children's hospitals what collaboration could look like, in 2012, we assembled a small team of ECS board members, national leaders in the home visiting field, the Pew Center on the States Home Visiting Campaign, and the Association of Children's Hospitals to explore avenues for collaboration. We based our proposal on our demonstrated experience with Cincinnati Children's and characterized home visiting services as a bridge between the hospital and high-risk children. We cited the benefits that would accrue for communities and families if these linkages could be more clearly defined.

In 2019, the Ohio Children's Hospital Association asked me to speak to their group about the benefits of partnership between home visiting programs and children's hospitals. Ohio at that time had two examples: Cincinnati Children's and Nationwide Hospital in Columbus. Again, we talked about the possibilities for sustainability, quality, better integrated community services, and successful families. I cited the trust that families have for children's hospitals and their pediatricians and suggested that home visiting should not be an entity unto itself, but rather part of an integrated team where scarce and precious resources are used in the most effective way—morally, ethically, programmatically, and economically—with the hospital at the center. We identified seven areas in which collaboration between home visiting programs and pediatric hospitals had potential value:

1. An avenue to help to integrate a pediatric hospital with the community
2. A joint commitment to high quality, innovative research, and evaluation
3. The development of interventions to further improve the health of at-risk families enrolled in home visiting
4. A focus on prevention along with treatment of disease and injury
5. An emphasis on actionable research
6. The use of quality improvement strategies in a community setting
7. Access to large data sets for further exploration and learning

We never got beyond the planning stage. Hospitals, facing a variety of pressures, were not interested in taking on new programs. Most other children's hospitals were using community benefit funds and in-kind resources for other priorities. In the end, we considered ourselves fortunate that the situation was different in greater Cincinnati. Again, an effort to change the nonprofit business model was not successful.

Collaboration with the Community: Our Learnings

Tiered Care Teams

The need for early childhood tiered-care teams underscores the importance of improved collaboration in our community and need for collaboration to achieve maximum gains for the population. ECS, along with others, has advanced the concept of creating care teams so that together, various disciplines could blend skills and resources without duplicating effort. Within the early childhood community, home visiting services have been delivered by home visitors, community health workers, doulas, home health care workers, lactation consultants, health care navigators at Cincinnati Children's and at the Hamilton County Department of Health, social workers at the Hamilton County Department of Job and Family Services, early care and education providers, and physicians and nurses at prenatal and pediatric clinics. Clearly, not all these functions overlap, but if roles and responsibilities for each of these disciplines were defined and opportunities for collaboration available, existing fragmentation and confusion could be minimized and barriers to implementation could be reduced. But saying that is easier than doing it. Long-term sustainability in the nonprofit role needs an organization or a group of organizations serving as a coordinator and offering incentives for collaborating. In the breach, programs have grown to serve their individual mandates even though working together would lead to better outcomes and serve more families.

The relationship between home visitors and community health workers offers a good example. As with other adjacent agencies and programs with similar target groups, both workers are valuable, and each provides a distinct service. But without a clear scope of work, both are often deployed to improve family outreach, engagement, resource and referral, and timely receipt of health and other services. Without coordination between home visitors and community health workers, services are duplicated, messaging confusing, and the strength of each diminished. Home visitors have a parenting and child development curriculum to deliver, while community health workers have expertise in outreach, community education, informal counseling, social support, and family advocacy. With careful planning they could work together, educating the family, encouraging good parenting, connecting with services, and creating community support.

> Long-term sustainability in the nonprofit role needs an organization or a group of organizations serving as a coordinator and offering incentives for collaborating.

Consistent with the importance of collaboration, as ECS negotiated with an MCO, we described the tiered-team approach to serving families. We explained that we were eager to launch a pilot project to demonstrate how a tiered team of home visitors and care coordination/community health workers could more effectively deliver services to pregnant women and families with young children by integrating two distinct yet related disciplines. Our plans for working with an MCO did not materialize, but we continued to refine the tiered-team concept. In 2019, we applied for and received a grant from Bethesda Inc. bi3 to examine the relationship between home visitors and community health workers, offering ideas for improvement. We ended our report with the following conclusion:

> A consistent theme is that systems and funding structures are not created to incentivize collaboration in the perinatal period. An example of the sometimes-contentious relationship that can result from years of this disjointed structure and funding emerged in one of the interviews. The home visitor reported that she entered the home of the client and was met by suspicion, not by the client, but by the community health worker. Incentives that reward one program over another in the perinatal space have resulted in competitive and occasionally awkward relationships rather than cooperative and synergistic ones. (Internal communication)

As an aside, by 2021, there was still not a clear or operationalized definition to describe how home visitors and community health workers can work together most effectively. With the growing movement to include doulas as part of the perinatal care team, another segment of the workforce has emerged. As we said in our proposal: "The integration of community health workers into existing home visiting practice is novel and holds promise for creating synergies and greater efficiency in service delivery while also fostering social networks and leveraging community assets." Yet, how home visitors, community health workers, and doulas each play a role has not been well articulated in public policy or local action. Collaboration needs to be a value at all levels of organizations to build a continuum of services from prenatal to age three that uplifts mothers, their children, and their families. The opportunity for teamwork is great. The potential for creation of an effective continuum of support for families, providing the opportunity to better address their social determinants and supporting good parenting and life skills that will result in positive child development. Encouraging and operationalizing this particular type of collaboration is increasingly important as the federal government spends millions of dollars to both expand home visitor roles and increase the number of community health workers available as part of the response to the COVID-19 public health emergency.

StartStrong

StartStrong was a geographically focused initiative to redesign health-care delivery in the Avondale community adjacent to Cincinnati Children's. The project to reduce preterm birth rates was a collaborative effort among Cincinnati Children's, Good Samaritan Hospital, and ECS. The Avondale community had one of the highest infant mortality rates in Ohio. But following the focused StartStrong work and with dedicated and place-based efforts, at the end of the three-year grant period, the rates were better than the countywide average and no very preterm births were reported for 2015 to 2017.

Our engagement with the StartStrong project began with a request from a potential funder. Both ECS and Cincinnati Children's had made application for grant funding from Bethesda Inc. bi3 to address the high incidence of preterm birth in two low-income communities. The funders liked our proposals but asked that we combine them—exactly the right advice to encourage cooperative work. Through the three StartStrong years, we not only developed new strategies and alliances but also realized the benefit of working together with our partners Cincinnati Children's, Good Samaritan Hospital, and later the University of Cincinnati Medical Center and Cradle Cincinnati. Funding came from both Bethesda Inc. bi3 and Cincinnati Children's.

Community engagement and redesign was at the center of this effort. With the support of Bethesda Inc. bi3, three core areas were explored: 1) engaging the community to support pregnant women and their young children and to begin prenatal care as early as possible; 2) improving the referral and enrollment process to seamlessly connect women to community home-visitation programs and service agencies; and 3) improving the experience with healthcare and community support programs to increase mutual trust and communication.

Our primary takeaways were five: 1) an infrastructure is needed to support quality improvement training and data collection/analysis and to standardize best practices in prenatal care, 2) community outreach tools (family strong dinners, parent groups, block-by-block activation) make a difference, 3) transformation of prenatal care at clinics led to verified reduction in preterm birth, 4) ongoing innovation was necessary and 5) the social service referral system was inefficient.

Although our start-up year took longer than we had anticipated, by the end of the three-year period, we had good approaches in place to address the key issues and had collected sufficient data to verify what was working. We knew that leadership champions were required for success; that the systems, rather than just the people, needed to change; that opportunities existed to form cohesive partnerships; that competition among agencies delayed progress; and that common goals and regularly reported data were essential to engender trust and to ensure buy-in from all parties. However, not atypically, by the end of year three, funding was no longer available, and the formal work ended. Parts of the change that we had effected could be continued, most notably improved coordination within hospital prenatal clinics and improved customer service for mothers coming to the hospital for prenatal care. At ECS, we were able to use our StartStrong perinatal curriculum as a part of our overall work with perinatal moms. These were significant and important outcomes, but there was much that was lost.

Bethesda Inc. bi3 produced a StartStrong report as a part of its bi3 Learning Series to capture what happened with the project and to document what their investment produced. StartStrong is to be credited with truly focusing attention on infant mortality reduction in our community, as previous efforts, albeit well-meaning, had been scattered and episodic. Its funding commitment, augmented by Cincinnati Children's, and the work initiated over the three-year period, is viewed by Bethesda Inc. bi3 as germane to garnering public attention and leading to the current low infant mortality rate in Hamilton County.

What happened with StartStrong represents a typical challenge in community-level change. Philanthropy funds a project—for example, initial piloting or dissemination of a new strategy or evaluation of a new approach—the work occurs, and learnings are identified, but little really changes at the population or community level. The new approach and its demonstrated impact may become the subject of a professional journal article or a bullet point in an annual report. The gap is not closed between the philanthropic initial investment and the major public or private investment needed to sustain change and take the program to scale. Systems development or service transformation doesn't take hold. This failure to institutionalize positive changes also continually undermines the trust of families and communities. They become increasingly less likely to invest in community partnerships with nonprofit and governmental organizations, less trusting that their time and other resources will result in sustainable change.

Avondale Community Partnership

The Avondale Community partnership was one of the important collaborations in ECS history. By engaging the community of Avondale, we enhanced engagement in our program. It also gave an opportunity to understand how a focused effort in partnership with the community made a difference in program participation, mother-baby relationships, and levels of community support. Yet despite measurable success, we were never able to expand the funds to spread this partnership approach to other communities.

The Avondale partnership—and we deliberately called it a partnership—was launched in 2007 with private-sector funding obtained by then Cincinnati Children's and ECS board members Lee Carter, Thomas Cody, and David R. Walker. Our goal, over three years, was to build upon the success of Geoffrey Canada's Harlem Children's Zone by designing special community and collaborative programming for Avondale, the community that was home to Cincinnati Children's, ECS, 65 churches, and a population of approximately 10,000. Our idea was to concentrate on a community-based approach. We would partner with Avondale churches and other organizations serving challenged families to eliminate our Avondale waiting list and to enroll all eligible moms living in that city neighborhood. We would offer them not only home visiting but also links with a full range of services, everything from medical care to nutrition to safety to social connectedness and employment.

As we began to build relationships with the families, we were sobered by the daunting social, community, and system challenges they faced. Financial pressure, limited formal education, lack of employment opportunities, inadequate access to food, transportation, and affordable housing, exposure to drug dealing and violence—all were obvious obstacles to effective parenting. We were fortunate that Reverend Clarence Wallace, pastor of the Avondale Carmel Presbyterian church; Anita Brentley, ECS community coordinator; and CAA were energized by the possibilities the Avondale Partnership represented, and they skillfully led the initiative.

Through monthly moms' groups, a caring network pantry, health fairs, community walk-throughs, individual family follow-ups, frequent text messaging, the indefatigable work of community leaders Brentley and Wallace, ECS home visitors, and the CAA, we were able to enroll 85% of eligible Avondale moms, 70% of them prenatally. A detailed study of the community-based enrichment effort found a significant improvement in participation in home visiting among more than 2,000 families, compared to a group of peers who were not touched by this effort. Families reached by the community-engagement efforts stayed in the program longer, participated in a greater number of home visits, and lived in homes with children in stimulating environments for learning and development. Parents were acquiring new parenting skills, and it was truly exciting—and fun (Every Child Succeeds 2016; Folger et al. 2016).

A poignant conversation offered additional insights and opportunities for action. Brentley asked me to speak at one of the moms' group meetings to thank the many volunteers who showed up each month to make dinner, help with the babies, or lead a conversation group. After my talk, two young mothers with strollers approached me with their question: How can we volunteer too? We want to help. Here were two women with unimaginable stress and few financial resources offering to help others, to bring their lived experience and wisdom to our effort. Their question caused me to reflect and compare them to other women with too much time on their hands and too many resources, not able to get out of bed before 10:00 a.m.

Each moms' group meeting was an affirming event—the interaction among moms, home visitors, church members, and ECS staff was thrilling, people were happy and engaged, attendance ranged from 60–80 moms each month, church volunteers prepared dinner. Brentley believed in celebration, and we had ceremonies with presents for babies showing new teeth or taking their first steps, moms who continued breast-feeding or got jobs or attended school, dads who attended the moms' group meetings, dads who helped with parenting. We were building connections and fostering relationships, with parents and between parents and babies. The incidence of preterm births plummeted.

As manager, Brentley worked with the moms to create a mission statement for their moms' group. It took several meetings and careful thought but the words that they agreed upon are these, and they used this short statement to open each meeting: "Starting prenatally, we want healthy, happy babies. We want to become resourceful and instill goals and values in our children that will carry them into adulthood."

We were able to secure some special United Way funding for what they termed a Place Matters initiative. With those monies we hired some of the Avondale moms who participated in ECS to be community liaisons and present the services to other women in their community. Words from one of our liaison moms:

> One day Ms. Anita called to ask if I'd be interested in working part time for ECS as a community liaison. This is the perfect job for me—it is close to my home; I can bring my son and it involves recruiting first-time moms to be part of ECS. I like working in the pantry too. Some of our moms are really in need of the pantry, and I am glad that it is there for them, this is a beautiful program and I'm happy I'm in it. It's helping me raise my son to be somebody and succeed in life. I saw our pediatrician a few months ago and thanked him for referring us to ECS.

So, you might ask, "What happened?" Why wasn't this positive work continued in Avondale and other neighborhoods? The answer, like so many others, is simple—the money ran out. Without sustainable funding for our community work, the work had to end. Grant money most often is episodic. It is welcome, certainly, and provides opportunities to learn about new services or programs or to grow services. But there are few if any private-sector funds committed for long-term support, and public money typically pays for a basic service such as home visits but not much beyond that.

Even though we were able to document the success of the community engagement in Avondale, eventually the moms' groups were discontinued. The pantry closed, and our intensive ECS community focus ended. We wrote a community engagement manual for other communities to use, and we offered consulting services, but other communities faced the same problem that we did—recognition of the importance of community engagement but no funds to support it.

Ironically, evidence has continued to accumulate documenting how social determinants of health—neighborhood, income, family and household structure, social support, education—have an impact on health and healthy development. The US Department of Health and Human services reports on how social determinants of health also contribute to wide health disparities and inequities by race, income, and other factors (the website of the US Department of Health and Human Services, Office of Disease Prevention and Health Promotion, "Social Determinants of Health").

Who Is Poised to Be the Backbone of an Early Childhood System?

United Way as a Backbone Organization

United Way had been operating in the greater Cincinnati area for many decades when the ECS initiative was launched (United Way of Greater Cincinnati, LinkedIn). United Way of Greater Cincinnati, which partners with hundreds community-based agencies and nonprofits (website of the United Way of Greater Cincinnati, "Welcome to Our Nonprofit Portal"), began an intensified focus on young children and a program strategy based on collaboration by heeding the challenge from Pepper to the Haller task force to the steering committee. In many ways, United Way of Greater Cincinnati, with campaign contributions in excess of $50 million annually (UWGC 2020 *Annual Report*), was the logical organization to guide improved program integration community-wide. But one could also make a case for Cincinnati Children's or a new "backbone" organization or a large community organization with a strong community footprint. Whatever the structure, community will, accountability, transparency, visible and effective leadership, and a path to sustainability are essential. But most important, the focus needs to be clearly defined and maintained.

A focus on neutrality was critical going forward, because the mandate from the original work of the Blue Ribbon Task Force on Focus called for creating a framework so that all groups funded by the United Way and providing service to children would be asked to coordinate their work through an umbrella organization, and create interlocking sets of services for our community's children. The organization would have been required to analyze all the groups' work and report outcomes with precision and transparency. This would threaten agencies that would have difficulty meeting high standards, not only locally but also with the national shift toward greater government accountability and evidence-based practices.

One of the most contentious meetings I attended during my entire career was held by United Way to alert its 135 agencies to the new requirement to collect and report data—good, sound, verifiable data. ECS was set up to meet those requirements from day one, but many other groups had not collected data, didn't have anyone who knew how to do it, couldn't afford to hire additional staff, and generally were intimidated, wondering why, if they were doing good work, this was necessary. The audience erupted even though the United Way offered to provide technical assistance if needed. It was an emotional afternoon. The United Way president and board chair conducted the meeting and explained that donors were not only asking for validation for program outcomes but also would begin to require it. Long gone were the days when a philanthropist would be willing to send in a check to "do good" without feedback and/or evidence of outcomes effected by their contribution.

Nonprofit boards and senior leadership have a responsibility to hold agencies accountable for documenting effectiveness, which includes not only defining outcomes but also on occasion trying new strategies with the potential to achieve better outcomes.

Cincinnati Children's as a Convener

Nonprofit boards and senior leadership have a responsibility to hold agencies accountable for documenting effectiveness.

Having a major community institution as a convenor, patron, or parent organization can benefit nonprofit organizations in multiple ways. Considering Cincinnati Children's as the convener for this work reflects in principle what Children's itself has long advocated. Although as a free-standing pediatric hospital, Cincinnati Children's concentrates on clinical expertise, its leadership strategy has consistently emphasized a community commitment and the importance of community partnership. Its position has been to participate but not lead, understanding that no one knows what the community needs better than the community itself.

With its support for ECS and led by its former president, Michael Fisher, Cincinnati Children's has intentionally characterized its role as a partner, not the leader. It operates in a partnership with a willingness to bring formidable resources and expertise to the table, acknowledging that it does not have all of the answers. In other words, it sought to be a great collaborative partner even though it was understood that in many ways Cincinnati Children's is larger and more influential than the rest of us put together. Cincinnati Children's brings sizable resources, including in-kind services and access to the science, the rigor, the excellence that is emblematic of that organization.

Fisher's history with this expansive thinking extends over decades, beginning with his service on the United Way board, his role in the United Way 1999 major gifts campaign, his co-leadership of the 2003 United Way campaign with his wife, Suzette, and his willingness to make home visits with our families so that he could experience ECS's methods for himself. Fisher often describes sitting on the floor with the mom and the home visitor, hearing her story. He continued the example set by Cincinnati Children's leadership including prior CEO Jim Anderson and board members Lee Carter, Thomas Cody, Jane Portman, and Mark Jahnke, expanding the organization's commitment to the community.

When we began the journey that led to ECS, Anderson was president of Cincinnati Children's, and Carter was board chair. The two men initiated support for our endeavor with zeal. Fisher and subsequent board chair Jahnke advocated not only for the ECS outcomes but also high-quality program delivery, evaluation, and research. They had a good understanding that evidence-based home visiting is part of a solution to a complex problem that has been festering for generations—how to increase the life chances and opportunities of every child. Or, as longtime ECS board member and P&G CEO Pepper once told us, "Our situation (in the US) is morally and ethically wrong."

Lessons

1. See and seize opportunities for collaboration and systems building. Identify joint, mutually endorsed, and defined goals. Know that collaboration requires true and not perfunctory mutual decision-making. Sustained partnerships require synergy, shared interests, trust, and cooperative action.

2. Engage strong leadership. Brave, diverse, and strong leaders have the credibility and political clout to bring key partners together. Partners should include the families, the other consumers of your services, the workforce who delivers the services, and other nonprofit agencies, advocates, and policymakers.

3. Avoid territorialism. Encourage funders, policymakers, and program leaders to make decisions that encourage collaboration. Competition for scarce resources is an enemy of

collaboration. Press for resource allocation that leads to shared interest, effective collaboration, and sustainable outcomes.

4. Build a system, not a program. Use leadership and partnership to link programs more effectively in order to reduce balkanization, improve transparency and accountability, and create an accessible and equitable continuum of services for families.

5. Focus on long-term sustainability. Recognize that sustainability is not only dependent on predictable funding but also on wise leadership, program coordination, data sharing, mutually agreeable outcomes, and demonstration of value. Trying hard to do good is not enough. Results matter.

Chapter 6

Working with the Private Sector

Business Community Partnerships

ECS had the right team when it came to funding, professional development, business guidance, and decision-making. This was ECS's important advantage: Our business community supported us and was critical to our success in a variety of ways. When Pepper made Frank Smith, a senior P&G executive, available to us for a year to help us launch our program, we put processes and clear strategies in place that became the foundation for how we operated. What we knew then is that a nonprofit must have a strong business foundation to be successful and accomplish its mission. In the argot of the early childhood world—not only to strive but also to thrive.

Examples included tools for systematizing planning and priority setting by identifying the compelling improvement need—the value proposition—the killer issues and the reason to believe. Focus is essential not only in asking the hardest questions but also being clear-eyed about the answers. We had strategic OGSM analyses (objectives, goals, strategies, and measures) and STAR diagrams (structure, people, incentives, information sharing/decision making, tasks) for the more tactical work.

We used these tools to guide decision-making and were disciplined about our willingness to go back to basics when a problem or an opportunity arose. We committed ourselves to unifying our long-term direction, providing visible accountability, continually improving and learning from mistakes. In short, we accepted the challenge to assess our position, renew our commitment on a regular basis, and be courageous enough to make changes when they were warranted.

Walker, in his role as both ECS board chair and mentor, asked questions that were pointed and strategic. He wanted to see plans and proposals concerning agency profitability, maintaining quality, the real cost of service, the ability to build capacity internally and externally, the availability of government funding, and whether we were separating long-term strategic choices from near-term decisions.

Our for-profit business guides nearly always led with an admonition: run ECS like a business with market knowledge, subject expertise, data, and measurement. Ask the right questions, the hard questions. Identify the "killer issue," get to root causes, continue to explore and clarify our value propositions, reject facile explanations, focus.

Examples from a senior P&G executive and ECS board member included these questions more than once: What are the most critical ECS goals that we absolutely must achieve over the next twelve months, over the next three-to-five years? What are the most foundational priorities—the no-miss action plans? What are new capabilities that we may not have today but that need to be developed? What are ongoing optimizations/improvements for what we are already working on today? Are we, as a board, and as a program, organized and structured to implement the most foundational actions we need in the next three-to-six months?

And from our P&G colleagues, we were encouraged to confine answers to one page and never use more than seven words on a slide in a presentation. If people are reading your slides or you are, the audience is not paying attention to what you would like them to know.

Another board member described our situation this way: We do not have laurels to sit on. Actually, no sitting is allowed.

The need for leadership that was focused, analytical, coura-geous, and thoughtful led to three recommended questions—call them "join-up" topics for potential board members or for anyone who might become the voice or the face of ECS in the community:

1. What are the three most important things that you would like to see ECS accomplish over the next two years?
2. And for you, personally, what would you like to do over roughly the same time period?
3. What do you think are the top one to three problems that ECS faces and what are the three opportunities?

Here is an example of how we applied those questions to our operation: When community pressure arose about reaching all mothers in the community or providing services beyond home vis-itation, Walker, as our board chair, effectively brought us back to the massive work we had already promised to do, letting us know that our focus was on the big assignment that we had accepted but not yet accomplished. We quietly but emphatically rejected those community requests, mindful of the P&G saying, "Make a little, sell a little, learn a lot." The point being that we needed to get experience on a small scale, learn what works, and expand that later. That is what we did.

But the help and guidance didn't stop with P&G. There was an entire group from our business community who stepped forward and, as I told *The Wall Street Journal* for an article that appeared on page one June 20, 2006, brought us time and ideas from the kinds of minds we couldn't afford to buy. As a leader I have always welcomed a strong management team, people smarter and more accomplished than I am but who also bring the same work ethic and are focused on the same cause. With our business-minded partners, we were able to amplify our ideas and receive new ones, making the partnership the best of both worlds.

Acknowledging that we would probably always be swimming or rafting in "permanent whitewater," we focused on our mission, made solid decisions even when they were difficult, documented our progress, and ensured that the investment made in us was well founded. Our friends in the private-sector world provided invaluable guidance.

There is a story here, too, from Walker, who let us know why he has spent nearly 40 years volunteering at senior levels for non-profit organizations and making sizable financial contributions. He explains it this way:

> I am a firm believer that people with business skills should become involved in helping their communities become better places to live. This value was impressed upon me during my career at P&G. But sometimes, people leave some of what they know at the door when they get involved in community work. We accept conditions in our communities which are not acceptable—assuming the problems are just too big and too persistent to be solved. I don't accept that—never have and never will. So, I hope that my legacy with nonprofits I worked with is that I pushed myself and everyone else around me to make a larger difference than we have before.

An essential lesson for any nonprofit is this: An initiative must be able to survive as a business to even begin to deliver the social mission. We were fortunate to have outstanding guidance; to our credit, we were able to maintain our focus for more than two decades. Following recommendations and guidance from the business community allowed us to create a nationally recognized and applauded program. But even with our good advice and our entrepreneurial spirit, there is an essential limiting factor: Nearly unsurmountable challenges placed upon nonprofits frequently cause them to be unable to deliver on what they know to be true. Remedies come in the form of funders who demand verifiable outcomes, improved coordination among organizations working on the same problem, and funding that supports research and development rather than just service alone.

Strategically, the close relationship with our business community brought foundational design, growth, and systems development

> An initiative must be able to survive as a business to even begin to deliver the social mission.

based upon best business practices. Among the advantages and knowledge our partnership provided and nurtured:

- The importance of clearly defining the problem to be solved and using a stringent, candid structure to ensure that the root cause is clearly identified
- The opportunity to access the "kinds of minds we couldn't afford to buy"
- The open doors for meetings with people influential in the community and the fertile ground for the development of community will
- The emphasis upon accountability and return on investment
- The willingness to stop something that isn't working
- The ability to leverage public money with private dollars to enhance program quality, and be as innovative as funds allow
- The respect in the community that comes with support and approbation from business leaders
- The integration of the need to find creative solutions rather than saying no to opportunities
- The significance of collaboration and a systems approach to solving problems

Our business partners taught us skills of negotiation and demonstrated tools to manage our work: Red Green Charts for quality assurance, dashboards and data requirements identifying the crucial numbers and information needed for good decision-making, and the benefits of understanding our competitive advantage and our outcomes. Crucially, our friends in the business world continued to let us know that our work mattered and that, regardless of the internal and outside pressure, we must never give up.

Deloitte Organizational Assessment

In 2000, soon after we opened our doors, and with the recommendation from our founding partners, the Health Foundation of Greater Cincinnati (now Interact for Health) commissioned

Deloitte, a leading business consulting and professional services firm, to conduct a "thorough organizational assessment of (our) management structure and span, critical business processes, provider relationships and performance metrics." In its report, Deloitte commended the community leaders who committed time and energy to develop ECS and who envisioned a quality program supported by a collaboration of business, nonprofit, and academic leadership. Their assessment included the following key findings:

1. Exceptional progress has been made in a short time.
2. Collaboratives can be beneficial but require respect, trust, and nurturing.
3. Agency growth will require more clear definition of management roles and responsibilities.
4. Sustainable funding and demonstrable outcomes are key.
5. Detailed business planning, including capacity and utilization, are vital to success.
6. Process and outcomes measures need better definition and presentation.
7. Subjective and informal measurements are implemented more often and consistently than are quantitative measures.

The assessment from Deloitte came after we had been operational for about 18 months. It reinforced what we knew and offered a valuable critical appraisal as well as ongoing guidance for our work.

IDEO

In 2010, as a result of my receipt of the Purpose Prize, I had the opportunity to attend a session with the IDEO group in California. Long recognized as a leader in human-centered design, IDEO provided a context for me to think about how we at ECS could clarify problems that needed to be solved. Remembering our P&G guidance about addressing the killer issue and solving the most limiting factor first, I was eager to better understand the logic model employed by the IDEO group.

Working with them was fun and thought-provoking as we moved away from the constraints and restraints that too often control us, and try to find creative but realistic solutions to problems. Basically, what I learned was this: Study how people behave in their environment, go out and actually see it. Tell stories about what you saw and felt, break down the stories into manageable pieces—a concept that, like Goldilocks found in the Three Bears' home, is not too big but "just right." Actually, create a prototype that you can walk through. For me that meant going through every step of the process in my mind, maybe creating a roadmap, maybe using props, but in some way putting myself in the shoes of one of our moms or one of our babies or one of our referring counselors. And finally, present ideas as experiments, allowing co-creation. In our case, the solutions must always include wisdom and guidance from our families.

Focus

If there is one single message here that has been the underpinning of our success, it is *be focused*—be clear about what we planned to do, how we planned to do it, and why we chose this path. What we learned early on is that if goals are not clearly defined—focused— there always exists the tendency to broaden the lane and move a little beyond the plan for funding sources, for "mission creep," for joining a new initiative. The guidance about focus came from P&G but also from our longtime advocate and board chair, Jim Spurlino. As a successful small businessperson with a fervent interest in early childhood, Spurlino exhorted us to always go back to the original questions: the Toyota "five whys," ensuring that we were remaining committed to our original purpose and staying in our lane.

In his book *Business Bullseye*, Spurlino explains how to "take dead aim and achieve great success," a concept applicable to nonprofit and for-profit enterprises alike. One graphic example of Spurlino's thinking continues to be part of his public comments. His business, building materials, concentrated on concrete

> If goals are not clearly defined—focused— there always exists the tendency to broaden the lane and move a little beyond the plan.

foundations for large structures. When he talked about early child-hood and ECS, he often used good construction as a metaphor for the importance of the early years, the foundation laid during the first 1,000 days of life. This was both a visual and true depiction.

In another indispensable way, Spurlino, from a small-business perspective, provided an important lesson—just saying "no" or offering an excuse is almost never the right way to solve a problem. Rather, before closing the door to an opportunity, be creative about how to address it or find another way to make it happen. An example is text messaging with families when phone minutes don't work or meeting a family at the library when going into the home isn't advisable. Our pandemic response was testament to our ability to find new ways to serve families when going into the home or being together wasn't possible.

The Strategic Business Plan

The business plan that we wrote for ECS provided the blueprint for how the work would occur and who must be involved—the partners, the board, the funders, the agencies, the community members, the challenged families. We knew that guidance from our colleagues in the business community was essential for success. Involvement of large and small business leaders allowed ECS to be constructed on a firm foundation using the best principles of private enterprise so that we could respond to vagaries in the marketplace, the advent of competition, and opportunities for growth. Sometimes we say that there is P&G DNA in ECS and it has made us infinitely stronger. We have always been exhorted to clearly define our "unique selling proposition" and "reason to believe," advice from the world's largest and highly successful marketer.

The business plan that we presented in April 1998 had seven key components: the implementation strategy, the partners, the structure, the funding, the evaluation process, the marketing, and the timing. Those elements formed the blueprint for our work going forward. We characterized our work as moving away from incrementalism and focusing on prevention and celebrating children and their ultimate success.

By October 1998, we had a good list of the critical tasks that we needed to accomplish to open our doors for families. They were meticulously crafted, well researched and community informed. The tenets in the April 1998 business plan resulted in a strong program launch in March 1999 and their relevancy endures:

1. Contract development with multiple service delivery organizations and the states of Ohio and Kentucky

2. Quality improvement (QI) and evaluation protocols focused on both program operation and family outcomes

3. Funding and fiscal management structures to support internal operations and budgets, legal and IRS requirements

4. Marketing to create community awareness and boost voluntary enrollment of moms

5. Board identification to develop and delineate roles and assignments

6. Provider council (now lead agency) to begin engagement and collaboration process

7. People/staff to secure consultants where needed, hire staff, and determine which services will be provided by partners

8. Program to inventory referral sources, set up proper training, determine the best program elements, and make neighborhood/agency assignments

9. RFPs for program to determine which agencies want to operate the Nurse-Family Partnership and Healthy Families America models (other models ultimately used as well)

10. Outcome monitoring and information systems to describe primary and secondary outcomes and the computer hardware, software, personnel, and facilities for home visit service coordination, training, and outcomes assessment

The Public-Private-Sector Partnership

In other chapters, this book provides further detail to amplify and describe how ECS was able to construct and maintain the public-private partnership that allowed us to go beyond the basic public-sector funding and do—albeit in a small way—what Pallotta compellingly urges in his book *Uncharitable* (2008). Our nonprofit organization benefited from our public-private partnership but was still constrained by our inability to benefit from the opportunities that free-market capitalism allows. For a variety of programs that we piloted and demonstrated as effective, we could not secure funding to keep them going. In some of these, learnings and opportunities were lost, and money was not well invested. We did not sufficiently build upon what was working and failed to keep commitments that could have built more trust with the families and communities we aimed to serve.

Linking Home Visiting with Pediatric Primary Care

An attempt at improved program coordination was illustrated through a proposal we wrote to develop mechanisms to link home visiting more closely with pediatric primary care. Even though research studies and national recommendations pointed to the potential positive impact of such an alignment, it had not been widely implemented. ECS could be, we argued, a good resource for a busy pediatric office where the doctor typically has only minutes to spend with each patient. If the physician were able to use ECS as a resource, and refer the child to a professional home visitor, that home visitor could address nonclinical issues—the social determinants of health—as well as support the family in using recommended health services. By maintaining close links to and accountability with the health provider, the result could be improved service by the home visitor who would have additional information about the family to guide her work. Such links could also be a reliable resource for the pediatric primary care provider to address issues that couldn't be managed in an office setting.

A few small-scale research studies elsewhere had identified opportunities for improved engagement to better integrate services and systems, support the medical home, focus on healthy development and two-generational well-being, optimize existing capacity, and engage and empower families. Using our private-sector resources and the support of pediatric care leaders at Cincinnati Children's, we began designing small tests of change (e.g., getting family permission, using the medical record, sifting workflow), and we were successful.

We prepared a proposal for a project called "Integrating home visiting and primary care to improve child and family outcomes." Its purpose was to increase the efficiency, effectiveness, and quality of both home visiting and pediatric primary care through service integration. We then approached several national, state, and local foundations to seek funding for a demonstration project but were unsuccessful. The health foundations said they did not fund home visiting efforts, while those funders committed to home visiting told us they did not fund primary health care projects. We could identify no philanthropic sources of funds willing to step away from their siloed investment portfolio. We also could not identify a way to use government home visiting funds, other than public grants or Medicaid dollars, to launch this effort. While national expert recommendations continue to call for greater collaboration and linkage between home visiting and primary care, the promise of such efforts has not been fulfilled in greater Cincinnati or on a wide scale elsewhere.

University of Michigan Ross School of Business

The involvement of the business community and our business orientation was highlighted again in 2006, when we were asked by the University of Michigan Ross School of Business to present at a conference for graduate students enrolled in the nonprofit management curriculum. Al Spector, retired P&G executive and longtime ECS volunteer, and I made the trip to Ann Arbor to participate in the university's social-enterprise symposium, "Quantifiable Outcomes to Support Funding Requests." Our topic was: "Real People, Real Issues, Real Solutions." The symposium leaders were intrigued with our close relationship with the business community and our focus on evidence-based decision-making. They told us we were 10 years ahead of our time. We were honored to be included.

The keynote speaker, Bo Burlingham, then editor of *Inc.* magazine, talked about his new book, *Small Giants: Companies That Choose to Be Great Instead of Big* (2005). The book focused on businesses who decided to remain small and, one would imagine, more manageable. Fortunately for all of us, one of the businesses he highlighted was the Katzingers Group in Ann Arbor, purveyor of a variety of wonderful food products and services that they liberally shared with us. Burlingham let us know that Katzingers was an outstanding example of why unbridled growth, as appealing as it may look on paper, is not always the best strategy to maintaining quality and control.

Spector and I focused on our relationship with private business—how it happened and why it mattered. We were gratified when the Michigan group complimented us, saying that we were far ahead of most social service organizations in terms of applying principles of entrepreneurship to a nonprofit organization.

To provide experience for their students and to help nonprofits, the Ross School created what it called a "domestic corps" so that organizations like ours could apply to have an MBA student assigned to us for a summer internship. Ethicon Endo-Surgery paid for the engagement with Ram Kapadia. We applied and were fortunate to have Ram Kapadia work with us in Cincinnati to create a financial model for ECS. His assignment was to analyze growth opportunities, including fiscal and personnel requirements, and at the same time, provide answers to a central question: What is a principled approach to growth, and what are the challenges?

Marketing: Procter and Gamble and Others

Nonprofit Marketing

As we considered how to best market our program, a single image became ubiquitous—a simple side-by-side illustration compared the brain of an infant swaddled and not stimulated and another infant with many sensory opportunities. In one brain, there were large dark spaces where synapses failed to close. The other was vibrant and full. From the beginning we emphasized that professional home visiting was vital to support many families to help their children achieve their best possible start. We used the dual brain image on publications and slide decks, in videos and as a part of most of our presentations, because there in stark contrast was the actual picture of why our work was so important. We could see the visible effect of early stimulation and exuberant brain development for an infant. Effective home visiting was viewed as a way to promote optimal brain development and the foundational relationships that support parents and children for a lifetime.

Our initial public awareness campaign worked, and we had extraordinary free and voluntary support, but what happened to us early on was only one component of larger marketing/branding difficulties for ECS and arguably for most nonprofits.

Marketing and messaging at ECS had two broad audiences. The first was the public at large, including the stakeholders, the funders, and the families we were working to enroll. Then there was the internal audience, the moms who are part of ECS, the home visitors who serve them, and the organizations that refer to us.

Unfortunately, marketing and branding are two areas that rarely get the attention that they need at nonprofits. Seen as too "commercial" or expensive or money spent on something other than the direct service, marketing budgets are too small and/or the first to be cut when a budget adjustment is needed. Further, marketing money does not come from public sources; rather, it requires grants or philanthropy or other nonpublic sources.

Compelling Words and Frameworks

We have been aware, since soon after the launch of ECS in 1999, that the language we were using to describe our work and its importance was not always compelling and was not reaching the people we needed to reach—moms in the community. Further, we knew that we had to do a better job convincing funders from both the public and private sectors that investment in evidence-based home visiting programs was a sound choice.

In 2018, David Willis, MD, with support from the Perigee Fund, launched a national initiative focused on early relational health. Among other things, Willis worked with the Frameworks Institute to better describe the "what and the why" of early relational health and to create a framework that would allow improved communication with the general public. Through the Frameworks' early relational health survey, we were able to identify word and concept choices that would resonate with our stakeholders and our families as we worked to encourage support and enroll moms. Frameworks reminded us to emphasize the following in our messaging:

> The foundational relationships that babies and toddlers experience with all of their caregivers provide the stability and supports needed for their health, development, and well-being. When we focus on this foundation and foster stronger early relationships, children and their caregivers thrive. The two-way nature of early relationships affects two-generational health and well-being in the moment and long term. (Willis and FrameWorks Institute 2020, 5)

The work by Willis and his colleagues at the Center for the Study of Social Policy and previously at the Perigee Fund and in federal government roles urged us always to keep two essential questions in mind: How is the child doing? How is the parent doing? Then tell the stories that reflect recommendations from Willis and our P&G marketing consultants—show how relationships are joyful and gratifying, and focus on the positive, early and often. Be concrete and be alert to what we as a program can learn from parents.

Defining the Reason to Believe

We were fortunate in greater Cincinnati, because we not only had the approval of the business community but also guidance from P&G. The P&G folks understood messaging for both the groups we needed to reach. They let us know that we needed strong and recognizable external branding that emphasized the reason to believe in our work and to clearly define our role and our key outcomes. We needed to let the community know how we were making a difference and needed to highlight our key strategic partners. This would encourage participation by other groups and organizations.

In 2010, we were able to meet with one of P&G's senior marketing directors, to help us plan both our messaging and our strategy. With him we concentrated on how best to touch and improve lives for our moms, to have the consumer value and benefit from the product. He urged us to emphasize the positive: encourage and celebrate success, rather than highlighting developmental problems or something that isn't going well. Among his recommendations were: Let mom know that she is making progress, use rewards, and most importantly, build in delight for mom and child, continually reinforcing what is good.

He urged us to get clues and guidance by paying attention to what a mom says or doesn't say or when she doesn't respond. The nonverbal cues and clues matter, he made clear. He encouraged reviewing the data, of course, and keeping the objective measures in mind. Most important, he encouraged us to establish trust and generate confidence by responding to what moms need and celebrating things large and small.

Remember, this experienced marketing executive cautioned, the mother is never wrong, even if she isn't doing the right thing. The role of the home visitor—and it isn't easy—is to begin with respect for the mother and her ideas and to weave her accomplishments into the program and curriculum each day.

He further suggested that we think about our outcomes/ achievements with families in three-month rather than one-month segments, because the longer time period offers a better gauge of progress. Again, part of the role of the home visitor is to celebrate accomplishments, and having real, sustainable changes to talk about adds credence to the relationship. Finally, he told us that there is a difference between an expert system and a system run by experts. It is the expert system that can be scaled, and at ECS, he said, we had developed the expertise and now needed the expert system.

Belonging

Because we understood the significance of delight, celebration, and positive reinforcement in the relationships we encouraged with the home visitors and the families, we began to concentrate on promoting a concept of "belonging" for our mothers. We were aware that most people want to be part of something larger than themselves. We hoped to address the social isolation endemic with ECS families and the stresses that come with unsafe neighborhoods, too little income, racism, single parenthood, and other challenges to family well-being and relational health. So we began offering safe, positive group experiences, as well as themed logo wear and purple bags to give tangible reminders of being connected. Our messaging emphasized not only our services and our availability but our caring and our belief in our moms. Our message was: We are here for you, we care, and you belong.

Parents and children today are often separated from their biological families, and they welcome the opportunity to create a new extended "family." Each month when the Avondale Mom's Group met, young women who lived close to one another but were often unacquainted, became friends through the group. It was fun to see them arrive together, pushing strollers, animatedly talking and laughing, finding friends and social support—being less alone.

These experiences taught us the power of connection, belonging, and relationships.

Joining ECS meant that families were willing to share their time with us and to accept the vulnerability that comes when a new person wants to visit with them in their homes on a regular schedule for up to three years. The newness part disappears quickly as the mother and the home visitor develop their relationship. And to the mother's credit, she begins to participate in the home visitor sessions, trying new ideas, using new resources, and providing information. Slowly, with open and honest communication, our mothers tell us that they begin to feel that they belong to a group that values her and her child. None of this happens without trust and valid connection.

The mothers frequently talked about belonging to ECS and about feeling safe and protected. During the pandemic, the mothers called their home visitors their lifelines.

What did this concept of "belonging" mean? For ECS, and no doubt for many other nonprofits, it meant making promises to those we served, promises of respect and caring, safety and trust—and keeping them. Whether mothers with new babies, seniors aiming to stay living in their homes, vulnerable youth, or another population served by a nonprofit, community-based organization, building trust, increasing safety, and keeping promises is fundamental to success.

The families prioritized the well-being of their children, were willing to learn and act on it in their daily lives, and wanted to be part of something bigger. They wanted to advocate for their children as they became more confident as parents, creating a good support system for themselves and their children. Families in ECS were wonderfully resilient, and by belonging to ECS, they were able to amplify their strengths. Moms voluntarily joined ECS because they wanted to learn and grow with a group of like-minded women, and they believed that becoming part of ECS had value. The ECS role was to ensure that their engagement with us met their expectations.

The Branding Issue

By 2018, we determined that it was time to refresh and reexamine our brand strategy and positioning in the marketplace. The environment had changed with new programs, improved program offerings, and funding opportunities from both Ohio and Kentucky health agencies. ECS home visits and enrollment had gone down 20% since 2016. We wanted to improve the appropriateness of our referrals, reduce the time from referral to engagement, and retain more families in the program once they joined. We saw our primary task as finding and engaging families.

Kay Johnson, consultant extraordinaire, quoted from Laurel Cutler, a branding leader, futurist, and advertising executive—in 1987 called by *Inc.* magazine one of Madison Avenue's most powerful women (website of *Inc.*, "Futurist Laurel Cutler")—explained branding this way: "A brand is more than a visual identity, the name, logo and graphic design used by an organization. A brand is a psychological construct held in the minds of all those aware of the branded product, person, organization or movement. Brand management is the work of managing those psychological associations. In the for-profit world, marketing professionals talk of creating a 'total brand experience.' In the nonprofit world, executives talk more about their 'global identity' and what and why of the organization, but the point in both cases is that branding goes far beyond the logo."

Challenges to Moving Forward with Branding

We felt ready to move forward and naively thought that we could base our next steps on what we thought were the answers to three primary questions:

1. What is the problem we are trying to solve?
2. What is our competitive advantage?
3. What strategies must we employ to regain awareness and market share?

But a candid and cautionary advisory email from two ECS board members with extraordinary marketing insight, Fama Francisco, CEO of Baby and Feminine Care at P&G, and Bryan Hamilton, formerly at P&G and now vice president of marketing and communications at Cincinnati Children's, caused us to step back and reconsider what to do next. The P&G duo told us that we had two significant challenges to face before we began redesigning our communication materials—which should be the last step in the process, not the first. Addressing the killer issues was basic to the program and the board needed to be involved in decision-making.

The first killer issue was inadequate program funding. Like most nonprofits, funding streams cannot be taken for granted; new streams need to be identified and cultivated long before they may be needed. Could we find new sources of funding in the next six-to-18 months? Could we partner with another agency, privatize part of the service, determine how to do more with less, assume a smaller organization serving fewer families, something else?

The second killer issue was how to widen the funnel that brings new moms to us. In order to capture the target audience, an organization must cast a wide net. This should be done knowing that every contact will not end up in a successful partnership, but that those who are served by your organization need to move through smoothly. Do we understand what the current funnel looks like and why? Do we know how many moms we can really serve in a year? Do we have sufficient staff capacity? Are there other agencies or partnerships that could help to widen the funnel and achieve a win/win? Without clear answers to these questions, new communication materials would have limited impact. Further, they advised, when we do revise our marketing materials, they must be more consistent, have a more visible identity, use program language that isn't so academic, that speaks to our target moms, and is crisp and actionable. The P&G pair urged a brand that is simple, differentiated, and unified.

> Your brand needs to be simple, differentiated, and unified.

We followed their advice, engaging the board and defining a path forward. On the money side, the Ohio Department of Health was willing to raise its funding rate, a small increase but an increase, nonetheless. We launched a successful philanthropic fundraising campaign and raised over $4 million, ending just as the COVID-19 pandemic began (website of Bethesda Inc. bi3, June 15, 2022).

For the referral piece, we renewed and expanded our efforts to engage moms both by working more closely with referral sources and improving our internal processes for enrolling moms once we had received their names. Limits on capacity, especially in a small organization, can have crippling effects on outcomes and success rates. Having enough home visitors continued to be a problem, and that was probably the single biggest operational deterrent to growth.

Following Francisco and Hamilton's marketing guidance, we prepared a request for proposal (RFP) to hire a firm to help us create a consistent and easily understood ECS brand presence. It would be one in which our communication materials offered uniform language, logo, and messaging. We hoped to stand out among competing service providers and resonate with families eligible for our home visiting program and with our referral and funding sources.

The admonitions from P&G were apt and continued to guide not only what our marketing materials said but also to inform program growth. We could not promise what we could not deliver and without enough home visitors, mothers would be put on a waiting list. This would amount to poor service for the mother who wanted help now and would discourage referral sources who had been asked to make more referrals. This could amount to disappointing messages to a community whom we had asked for support.

The next step was creating the strategy to regain our leadership role. That is where hiring an agency became paramount. Like many other nonprofits we had limited money to spend on marketing/communications, and our dependence upon our own staff, freelance workers, and volunteer hours had led to the confused ECS image so clearly visible to our P&G marketing advisors. We determined that we needed to move beyond our piecemeal

Basic Questions and Answers

We looked back to the three basic questions and had some answers: 1) We knew what the problems were that we were trying to solve; 2) We could identify our competitive advantages; 3) We offered eight strong reasons to believe in us, our competitive advantages:

1. Families were happy and satisfied.
2. Home visitors were experienced and empathic, helping families deliver on their life goals.
3. Board members were active and committed.
4. Cincinnati Children's, the CAA, and United Way continued to be supportive.
5. The ECS brand had some national recognition, emblematic of quality and collaboration, especially in the home visiting field.
6. Eight provider agencies had been with us for 20 years, working in a transparent, mutually beneficial way.
7. We had documented outcomes from 28,000 families and over 700,000 home visits.
8. ECS was seen as helping to create responsible citizens, healthy children, and a strong workforce.

And the problems that we needed to solve:

1. Private philanthropic support had decreased.
2. ECS was meeting less of the need for its services.
3. ECS (and home visiting generally) was complex, multi-factorial, and difficult to describe.
4. Home visiting has been shown to have pejorative connotations as moms are concerned that children will be removed from the home and/or the home environment will be reported to authority figures.
5. Hiring home visitors and maintaining a full complement of home visitors is an escalating problem.
6. The words *home visiting* and *home visitor* do not test well and are being used generically.
7. ECS was not using social media effectively to engage moms for whom social media is how they communicate.
8. The marketplace was now highly competitive and other splashier organizations are more visible.

work to something more impactful and reflective not only of our achievements but also the services that came with joining ECS.

Time Warner

In the early days, television and radio stations would often accept public-sector social service messaging, but the nonprofit had to be able to create the video or the audiotape to be placed on the various channels. We didn't have the money to even create what could become a public service announcement to send our message out into the wider world.

Soon after we opened our doors, Time Warner Cable (now Spectrum) stepped in to help. They produced four different public service announcements (PSAs) for us and aired them on a frequent and timely schedule. We estimated that the annualized value of the contribution was close to $300,000. We used their warm, nurturing spots to generate emotional appeal, making them part of a series so that one message could build upon another. The objective: Encourage moms to enroll in ECS and educate all moms in the community about the value of early nurturing for babies. As the PSAs were included in the Time Warner viewing schedule, two to three moms each day let us know that they learned about ECS through our public service announcements.

In addition to sponsoring our first annual ECS Mother's Day party with hundreds of moms in attendance, Time Warner proved to be an exceptional conduit to TV channels, media coverage, Roadrunner, and other early forms of internet access. They helped us get coverage in *Parenting* and *Baby Talk* magazines and their own large monthly Time Warner printed (then!) TV schedule. We were even featured on the cover.

Time Warner joined other major Cincinnati area businesses, including P&G, the Kroger Company, Federated Department Stores, and Cincinnati Bell to support what became our large regional partnership. All of these companies and more were leaders in promoting a high quality of life in greater Cincinnati, and they saw ECS as a key to what we needed to do for families.

Dissemination of ECS to Other Communities

In 2007, as we began to assess our success and think about how we could expand our reach, we explored the possibility of taking our ECS program to other communities as our national presence grew, and other communities approached us about replicating our program. We couldn't really call ourselves a "model" because we were not a model in the sense that the Nurse-Family Partnership, Healthy Families America, or Parents As Teachers were home visiting program models. But how else to describe our work? What we had was a regional operation delivering enhanced evidence-based home visiting through multiple community-based agencies. We had built what we had on the strength of what the model developers and other researchers had learned, and we hoped to make the services even better. One of our then board members and later board chair explained as we deliberated our dilemma that it was like putting good chocolate and good peanut butter together and creating something even better—the Reese's Peanut Butter Cup.

We talked with contacts that we had at the Arkansas Children's Hospital and made several trips to Little Rock to exchange information. Excitement was high. There seemed to be an opportunity to grow the existing Arkansas program using elements from ECS. We offered as benefits the business approach, the management structure for billing, marketing, data collection, evaluation, quality and system improvement, program and curriculum development, training, robust research, compelling outcomes, and the advantages of public-private funding. And the "products"—Bringing Literacy to the homes of birth-to-three-year olds, success priorities, maternal depression treatment, medical home protocol, and ECS enriched curricula.

Arkansas's clinical pediatric leadership was especially intrigued with the involvement of our Cincinnati Children's and how that relationship supported the medical center's teaching mission, as well as research and community care. Ultimately, funding wasn't available from private sources for either program delivery or administration, and the state policy makers decided to stay with the traditional models, even though there were significant reasons to make changes. Therein lies a challenge in the nonprofit world.

We also explored collaboration in our neighboring state of West Virginia, because its private-sector banking and community organizations approached us and were interested in what we were doing. I grew up in West Virginia, my father practiced pediatrics there for decades, and when he retired from private practice he became the state's Director of Maternal and Child Health. I had written the West Virginia emergency medical plan as a graduate student. The West Virginia business leadership was seeking new programming for young children. Again, there were meetings, visits, and information exchanged and promises made. We had learned with Arkansas that we needed to be better prepared to ask the right questions:

1. What home visiting programs do you have that are designed to serve pregnant women and parents with children ages birth to three? What geography do you serve? Who is the organizer? How long have the programs been in existence? Are they affiliated with the national models? How many families are being served? How many home visitors? What is your annual budget and the sources of funding?

2. How has the state used the federal MIECHV funds to structure a home visiting system? What models are being funded with federal/state dollars? What requirements does the state have for local home visiting programs?

3. What is the level of need? How many at-risk moms? First-time moms? What is the infant-mortality rate in the geography you serve?

We moved forward at both sites with guidance and requirements from our board and our business advisors: Make sure that all costs are covered by the new communities, be sure that there will be no impact on the local program as we continue to grow our ECS approach. Do not add staff without a funding source, and be extra careful about how and when to formally transfer knowledge. Most important: make sure that there is tangible benefit to ECS-Cincinnati, preserving the quality of the ECS brand and ensuring that the organization will willingly comply with our transparency and data collection protocols. Measure performance and monitor standards.

What could we offer the new location? Surely, our know-how and best practices; our concentration on a system approach rather than on piecemeal components; research and scientific direction; a continuous quality improvement system; capacity to deliver multiple evidence-based home visiting models; the ECS service model, program, training and course materials; the eECS data platform; and the use of the ECS trademark and logo along with ongoing consultation and centralized shared services, just as we were doing with our disseminated but centralized ECS provider agencies.

A tangible benefit to ECS would be the ability to share central office costs, thereby freeing dollars to expand the number of families we could enroll in Cincinnati. We examined types of fee structures or a form of a franchise model, and although any profit margin would be small to nonexistent, we would be able to share overhead and thereby expand the number of families.

The value proposition was clear: The new community would receive a turn-key home visiting system with demonstrated best practices, established credibility, program enhancements, reduced start-up costs, and the centralized administrative functions at a fraction of the cost. For Cincinnati, we would have all dissemination costs covered, shared support for centralized functions, reinforced credibility for the ECS program itself, and opportunities to use additional national, state, and local funding sources.

We had proposed pilot projects in both Arkansas and West Virginia. But to move forward, the states needed to receive their appropriate approvals, and we needed to find a $300,000 grant to ECS to fund upfront costs for our first community (dissemination costs per community would decrease as more sites were added) and to hire an ECS business-development director to initiate dissemination tasks and to assemble a dissemination advisory board.

That did not happen because we could not find the $300,000 in seed money needed to get the project off the ground. The situation represents a good example of why nonprofits are typically unable to fulfill their potential for growth even when validation and opportunity are established and the need is clear. The funds were simply not available to us to go forward.

Program replication/scaling is not without enormous challenge. In Spring 2003, the *Stanford Social Innovation Review* published what I continue to view as the seminal work on the subject, "Going to Scale: The Challenge of Replicating Social Programs" by Jeffrey L. Bradach (2003). Here are two excerpts:

> The nonprofit sector in the United States is comprised of cottage enterprises—thousands upon thousands of programs, each operating in a single neighborhood, in a single city or town. Often, this may be the most appropriate form of organization, but in some—perhaps many—cases, it represents a substantial loss to society overall. Time, funds and imagination are poured into new programs that at best reinvent the wheel, while the potential of programs that have already proven their effectiveness remains sadly underdeveloped.
>
> One impediment to replication is the prevailing bias among funders to support innovative "breakthrough ideas". . . The objective is to reproduce a successful program's results, not to slavishly recreate every one of its features. (Bradach 2003, 19)
>
> . . . The fact that dollars seldom follow success is one of the most vexing challenges nonprofit leaders face. Proven solutions to pressing problems do not spread . . . for the most part, the funding patterns of the nonprofit sector—small grants, for short durations, focused on program work—conspire against building strong organizations. (Bradach 2003, 24)

Even when validation, opportunity, and need are established, lack of funding often stands in the way of expansion which can lead to economies of scale and a thriving organization.

ECS has been driven by an entrepreneurial spirit from the beginning. I credit our private-sector guides for helping us to view the world with innovative ideas and creative problem solving. We always were looking for new information to improve our work and for new ways to share what we were learning with our colleagues. Certainly, our attempts to disseminate ECS to Arkansas and West Virginia are examples. There is a strong economic motive as well. Having new sources of revenue that are not dependent upon grants and donations means that the organization itself, in this case, ECS, could begin to move toward independence, at least in part. A program like ours will always need public monies for the service and private monies to augment the public funds. However, when there is an opportunity to generate new and additional revenue by selling a product or a service, the organization thrives, and its good practices are spread.

An Entrepreneurial Approach

> Moving toward independence requires public monies for service and private monies to augment public funds.

As early as 2004, our business colleagues urged us to consider identifying and then leveraging ECS intellectual property that would be of value to others. By creating a strategy to sell the product or the process to other home visiting programs, we could generate new revenue for ECS.

As nonprofits struggle to find money to support their initiatives, they seldom can turn what they learn or what they create into products that they could provide to another organization. There is money (limited) for provision of direct service from both public and private-sector sources and sometimes there is money for operations (even more limited) but rarely is there funding for the seed money required to take expertise or a product to market and do two things: share something that is valuable and has been proven and/or create a new revenue source for the organization.

ECS faced this many times over the two decades when I served as president. Multiple times we sought to create products and/or programming that would not only bring new revenue to ECS but also disseminate findings that would be useful to the home visiting and early childhood system fields writ large. Examples of such products and services include workshops, training, consulting and mentoring services, manuals and tools for program planning and launch, and ongoing operation support. In addition, five programs we developed had the potential to improve and/or enhance other home visiting programs: the eECS data platform, the maternal depression treatment intervention called Moving Beyond Depression, the StartStrong community focus and activation strategy, the early literacy curriculum called Let's Talk Baby, and the child development/parent awareness plan, Pampers University.

Moving Beyond Depression

Early into the deployment of ECS and as a result of our comprehensive data collection, we noted that nearly one-half of our mothers had measurable signs of clinical depression. Further, we knew from decades of research that when the mother was depressed, it was difficult for her to parent effectively; to be attentive, nurturing, and responsive to her child's needs; to take care of her own needs; and to create a dynamic relationship with the home visitor (Ammerman 2017; Folger et al. 2017; Ammerman et al. 2012; Ammerman et al. 2010). Early relationships and, in turn, child development were affected, sometimes seriously. Too often, these moms lived in an environment where poverty, violence, underemployment, and social isolation were not only common but pervasive. Few of these mothers were able to receive treatment in their communities, even if sought, because of limited access to mental health services. In addition, many new mothers lost health coverage from Medicaid 60 days after the birth and had no means to pay for mental-health treatment. And even if there were a way to pay and a treatment was available, it was nearly impossible for the mother to even keep appointments given the real-life challenges of transportation, time off from work, and childcare availability.

A few years into our development, ECS scientific director Frank Putnam and ECS evaluation director Robert Ammerman began the work and the grant writing that led to the creation of our national ECS Moving Beyond Depression program, which linked effective treatment for depression with home visiting (Ammerman, Putnam, et al. 2012; Ammerman, Putnam et al. 2009). This new in-home cognitive behavioral therapy approach was designed to work in tandem with home visiting programs and had demonstrated significant positive results. ECS obtained funding from the United Way, three local foundations, and the National Institute of Mental Health for the research startup, two randomized clinical trials, and the creation of the infrastructure for program delivery.

Results for the mothers were gratifying, with 85% of mothers served experiencing a substantial reduction in depressive symptoms following the sixteen in-home treatment sessions (Ammerman et al. 2017; Ammerman et al. 2016; Ammerman et al. 2015; Ammerman et al. 2013; Ammerman, Peugh, et al. 2012; Ammerman et al. 2011; Ammerman et al. 2009).

Over time, with the effort in Cincinnati as the national model, programs in 11 states signed on to include Moving Beyond Depression as a part of their home-visitation offerings. However, the programs who purchased Moving Beyond Depression from us had trouble finding financial support. They used a variety of short-term solutions; they reported that the mothers, the therapists, and the home visitors were all pleased with the program results; but the organization simply had no way to pay for it. For ECS, we were not able to hire staff to find new clients, train the therapists, maintain the data file, and provide the frequent communication and training between ECS staff and off-site purchasers. Repeated visits with elected and appointed officials were disappointing, even as we explained why the service was needed and how effective it was. Invariably, they expressed support, but did not make money available and were unwilling to include Moving Beyond Depression as a part of the state-level supported home visiting programs in Ohio and Kentucky.

While some initially used the federal MIECHV program dollars for a short period, Moving Beyond Depression was disqualified as an evidence-based home visiting program under MIECHV, as other evidence-based mental health models have been, because it was considered more of a mental-health intervention. As a result, states were asked to stop using those funds. In addition, Moving Beyond Depression was being poorly accepted by public mental health authorities as an appropriate use of their funds because it was delivered in homes rather than in clinical settings. Further, as mentioned previously, in many states 50% to 60% of women who had a Medicaid financed birth lost their coverage at the end of 60 days following the birth (postpartum) and had no health coverage for this or other mental-health treatment. While many states were launching early childhood mental health projects, most did not include the pregnant women in these efforts (Willis et al. 2021; West et al. 2020).

This was another opportunity lost for those who needed the service and the children who needed engaged parenting. Optimistically, we can see that as states use their option to extend postpartum Medicaid coverage to one year, perhaps a new window of opportunity is opening to deliver Moving Beyond Depression and successfully treat perinatal depression in conjunction with delivery of home visiting model services.

StartStrong

The StartStrong program (as described in Chapter 5) tells a different but similar story. In 2018, ECS and Cincinnati Children's responded to a request for proposal from the local foundation Bethesda Inc. for a bi3 grants initiative to transform health. They were offering sizable funding for organizations who could engage families, communities, health systems, and physicians to transform the current system of care and improve birth outcomes.

We felt this work was just right for us at ECS and so did the community component of Cincinnati Children's. Unaware the other was making similar proposals, the Perinatal Institute at Children's and ECS both wrote proposal letters. Upon receipt of the two proposals, a representative from the funder, Bethesda Inc. bi3, wisely came to each of us asking, "Why can't you work together?"

An Example of Nonprofit Innovation Focused on the Aging Population

The Council on Aging of Southwestern Ohio (COA) has always been an innovator in its role as a nonprofit. In fact, "Innovation" is one of their six organizational values. Why? The answer is simple . . . they want to make the lives of seniors better. They want to push the boundaries of service delivery, so seniors get the best!

COA always had very few discretionary funds since funding is mostly from government sources and has always been reimbursed based on costs incurred, rather than by grants or other funding mechanisms. With changes in state programs, COA had the opportunity to move to a revenue model that was risk based—if they spent more than taken in, they lost money but if they spent less, COA could keep it. They embraced this model and began developing programs to market to health plans to address their respective pain points. They would build a profit margin into these programs, which, again, allowed growth in the funding base.

In 2018, COA began to see the effects of a declining home care workforce and began to implement pilot programs aimed at addressing this challenge. When there is no home care staff, their mission of keeping seniors independent at home is threatened.

After doing pilot projects focused on increased wages and seeing no impact, COA decided to take a comprehensive approach to identify the systemic issues. They joined a nonprofit design thinking organization called The Livewell Collaborative to assist in identifying how to expand the home care workforce.

Four years later, they are rolling out an app, AddnAide, which is designed to disrupt the existing model by allowing home-care aides to set their own schedules and maximize their client volume by being able to select clients in the proximity of their homes or clients they are already serving. The app has features that will allow clients and aides to "match" one another based on needs, schedule, and special attributes (nonsmoker desired, etc.). The app also provides safeguards so that we know the services have been delivered. Once services are provided and approved by the client, COA can authorize payment through the app and an aide can get paid weekly.

This is a large innovation and required substantial resources. COA invested $1.8 million in development of the app. This year they applied for and received $1.65 million in federal funds for marketing and app development. COA is currently rolling out the app in our community programs.

Once local implementation is complete the focus will be on dissemination, to license the app to other organizations that have the same workforce issues. The possibilities for this seem great, as it would work for private home care agencies, State Medicaid departments, MCOs, hospice organizations, and others. The funds raised from selling or licensing the app will allow COA to continue to invest in innovative products and services that will make it easier to age in home and community settings.

The commitment to innovation is what sets COA apart and allows them to be a national leader in the aging network. The ability to secure public funds for research and development will translate into major progress in their service capacity. The experience of COA is an example of the creative response to a widespread challenge.

Of course, they were correct (collaboration again). We revised our two proposals into one and received a three-year $3.2 million grant, and Cincinnati Children's agreed to match the Bethesda Inc. bi3 contribution.

Partners for this collaboration included Cincinnati Children's, ECS, and Tri-Health/Good Samaritan Hospital. The goal was to determine how to bring down the unacceptably high infant mortality rate in our community.

It took nearly the first year for us to determine how to work together—new leadership, new committees, new work plans—coordinating data systems, identifying outcomes to be monitored, materials that would be needed, and sites where the work would occur. The activity was neither rancorous nor obstructionist. Rather, to paraphrase from Johnson's ECS Occasional Issue Brief, No. 4, August 2018, "The planning was complex with many players and partners . . . establishing the structure, the roles and responsibilities had to happen before we could begin delivering the program." Besides and ironically, we had to agree on a name, and that took longer than one would expect, but StartStrong eventually won out.

As year three ended, the program was running smoothly. We were coordinating our approach to engaging families, communities, health systems, and physicians. We were transforming the system of care and reversing trends in birth outcomes in the Avondale community by using dedicated nurse managers, evidence-based home visitors, trusted community health workers, physician champions, and supportive hospital administrators. Families played a more active role in defining what they needed and wanted. Focused on the perinatal period, we were positively impacting the lives and health of mothers and babies, making care more person-centered.

Results? The Avondale infant mortality death rate dropped from 21/1,000 live births to 8.6/1,000 live births. There were fewer preterm births in Avondale and no extremely preterm births (less than 28 weeks) in the two-year period. Costs for hospital care for preterm birth were reduced by more than $1.3 million over the three years.

So, the logical questions include: What happened next? Did this grow? Were learnings reapplied? The answer to the latter questions is no, with a few exceptions: families were more often placed at the center of the planning, structural changes at the hospitals continued, ECS incorporated the perinatal curriculum we wrote for this project home visitors, and community health workers continued their cooperative relationships where they existed. But the funding ended.

While StartStrong continued to exist in name, the program effectively closed, and a great opportunity was missed. We had planned to add a second community, Price Hill, but that work barely began when year three ended and the funding door closed. The gains did not hold.

However, and this is important, Bethesda Inc. bi3 leadership highlighted the long-term positive effect of the StartStrong program that led almost a decade later to lowered infant mortality rates in Hamilton County. This accomplishment, they stated, stemmed from the work that began with StartStrong.

So, Bethesda Inc. bi3 did two remarkable things: first, they insisted that two like-minded grant applicants work together, and second, they worked with Cincinnati Children's to provide sufficient funding for the grant to identify and implement strategies that could be reapplied across our community. Grants are not meant to sustain programs over time, rather, they are there to provide the seed money for testing, for piloting, for determining what can work. Would we have liked another year or two of grant-funded activity? Certainly, but we learned enough in those three years to make a difference, and that counts.

Once the work was complete with the private sector, the public sector could have stepped in to build upon what philanthropy allowed us to demonstrate. We kept good records. We validated our experience and our findings. We knew what to do next and we were eager to teach others. We responded to a need, and we found solutions. As with the home visiting and pediatric primary care partnership, this innovation, in the form that we delivered it, fell into the cracks between siloed systems.

> Grants are not meant to sustain programs over time, rather, they are there to provide the seed money for testing, for piloting, for determining what can work.

Philanthropy did its part, allowing us to test and pilot, but even though we had robust health and economic outcomes, we had no way to grow the program and allow more families to benefit.

As maintained throughout this book, health and social-service problems cannot be solved with funding from short-term philanthropic contributions or government siloed and limited resources. Even with new payment approaches in health care, such as accountable-care organizations or value-based payments, it is not clear that something as broadly conceived as our StartStrong demonstration project, or the primary care and home visiting collaboration, will be funded with payer dollars from health plans. Federal policy proposals for locating child development experts in primary care clinics might result in new funding and make a difference. But even with new investments in childcare, the focus will not be on improving the quality of parenting and relationships in the first three years, and there is still not a focus on expanding home visiting federal dollars.

Let's Talk Baby and Pampers

The Let's Talk Baby project began as a part of our scientifically researched early literacy program and provided language and literacy training for all ECS families via their home visitors. We wanted to make sure that ECS parents not only understood the importance of language and early literacy development for their children, but also were encouraged to talk with their children early and often, reading to them at least three times per week. Through our volunteer-initiated Bringing Books to Babes program, we were able to ensure that there were age-specific books in the home by distributing more than 14,000 developmentally appropriate books each year to ECS enrolled families. The home visitors were asked to observe and document language and literacy skills as a part of their regular visits, and many of them reported back that the toddlers greeted them at the door and were eager to get their new books.

In 2014, we developed Let's Talk Baby, an early language-learning app to promote parent-child interaction and optimize early childhood development during the critical period of brain development, birth to age three. Parents received two weekly activities on their mobile device or computer. The app had a mechanism to provide feedback to the parent. P&G funded the development of the app, and Cincinnati Children's supported the creation of the web platform. The plan was to test the app with Pampers' rewards members. Our promotional video described it this way:

> Let's Talk Baby offers guidance to enable parents to gauge child literacy growth and validates their efforts to be great parents. Let's Talk Baby affirms that parent-to-baby interaction, talking and reading impacts brain development and cognitive growth. These are essential for a child's success in reading and in school.

Informed by research and backed by ECS's proven track record for positively influencing parents and young children, Let's Talk Baby was a tool to help parents create a nurturing and stimulating relational environment, essential for the first three years of life and beyond. Parent Talk Tips, activity handouts coordinated with the Let's Talk Baby app, were provided to families by the home visitors at every visit, beginning with the first infant visit at week one. Each parent tip had three elements: the suggested activity, an example for the suggested activity and age-appropriate developmental information for the parent. Parents were encouraged to talk and talk and talk with their child—it is never too early. Narrating life to a baby matters. Hearing words matters. Reading is crucial.

As we began to work with P&G to consider how Let's Talk Baby and the Parent Talk Tips could be coordinated with Pampers sales, we were excitedly optimistic. Suddenly we saw ourselves as a provider of information about early childhood conveyed through national, even international sales of Pampers diapers—maybe messages on the boxes?—thousands of boxes with the ECS logo, maybe through a website, maybe through the Pampers Rewards program, maybe cited as an authority for the "your baby's stages of development record book" that Pampers distributed to their moms.

We had a good product that had been professionally developed and tested with our ECS home visitors and moms. In my mind I was calling this Pampers University and the curriculum was Literacy 101. We had reasons to believe that a personalized literacy curriculum would be appealing to parents at all economic levels because parents were telling us:

- "My life is too busy. I don't have time to figure out how to find resources to meet the literacy needs of my baby."
- "There is almost too much information on the web, in books and periodicals."
- "I need to know what to do for my baby on a regular basis, but not for babies in general."
- "I want a reliable source of information that is credible and of the highest quality."
- "I want to be the best possible mom."
- "For a small amount of money, I can make sure that my baby gets the best possible start."

Seeing the potential, we worked on this for months with a talented team from P&G. Eventually, to our disappointment, it didn't work for several reasons, but first among them was the fact that the ECS brand did not have adequate currency outside of our service area. P&G knew that what we were proposing together had value, but in the end, it wasn't compelling enough nor distinct enough to warrant further investment. Early literacy materials with our enrolled ECS families continued, but our dream of a wider play became simply that, a dream.

Home Visiting as a Benefit for Employees

Several years before I stepped down as president, we began to talk about the possibility of offering an ECS type product for employers. Understanding that middle-class mothers shared many of the child-rearing and development issues that we address with our challenged moms, we talked with several large employer benefit managers about purchasing ECS home visiting services and making them available to their employees as part of a benefits package. We were aiming for middle-to upper-middle-class moms who had jobs and, if they were married, so did their partner. They would have a new baby, probably daily day care, could spend limited time with their children, but like our moms, they wanted to be good parents. They wanted to give their child the best possible start. They wanted guidance and often lived far away from their own extended families. Some had their own adverse childhood experiences or stresses that they wanted to avoid with their own children. We had the experience, the curriculum, and the tools to help them.

Debbie Vargo, a retired P&G executive and a past ECS board chair, agreed to investigate the possibilities. I asked her to identify critical questions and possible strategies to determine whether employers and benefit managers would see an evidence-based home visiting option as a value for their employees and whether there would be a revenue opportunity for ECS.

Relying on her P&G background (Cincinnati is fortunate to have such people), Vargo developed a working-knowledge template that organized the key questions into the following categories: finances, population, selling proposition/concept, curriculum for paying parents, curriculum options beginning prenatally and continuing for three weeks, six weeks, twelve weeks, six months, a year? She suggested that we work with one of our provider agencies to test the concept. We agreed that offering the benefit through an employer was more realistic than trying to sell and serve an open-market population and trying to enroll one family at a time.

Vargo reminded us that her approach would be to address the killer issue first—the P&G approach to problem solving. Solve the hardest, most limiting factor first and don't address any of the easier issues until later. Vargo believed that the killer issue for this endeavor may be whether new parents would pay the relatively high cost.

We were never able to do even the preparatory work to pursue this concept. Our volunteers offered guidance, but again, we needed staff and seed money even to conduct a pilot. It was another good idea unfulfilled, both for the services that it could have provided for the target population and for the potential revenue that could have been generated to add more at-risk families.

Lessons

1. Focus, focus, focus. Write a realistic business plan to deliver services and to sustain the operation. The plan must be flexible yet stable. (The ECS plan, written nearly 24 years ago, was amazingly prescient and was guided by our business-leader partners.)

2. Find business sector partners who believe in your mission and will foster your success. Understand that dedicated involvement of the business community can accelerate success by emphasizing return on investment, entrepreneurial thinking, focused activity, accountability, transparency, and marketing.

3. Take advantage of private sector and business involvement when possible. Collaborate with like-minded organizations and people as often as possible. Seek partners that share your understanding of the mission and its value. Learn from people across sectors.

4. Don't automatically say no to new ideas and/or challenging opportunities. Weigh the potential advantages and disadvantages. Find a path for making changes that will improve services and outcomes. Get to yes.

5. Build upon documented successes and what works for your field, for your nonprofit. Stop doing what is not working. Document how and why things worked and use those lessons to improve. Do not over-promise but always strive to over-deliver.

6. Make investments to support the mission, not to make or save money. This distinguishes mission-driven nonprofit work from for-profit business endeavors. Many businesses are often accountable to shareholders and under additional pressure to generate a profit. Help your business partners and funders understand this distinction.

Chapter 7

Sound Measurement Is Key to Success

Centering Families

This section about sound measurement needs to begin with a reflection from our then evaluation/now ECS scientific director, Robert Ammerman, from a presentation he made to the United Way. Here is how he described the experience:

> I was armed with charts and tables, quantifying our work and our achievements. Also presenting was a mother enrolled in ECS. I was struck by the contrast between her poignant and earnest testimony about how ECS had helped her—being more confident as a parent, feeling hopeful about the future, anticipating the healthy development of her baby as compared with the numbers and lines on slides that comprised my presentation. Both of our presentations were important and helpful in describing ECS. I came away reminded of the human and personal impact of our work and a recognition that behind the numbers are stories of thousands of parents and children making meaningful changes in their lives.

With mothers and children at the center of the science and measurement paradigm, there were at least nine primary stakeholder groups across the public and private sectors that influenced the work of ECS: families themselves, our board and staff, provider agencies, home visitors, health care providers, the local community, the scientific community, governmental policy makers, and funders.

Measurement was not only a central focus for ECS, but it was also germane to our success and to understanding what constituted success for families. We believed in transparency and eagerly sought input from our families and our home visitors regarding what was working well, what wasn't working, and what questions needed to be answered. This work was grounded in the original stipulation from Cincinnati Children's then Chair of Pediatrics, Thomas Boat: Children's will only be part of the ECS home visiting initiative if it had a strong data component.

To that end, we aligned our performance and process measures with defined outcomes that we and our families wanted to achieve. We surveyed families to ensure that we were including the voice of the customer. We asked both the families and the ECS team: What surprises you? What is going well? What challenges exist? What could be done better? Community nonprofits should ask themselves and those they serve similar questions to increase transparency, accountability, and community engagement. Program participation and long-term success depend on delivering the right service to meet the expectations and needs of those they aim to serve.

In addition, over the years, we used information collected by our home visitors and our agencies about the needs, plans, and outcomes of families to make decisions about program operations.

To gauge progress, we monitored the performance of each agency in the organization. In the case of ECS, agencies knew in advance what we would be measuring, so each year when we reviewed their performance, there were no surprises. These periodic reviews were important as we worked to maintain system excellence and stability. Everyone understood that these performance review meetings were fundamental to delivering the ECS mission. Most of the meetings were opportunities to laud success and/or to look for new strategies to address a specific problem. However, on three occasions and after warnings and remediation, we did not renew contracts with agencies not performing at the level we set for the organization. Those were never easy discussions.

As an organization, there must be a willingness to confront adverse outcomes, be it a strategy that isn't working or an agency that isn't performing up to standards—standards that put the mission at the center of the work.

What We Did: Optimizing the "Three Faces of Measurement"

Measurement has been central to ECS from the day that we enrolled our first family, and that focus included aspects of measurement science brought to us by our partner Cincinnati Children's. Functionally, we committed to use what the Institute for Healthcare Improvement (IHI) refers to as the "three faces of performance measurement," that is, measuring for purposes of: 1) quality improvement (QI); 2) population-level performance monitoring (accountability); and 3) research and evaluation. These three faces of measurement are discussed throughout this chapter (Solberg et al 1997).

Based on the work of Leif I. Solberg, MD, a leader in quality measurement and an executive at HealthPartners Institute, the framework using three faces of measurement reminds us that the data we collect will be used for different purposes, toward different ends, and to demonstrate different types of accountabilities. So, for example, ECS used data collected by home visitors to design QI projects that would ensure families were receiving the intended components of a home visiting model or that would identify areas where additional training was needed. The same data used as population-level performance monitoring would tell us if our program was improving the rates of early prenatal care, immunizations, or breastfeeding, while reducing rates of smoking or depression. In addition, our data served as the basis for evaluation studies and helped guide development of research projects.

Notably, the Maternal, Infant, and Early Childhood Home Visiting (MIECHV) program is the only program for which federal law requires states to use all three types of measurement. Every state that accepts grants for federal home visiting must use the three faces of measurement. We were aligned with the federal approach and deeply committed to this approach. Our work on measurement met and exceeded these requirements for years before they became law. In the long run, this helped ECS and others who are supported by MIECHV funds.

ECS set out performance metrics, success criteria, forms-completion deadlines, quality improvement processes, systematic data collection and analysis. When possible, we added staff capacity to support this work, particularly people with QI skills, data analysts and researchers who could secure funds for projects to develop new knowledge and measure our efforts. Each component paid off for ECS and for the field of home visiting.

Our work on QI fit with the priorities of Cincinnati Children's and was supported and sustained by their expertise in this area of measurement. Then initiated and led by Uma Raman Kotagal, MD, Cincinnati Children's QI efforts in pediatrics were widely recognized as among the nation's best. It drove the work and training of home visitors, as well as many of our community partnership efforts and our work with primary care providers.

For population-level performance monitoring, we both collected our data and linked it to vital records and overlays of census-tract data to understand service utilization and impact on community/population-level outcomes. The data system designed by ECS (eECS) ultimately became the basis for an improved statewide performance-data system for the state of Ohio.

Our agenda and our work were complex and informed by all three types of measurement. During my 20 years with ECS, the list included collaboration efforts such as home visiting and primary care, community health workers and home visitors, community early childhood teams, and community moms' groups. We focused on measuring and improving the impact of our work on factors such as birth outcomes, parenting skills, child development, maternal depression, interpersonal violence, substance abuse, tobacco use, and readiness for pre-kindergarten and now, even early relational health. We pushed to understand precision in home visiting—what works for whom and how best to respond to the needs and plans of families. The measurement agenda also focused on aspects of program operation, including outreach and enrollment, participation and retention, home visitor training, equity and inclusion, and connections to other services. In each case, we used the tools of QI—performance monitoring and evaluation, and research—to advance knowledge of what works and to improve the work of ECS.

ECS operated with the understanding that "what gets measured gets done." Our first board chair, Gibbs MacVeigh, a retired financial officer, said loudly and clearly at least once a month that if something wasn't working, as shown in the data, we needed to stop doing it—whatever it was.

The key then was to know what wasn't working that could be made visible in the data. With our strong mandate from Cincinnati Children's to have robust data for QI, performance monitoring, and evaluation and research, our opportunity to hire an outstanding research staff, to collect reliable data into our unique data platform, and strong leadership from staff and advisors, we were in a position to know what needed to be improved.

> The key questions are: What to measure? How to measure? What constitutes evidence of success? What is actionable?

We measured to gauge quality, program performance, effectiveness, impact, return on investment, and to test ideas that had relevance to the home visiting field writ large. The key questions were: What to measure? How to measure? And most critically, what constitutes evidence of success and what is actionable?

How We Built the Measurement Approach

Scientific Advisory Committee (SAC)

Soon after ECS was formed, we assembled a Scientific Advisory Committee (SAC) to guide our research activities. It was initially led by James Greenberg, MD, co-chair of the Perinatal Institute at Cincinnati Children's and a longtime member of the ECS board. Experienced in all three faces of measurement, he was an excellent choice to chair this committee. Greenberg was joined by five other board members, community representatives, and affiliated faculty from Cincinnati Children's and the University of Cincinnati College of Medicine. The affiliated faculty represented the areas of behavioral medicine and clinical psychology, biostatistics and epidemiology, biomedical informatics, general pediatrics, and speech-language development at the Reading and Literacy Discovery Center. Staff work was provided by the ECS research and evaluation team, led by Putnam and Ammerman.

We deliberately included community and business representatives who were not part of our academic community in our SAC contingent—we wanted the voice of the for-profit and community perspective as well as the voice of professionals who brought academic content knowledge and strategies for study design. The charge for the SAC was to oversee the scientific mission of ECS, including identifying future projects, involving other investigators, validating research requests coming to ECS from other individuals and organizations, and working with staff to prepare and monitor the research agenda.

> Bring academic and for-profit community perspective together.

The SAC allowed us to highlight the ways in which the ECS focus on measurement, including QI, performance monitoring, and research, was synergistic with other activities at Cincinnati Children's. ECS brought valuable resources, including our family cohort, an extensive data file, research infrastructure, a collaborative approach, community contacts, and ability to obtain grants. We hoped to underscore our value to Cincinnati Children's and find multiple ways to work together.

The ECS board's challenge to the SAC was not trivial. We wanted them to help us generate research ideas and not just listen to us report about our current activities. They were asked to serve as emissaries from us to the Research Foundation at Cincinnati Children's and to their colleagues across the country, letting them know about our trustworthy infrastructure and our value to Cincinnati Children's and its research agenda. We were eager to foster additional collaboration and let SAC know that we needed their help.

At first, and as the group coalesced, their responses for us were largely observational, but as they—and we—learned more about each other, the recommendations, comments, and questions became more pointed and more challenging. They asked: Can you explain the what and why for findings that you highlight? Is your research work improving the home visiting field and/or improving ECS itself? Are you only examining specific outcomes or trying to understand why home visiting works? Do you know what level of service is needed to produce the outcomes you seek? Have you identified an investment strategy to fund ECS research and development, work that cannot be sustained without external funding? All were questions that focused on what can and should be done. The SAC developed a set of eight guidelines for proposals coming from scientists outside of ECS:

1.   The research must advance the field in a meaningful way.
2.   The proposed study must not put undue burden on home visitors and families.
3.   The research findings must be relevant to ECS and have implications for how we provide the service.
4.   The proposed study must not conflict with ongoing or planned ECS research.
5.   Expenses for the research must be covered by the grant.
6.   The scientific quality of the study will be high.
7.   The investigator and investigative team have a strong record of scholarship, grant writing, and publications.
8.   Working with the investigative team forges collaborative relationships that benefit ECS.

The SAC members debated whether a proposed study would be important for ECS, for funders, and for the home visiting field. They also debated whether obtaining the funds to do the work was feasible, whether the research line of inquiry was one where we had a track record and familiarity with the existing data, whether we had the infrastructure to do the work, whether we had or needed pilot data, and whether the ECS program and the home visitors would be able to support the undertaking.

They encouraged us to focus, to delve more deeply into a few home visiting areas rather than a wider range. But they, and we, knew that some of the questions we needed to answer were not optional, which meant that sometimes before we actually got into what we would like to pursue, we had to comply with mandates from funders.

Learning from Experts

The work of the SAC was supported by the ECS measurement team that monitored daily activities and the ECS evaluation committee, which was made up of representatives from ECS provider agencies. The agenda for the ECS measurement work was developed to meet the needs of the multiple constituencies invested in ECS and its outcomes.

In February of 2008, we contracted with Anne Duggan. Through her work based at Johns Hopkins University, Duggan had been a research and evaluation leader in the home visiting world for decades and served as the leader of the federally funded Home Visiting Applied Research Collaborative (HARC). We asked her to help us think creatively about how to address design and measurement issues for future ECS research. She understood that we were operating with a dual mission: high quality services for people in need and scientific rigor for program operation that would move the home visiting field forward. Duggan was one of the first researchers to reference what is called the "black box" of home visitation—what are the key elements needed in program implementation to ensure program success? Years later, there is still little agreement regarding what actually is in that black box.

Among Duggan's recommendations for us, three became a major part of our research activity going forward: 1) Answer the questions about how home visiting works, for whom and how effective models can be taken to scale with fidelity; 2) Monitor the process of service delivery and the completeness and accuracy of data collection; 3) Design observational and intervention research using factors that influence fidelity and promote fidelity. Substantial work is still needed in all three areas.

As we wove together the types of measurement with the questions posed by Duggan, we embarked upon the sizable task of identifying key success factors for families—what are the essential outcomes for a family in a specific time period? Who defines success? Why are we in business?

Defining Success

What Constitutes Success?

We aimed to define success, at least for ECS and our families. Certain performance indicators and outcome measures were required by the federal and state programs, based on a review of science. Local programs such as ECS had to put these into practice in real-time measurement activities, which was one of the most important yet continually challenging activities for our measurement team. In addition, we knew it was essential to understand and consider what families themselves would view as success, as well as what outcomes were valued by the community. Taken together, we created a template for what to measure and even how to measure. Yet most difficult to answer were the companion questions—which outcomes or conditions are predictive of future health and well-being? What matters?

Outcome data are important for families so that they can gauge their progress and work toward goals that they set for themselves in conjunction with their home visitors. As we began to think more intentionally about what information would be most valuable for families, we embarked upon an activity that sounded simple, but as we explored the possibilities, the complexity became obvious. Which were the right success criteria? Should they be considered by the age of the child? Were we collecting enough data to make a valued finding? We had many meetings to discuss the facets of the process, the outcomes, the priorities.

Being a somewhat-atypical nonprofit, we formed an internal-success-criteria committee, charged to create four groups of success markers based upon the age of the child: prenatal, birth to 12 months, 13–24 months, and 25–36 months. For each age group we identified two to three dozen possible criteria to include. Discussing the merits of each criterion became the agenda for a series of challenging meetings. All of the criteria were important. How to choose? Finally, we voted and used the results of our vote to create what we called the Success Priority Checklist. The list provided a framework for home visitors to know what to concentrate on for each time period. The home visitors were to ask themselves, "If you can accomplish nothing else right now, what should you focus on?"

The Success Priority Checklist became a useful and unique management tool for the home visitors. We produced a family success report for each home visitor and her caseload and then a separate individual Success Criteria Report Card for each family. Home visitors and families could see graphically how they were progressing.

We moved from creating a full list of the success criteria to taking a more holistic approach to prioritizing the criteria by age of child to identifying the measures that would allow us to document performance. For example, what needs to be achieved by age one: it sounds simple, but it was extraordinarily complex, as there are so many factors that lead to success at any age.

The success criteria were important for ECS, as we endeavored to make each home visit as meaningful as possible. And the measures played a role in our evaluation so that when data were accumulated, it would allow us to holistically answer questions for the program. In addition, the measures were intended to help the family understand how well they were doing. It focused attention on what the family and the program aimed to accomplish, charging the home visitors to partner with families to reach those aims.

We wanted to be sure that when a family ended participation in ECS, they left being aware—and proud, we hoped—of what they accomplished. As a part of our success priority program, each family received a gold embossed certificate with personal signatures for each completed phase of the program, emphasizing accomplishment and celebration.

However, late in my tenure at ECS, we had to discontinue this activity, because most of our data were being entered into state systems rather than our eECS system, and we were unable to generate the reports needed for the family success certificates. We lost a valuable part of our family celebration when the certificates were no longer available. And knowing that many of our families displayed the certificates they had been awarded in an honored place in their home, one of our board members suggested that we create a colorful and engaging chart for each family to keep in their homes to measure progress. This added a visible roadmap of success and celebrated accomplishments—going from a problem to a solution, in practical and program co-design terms.

The idea behind the success criteria was to begin to concretize, in a way that could be measured, what we were doing, where we were having success, and what we needed to do better. This type of iterative thinking, and even "five whys" questioning that gets to root causes and better responses and performance, has value. Thinking intensively about the questions is needed to clearly define the problem and the effective solutions. Any strategic planning and quality improvement activities need to be guided by this type of questioning. While in our case it was about children, this general approach could be used in any community nonprofit endeavor.

Quality Improvement

Within ECS, we wanted to employ QI strategies to determine how to effect change—to correct what wasn't working. But before we could even begin, we needed to make sure that we could obtain baseline data that was accurate and reliable so that we could identify gaps and problems. This meant that, in nearly all cases, the home visitors who would be collecting the data needed additional training because they were only nominally aware of QI methods. We engaged the agencies individually and as a group, sharing time for a woman from the Cincinnati Children's James M. Anderson Center for Health System Excellence to be our quality improvement consultant and to lead the work. The home visitors were being asked once again to look at their work differently, but to their credit they were enthusiastic about what they might be able to learn.

We were treading on new ground for quality improvement as well because we would be implementing it with community-based agencies rather than in a more restricted hospital or clinic setting. We were dependent upon the commitment of the agencies and the home visitors to embrace this new concept and deploy it thoughtfully, adding another dimension to their already complex work schedules.

The fact that these agencies had been working with us for multiple years, conscientiously collecting data, meant that they had experience in that aspect of what the QI work would require. Further, they trusted that what we were asking them to do was worthwhile and would allow them to add an innovative aspect to their experience as professional home visitors. Over time, the list of projects that ECS was able to address is testament to the home visitors' willingness to learn how to incorporate QI into their work and to help find answers to improve the program, and thus the family experience.

Many workers in a variety of community settings have now been trained by Cincinnati Children's to use QI strategies. But when we began, we were alone in implementing QI across eight community-based agencies, using our team of home visitors. Julie Massie was the ECS quality assurance specialist. She functioned as a liaison with the agencies and home visitors to explain what we were doing, secure their cooperation, and provide tech support as needed for this effort. She was perfect for this role—warm, friendly, smart, and well-trained in QI. If Massie asked you to do something, even if you really didn't want to, you did it rather than disappoint her.

She was patient as the home visitors learned a new skill, and she was always willing to demonstrate the value in what they were being asked to do. At the same time, she brought the methodological rigor and focus needed in a QI consultant or team leader.

In any QI project, a key to success is to involve those closest to the work in a process of testing and learning. We hosted teams of home visitors and supervisors who met on a regular basis, combining learning about QI methods and sharing ways to integrate them into their daily routines. The teamwork needed to be fun as well as educational so that the work was seen as an opportunity rather than a burden. The teams shared best practices at our training fairs and put together what they called Activity and Concept Tables to show other ECS agencies what creative strategies and materials had worked for them.

In addition to the teamwork and training fairs, we initiated Cafe Conversations, used QI Tips of the Week, and What's in Your Trunk where home visitors could show off what they were carrying around in their cars. They challenged each other to answer questions like, "What are ten things that you can do with a set of six blocks to encourage child development?" Or they played Grammy in the Room to share ideas about how to manage well-meaning friends and family who were providing incorrect advice for the mom and/or distracting her during the home visit.

> Mistakes can be gifts, not failures.

As our QI work began, we needed a way to track results visibly and clearly. The Red Green Chart was born, brought to us by private sector ECS volunteer Alan Spector, formerly of P&G and with a career focused on quality improvement in private industry.

He informed us that there were six keys to success in quality assurance: unifying long-term direction and strategy; driving improvement with data; data transparency/visible accountability; continual improvement and breakthrough learning from mistakes; periodic assessment; and renewal. It was Spector who taught us that mistakes can be gifts, not failures.

It was also Spector who helped us think through the concept of transparency. What data do we share with ECS' stakeholders such

as agencies and board members? Do we share cumulative numbers
for the full group of agencies or for each individual agency? We
elected to begin by releasing individual agency information at a
lead agency meeting. You can imagine the anxiety, ours and our
agencies. Was it data for accountability or data for improvement?
Across the top of the report were the agency names, and down
the left column were the performance metrics with targets. Color
blocks could be red, yellow, or green. Agency performance was
clear—nearly in technicolor. With credit to our managers, they
took the charts, which we updated quarterly, and used them as
we had hoped and intended as performance-improvement documents. Examples of those charts and figures are shown on the next
several pages.

Every Child Succeeds Sample Quality Indicator Charts
Q1 Trend Report Sample 2012

ECS Quality Indicator Report—Agency 1

Q1 = Jan-Mar, Run in May; Q2 = Apr-Jun, Run in Aug;

Q3 = Jul-Sept, Run in Nov; Q4 = Oct-Dec, Run in Feb

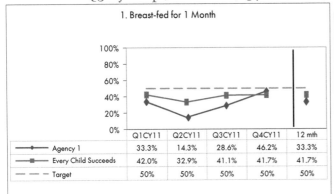

Agency 1			
Quarter	N	D	Rate
Q1CY11	1	3	33.3%
Q2CY11	1	7	14.3%
Q3CY11	2	7	28.6%
Q4CY11	6	13	46.2%
12 mth	10	30	33.3%

Every Child Succeeds			
Quarter	N	D	Rate
Q1CY11	29	69	42.0%
Q2CY11	26	79	32.9%
Q3CY11	30	73	41.1%
Q4CY11	35	84	41.7%
12 mth	129	309	41.7%

Developmental Period = 1

1. Breast-fed for 1 Month

	Q1CY11	Q2CY11	Q3CY11	Q4CY11	12 mth
Agency 1	33.3%	14.3%	28.6%	46.2%	33.3%
Every Child Succeeds	42.0%	32.9%	41.1%	41.7%	41.7%
Target	50%	50%	50%	50%	50%

2. Healthy Pregnancy and Delivery—Gestational Age

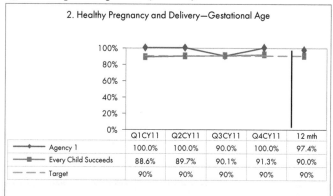

	Q1CY11	Q2CY11	Q3CY11	Q4CY11	12 mth
Agency 1	100.0%	100.0%	90.0%	100.0%	97.4%
Every Child Succeeds	88.6%	89.7%	90.1%	91.3%	90.0%
Target	90%	90%	90%	90%	90%

Agency 1			
Quarter	N	D	Rate
Q1CY11	9	9	100.0%
Q2CY11	15	15	100.0%
Q3CY11	9	10	90.0%
Q4CY11	4	4	100.0%
12 mth	37	38	97.4%

Every Child Succeeds			
Quarter	N	D	Rate
Q1CY11	93	105	88.6%
Q2CY11	96	107	89.7%
Q3CY11	100	111	90.1%
Q4CY11	95	104	91.3%
12 mth	394	438	90.0%

Developmental Period = P

3. Healthy Pregnancy and Delivery—Birth Weight

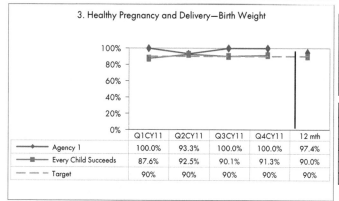

	Q1CY11	Q2CY11	Q3CY11	Q4CY11	12 mth
Agency 1	100.0%	93.3%	100.0%	100.0%	97.4%
Every Child Succeeds	87.6%	92.5%	90.1%	91.3%	90.0%
Target	90%	90%	90%	90%	90%

Agency 1			
Quarter	N	D	Rate
Q1CY11	9	9	100.0%
Q2CY11	14	15	93.3%
Q3CY11	10	10	100.0%
Q4CY11	4	4	100.0%
12 mth	36	38	94.7%

Every Child Succeeds			
Quarter	N	D	Rate
Q1CY11	92	105	87.6%
Q2CY11	99	107	92.5%
Q3CY11	100	111	90.1%
Q4CY11	95	104	91.3%
12 mth	394	438	90.0%

Developmental Period = P

4. Medical Home—Well Baby Check Up

	Q1CY11	Q2CY11	Q3CY11	Q4CY11	12 mth
Agency 1	77.8%	90.0%	90.9%	95.8%	94.6%
Every Child Succeeds	74.8%	78.5%	81.1%	86.9%	81.7%
Target	85%	85%	85%	85%	85%

Agency 1			
Quarter	N	D	Rate
Q1CY11	7	9	77.8%
Q2CY11	9	10	90.0%
Q3CY11	10	11	90.9%
Q4CY11	23	24	95.8%
12 mth	53	56	94.6%

Every Child Succeeds			
Quarter	N	D	Rate
Q1CY11	110	147	74.8%
Q2CY11	113	144	78.5%
Q3CY11	117	146	80.1%
Q4CY11	146	168	86.9%
12 mth	508	622	81.7%

Developmental Period = 1

5. Immunizations

	Q1CY11	Q2CY11	Q3CY11	Q4CY11	12 mth
Agency 1	77.8%	100.0%	75.0%	83.3%	85.7%
Every Child Succeeds	63.9%	65.3%	65.1%	72.7%	70.9%
Target	80%	80%	80%	80%	80%

Agency 1			
Quarter	N	D	Rate
Q1CY11	7	9	77.8%
Q2CY11	6	6	100.0%
Q3CY11	6	8	75.0%
Q4CY11	10	12	83.3%
12 mth	30	35	85.7%

Every Child Succeeds			
Quarter	N	D	Rate
Q1CY11	53	83	63.9%
Q2CY11	47	72	65.3%
Q3CY11	56	86	65.1%
Q4CY11	64	88	72.7%
12 mth	236	333	70.9%

Developmental Period = 2

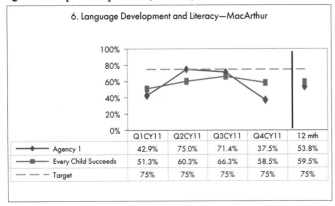

6. Language Development and Literacy—MacArthur

Agency 1			
Quarter	N	D	Rate
Q1CY11	3	7	42.9%
Q2CY11	3	4	75.0%
Q3CY11	5	7	71.4%
Q4CY11	3	8	37.5%
12 mth	14	26	53.8%

Every Child Succeeds			
Quarter	N	D	Rate
Q1CY11	39	76	51.3%
Q2CY11	41	68	60.3%
Q3CY11	53	80	66.3%
Q4CY11	48	82	58.5%
12 mth	184	309	59.5%

Developmental Period = 2

	Q1CY11	Q2CY11	Q3CY11	Q4CY11	12 mth
Agency 1	42.9%	75.0%	71.4%	37.5%	53.8%
Every Child Succeeds	51.3%	60.3%	66.3%	58.5%	59.5%
Target	75%	75%	75%	75%	75%

** Iteration changed from 24 months to 21 months of age.

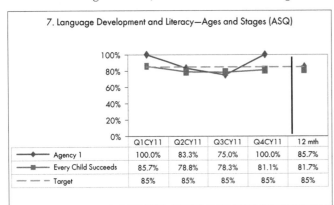

7. Language Development and Literacy—Ages and Stages (ASQ)

Agency 1			
Quarter	N	D	Rate
Q1CY11	4	4	100.0%
Q2CY11	5	6	83.3%
Q3CY11	6	8	75.0%
Q4CY11	2	2	100.0%
12 mth	18	21	85.7%

Every Child Succeeds			
Quarter	N	D	Rate
Q1CY11	54	63	85.7%
Q2CY11	41	52	78.8%
Q3CY11	36	46	78.3%
Q4CY11	43	53	81.1%
12 mth	178	218	81.7%

Developmental Period = 3

	Q1CY11	Q2CY11	Q3CY11	Q4CY11	12 mth
Agency 1	100.0%	83.3%	75.0%	100.0%	85.7%
Every Child Succeeds	85.7%	78.8%	78.3%	81.1%	81.7%
Target	85%	85%	85%	85%	85%

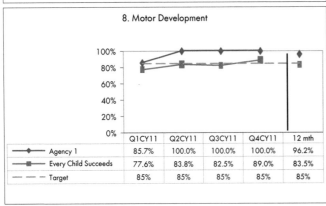

8. Motor Development

Agency 1			
Quarter	N	D	Rate
Q1CY11	6	7	85.7%
Q2CY11	4	4	100.0%
Q3CY11	7	7	100.0%
Q4CY11	8	8	100.0%
12 mth	25	26	96.2%

Every Child Succeeds			
Quarter	N	D	Rate
Q1CY11	59	76	77.6%
Q2CY11	57	68	83.8%
Q3CY11	66	80	82.5%
Q4CY11	73	82	89.0%
12 mth	258	309	83.5%

Developmental Period = 3

	Q1CY11	Q2CY11	Q3CY11	Q4CY11	12 mth
Agency 1	85.7%	100.0%	100.0%	100.0%	96.2%
Every Child Succeeds	77.6%	83.8%	82.5%	89.0%	83.5%
Target	85%	85%	85%	85%	85%

**Transition to ASQ 3rd edition July 2010. Data does not represent 12 months.

Q1 Trend Report Sample 2012 (*continued*)

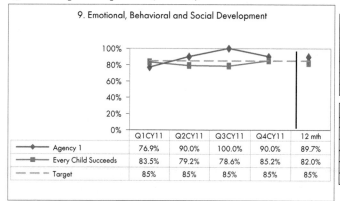

9. Emotional, Behavioral and Social Development

	Q1CY11	Q2CY11	Q3CY11	Q4CY11	12 mth
Agency 1	76.9%	90.0%	100.0%	90.0%	89.7%
Every Child Succeeds	83.5%	79.2%	78.6%	85.2%	82.0%
Target	85%	85%	85%	85%	85%

Agency 1			
Quarter	N	D	Rate
Q1CY11	10	13	76.9%
Q2CY11	9	10	90.0%
Q3CY11	7	7	100.0%
Q4CY11	9	10	90.0%
12 mth	35	39	89.7%

Every Child Succeeds			
Quarter	N	D	Rate
Q1CY11	116	139	83.5%
Q2CY11	95	120	79.2%
Q3CY11	99	126	78.6%
Q4CY11	115	135	85.2%
12 mth	432	527	82.0%

Developmental Period = 2, 3

Emotional, Behavioral and Social Development 24 months			
Agency 1			
Quarter	N	D	Rate
Q1CY11	6	7	85.7%
Q2CY11	4	4	100.0%
Q3CY11	7	7	100.0%
Q4CY11	7	8	87.5%
12 mth	24	26	92.3%

Every Child Succeeds			
Quarter	N	D	Rate
Q1CY11	64	76	84.2%
Q2CY11	59	68	86.8%
Q3CY11	67	80	83.8%
Q4CY11	74	82	90.2%
12 mth	268	309	86.7%

Emotional, Behavioral and Social Development 36 months			
Agency 1			
Quarter	N	D	Rate
Q1CY11	4	4	100.0%
Q2CY11	5	6	83.3%
Q3CY11	0	0	–
Q4CY11	2	2	100.0%
12 mth	11	13	84.6%

Every Child Succeeds			
Quarter	N	D	Rate
Q1CY11	52	63	82.5%
Q2CY11	36	52	69.2%
Q3CY11	32	46	69.6%
Q4CY11	41	53	77.4%
12 mth	164	218	75.2%

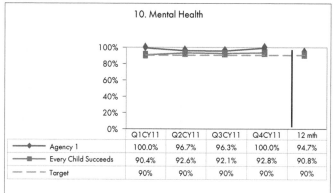

10. Mental Health

	Q1CY11	Q2CY11	Q3CY11	Q4CY11	12 mth
Agency 1	100.0%	96.7%	96.3%	100.0%	94.7%
Every Child Succeeds	90.4%	92.6%	92.1%	92.8%	90.8%
Target	90%	90%	90%	90%	90%

Agency 1			
Quarter	N	D	Rate
Q1CY11	22	22	100.0%
Q2CY11	29	30	96.7%
Q3CY11	26	27	96.3%
Q4CY11	11	11	100.0%
12 mth	90	95	94.7%

Every Child Succeeds			
Quarter	N	D	Rate
Q1CY11	244	270	90.4%
Q2CY11	238	257	92.6%
Q3CY11	268	291	92.1%
Q4CY11	257	277	92.8%
12 mth	1042	1148	90.8%

Developmental Period = P, 1

Mental Health—Prenatal (Edinburgh)			
Agency 1			
Quarter	N	D	Rate
Q1CY11	8	8	100.0%
Q2CY11	14	14	100.0%
Q3CY11	8	8	100.0%
Q4CY11	3	3	100.0%
12 mth	32	33	97.0%

Every Child Succeeds			
Quarter	N	D	Rate
Q1CY11	93	100	93.0%
Q2CY11	97	102	95.1%
Q3CY11	97	105	92.4%
Q4CY11	92	93	98.9%
12 mth	386	413	93.5%

Mental Health—Year 1 (Edinburgh)			
Agency 1			
Quarter	N	D	Rate
Q1CY11	14	14	100.0%
Q2CY11	15	16	93.8%
Q3CY11	18	19	94.7%
Q4CY11	8	8	100.0%
12 mth	58	62	93.5%

Every Child Succeeds			
Quarter	N	D	Rate
Q1CY11	151	170	88.8%
Q2CY11	141	155	91.0%
Q3CY11	171	186	91.9%
Q4CY11	165	184	89.7%
12 mth	656	735	89.3%

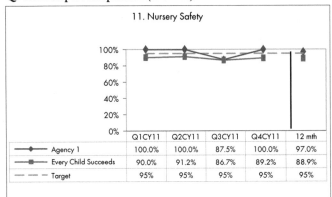

11. Nursery Safety

	Q1CY11	Q2CY11	Q3CY11	Q4CY11	12 mth
Agency 1	100.0%	100.0%	87.5%	100.0%	97.0%
Every Child Succeeds	90.0%	91.2%	86.7%	89.2%	88.9%
Target	95%	95%	95%	95%	95%

Agency 1			
Quarter	N	D	Rate
Q1CY11	8	8	100.0%
Q2CY11	14	14	100.0%
Q3CY11	7	8	87.5%
Q4CY11	3	3	100.0%
12 mth	32	33	97.0%

Every Child Succeeds			
Quarter	N	D	Rate
Q1CY11	90	100	90.0%
Q2CY11	93	102	91.2%
Q3CY11	91	105	86.7%
Q4CY11	83	93	89.2%
12 mth	367	413	88.9%

Developmental Period = P

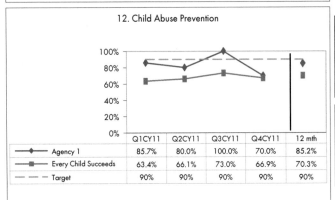

12. Child Abuse Prevention

	Q1CY11	Q2CY11	Q3CY11	Q4CY11	12 mth
Agency 1	85.7%	80.0%	100.0%	70.0%	85.2%
Every Child Succeeds	63.4%	66.1%	73.0%	66.9%	70.3%
Target	90%	90%	90%	90%	90%

Agency 1			
Quarter	N	D	Rate
Q1CY11	6	7	85.7%
Q2CY11	4	5	80.0%
Q3CY11	4	4	100.0%
Q4CY11	7	10	70.0%
12 mth	23	27	85.2%

Every Child Succeeds			
Quarter	N	D	Rate
Q1CY11	64	101	63.4%
Q2CY11	72	109	66.1%
Q3CY11	84	115	73.0%
Q4CY11	79	118	66.9%
12 mth	317	451	70.3%

Developmental Period = 1

13. Education

	Q1CY11	Q2CY11	Q3CY11	Q4CY11	12 mth
Agency 1	33.3%	36.4%	60.0%	50.0%	42.4%
Every Child Succeeds	44.7%	42.1%	57.1%	53.7%	51.1%
Target	50%	50%	50%	50%	50%

Agency 1			
Quarter	N	D	Rate
Q1CY11	3	9	33.3%
Q2CY11	4	11	36.4%
Q3CY11	3	5	60.0%
Q4CY11	4	8	50.0%
12 mth	14	33	42.4%

Every Child Succeeds			
Quarter	N	D	Rate
Q1CY11	21	47	44.7%
Q2CY11	24	57	42.1%
Q3CY11	36	63	57.1%
Q4CY11	36	67	53.7%
12 mth	121	237	51.1%

Developmental Period = 2, 3

Education 24 months			
Agency 1			
Quarter	N	D	Rate
Q1CY11	2	5	40.0%
Q2CY11	2	5	40.0%
Q3CY11	3	5	60.0%
Q4CY11	3	7	42.9%
12 mth	10	22	45.5%

Every Child Succeeds			
Quarter	N	D	Rate
Q1CY11	11	25	44.0%
Q2CY11	15	34	44.1%
Q3CY11	24	37	64.9%
Q4CY11	24	45	53.3
12 mth	77	142	54.2%

Education 36 months			
Agency 1			
Quarter	N	D	Rate
Q1CY11	1	4	25.0%
Q2CY11	2	6	33.3%
Q3CY11	0	0	–
Q4CY11	1	1	100.0%
12 mth	4	11	36.4%

Every Child Succeeds			
Quarter	N	D	Rate
Q1CY11	10	22	45.5%
Q2CY11	9	23	39.1%
Q3CY11	12	26	46.2%
Q4CY11	12	22	54.5%
12 mth	44	95	46.3%

Q1 Trend Report Sample 2012 *(continued)*

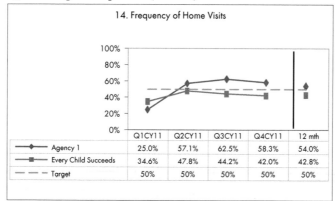

14. Frequency of Home Visits

	Q1CY11	Q2CY11	Q3CY11	Q4CY11	12 mth
Agency 1	25.0%	57.1%	62.5%	58.3%	54.0%
Every Child Succeeds	34.6%	47.8%	44.2%	42.0%	42.8%
Target	50%	50%	50%	50%	50%

Agency 1			
Quarter	N	D	Rate
Q1CY11	2	8	25.0%
Q2CY11	8	14	57.1%
Q3CY11	10	16	62.5%
Q4CY11	14	24	58.3%
12 mth	34	63	54.0%

Every Child Succeeds			
Quarter	N	D	Rate
Q1CY11	53	153	34.6%
Q2CY11	77	161	47.8%
Q3CY11	69	156	44.2%
Q4CY11	74	176	42.0%
12 mth	281	656	42.8%

Developmental Period = N/A

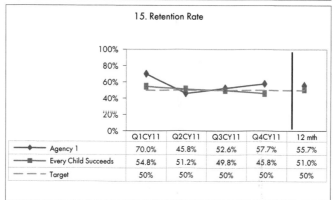

15. Retention Rate

	Q1CY11	Q2CY11	Q3CY11	Q4CY11	12 mth
Agency 1	70.0%	45.8%	52.6%	57.7%	55.7%
Every Child Succeeds	54.8%	51.2%	49.8%	45.8%	51.0%
Target	50%	50%	50%	50%	50%

Agency 1			
Quarter	N	D	Rate
Q1CY11	7	10	70.0%
Q2CY11	11	24	45.8%
Q3CY11	10	19	52.6%
Q4CY11	15	26	57.7%
12 mth	44	79	55.7%

Every Child Succeeds			
Quarter	N	D	Rate
Q1CY11	144	263	54.8%
Q2CY11	130	254	51.2%
Q3CY11	126	253	49.8%
Q4CY11	143	312	45.8%
12 mth	551	1081	51.0%

Developmental Period = N/A

16. Forms Completion

	Q1CY11	Q2CY11	Q3CY11	Q4CY11	12 mth
Agency 1	91.9%	96.2%	94.6%	94.8%	93.5%
Every Child Succeeds	85.8%	87.3%	87.8%	87.8%	85.1%
Target	75%	75%	75%	85%	85%

Agency 1			
Quarter	N	D	Rate
Q1CY11	580	631	91.9%
Q2CY11	602	626	96.2%
Q3CY11	562	594	94.6%
Q4CY11	544	574	94.8%
12 mth	1721	1840	93.5%

Every Child Succeeds			
Quarter	N	D	Rate
Q1CY11	7097	8269	85.8%
Q2CY11	7265	8324	87.3%
Q3CY11	7616	8670	87.8%
Q4CY11	7670	8731	87.8%
12 mth	22149	26031	85.1%

Developmental Period = N/A

QI Red Green Chart Sample 2012
Every Child Succeeds—Quality Indicators
04/01/11–03/31/12

		Target	Agency 1	Agency 2	Agency 3	Agency 4	Agency 5	Agency 6	Agency 7	Agency 8	Agency 9	Agency 10	Agency 11	ECS Total
1	Breast-feeding for 1 Month	50%	33%	43%	38%	100%	54%	18%	38%	57%	34%	33%	42%	42%
2	HP&D - Gestational Age	90%	94%	95%	95%	75%	88%	100%	82%	82%	79%	94%	100%	90%
3	HP&D - Birth Weight	90%	93%	90%	92%	80%	90%	97%	87%	89%	79%	93%	97%	90%
4	MH - Well Baby Check-ups	85%	84%	81%	85%	64%	73%	68%	68%	96%	91%	84%	82%	82%
5	Immunizations	80%	54%	67%	0%	38%	71%	93%	52%	86%	54%	79%	71%	71%
6	LD&L - MacArthur	75%	58%	59%	62%	47%	71%	93%	30%	71%	58%	58%	60%	60%
7	LD&L - Ages & Stages	85%	80%	79%	81%	86%	68%	64%	93%	100%	89%	80%	64%	82%
8	Motor Development	85%	82%	82%	62%	53%	79%	92%	60%	93%	94%	82%	92%	83%
9	Emo, Beh & So Development	85%	85%	75%	54%	48%	79%	86%	84%	93%	89%	85%	93%	82%
10	Mental Health	90%	84%	90%	96%	86%	96%	95%	85%	91%	95%	84%	87%	91%
11	Nursery Safety	95%	75%	95%	95%	75%	98%	94%	84%	85%	92%	75%	86%	89%
12	Child Abuse Prevention	90%	78%	67%	69%	100%	69%	74%	55%	62%	86%	78%	56%	70%
13	Education	50%	47%	33%	43%	45%	43%	85%	46%	33%	88%	47%	67%	51%
14	Frequency of Home Visits	50%	32%	45%	40%	9%	51%	42%	35%	65%	31%	32%	40%	43%
15	Retention Rate	50%	41%	59%	56%	26%	47%	52%	59%	51%	60%	41%	54%	51%
16	Forms Completion	85%	83%	83%	91%	80%	86%	89%	83%	74%	94%	83%	91%	85%

- Results meet or exceed established target
- Results do not meet established target
- Insufficient population – Denominator < 10

The QI Red/Green Chart is an internal quality improvement document for use by ECS administration, agencies, and home visitors. It is not for general distribution outside of ECS, and it should not be interpreted as a summary of ECS outcomes. © Every Child Succeeds, Inc., 2012

JM 6/12

At the time, that simple chart was revolutionary because, for the first time, we were recording the performance of our agencies on key metrics, and we were doing it quarterly, noting trends and progress toward the targets we had established for ourselves and sharing results. We built in an active feedback loop providing information to agencies that was specific for families, caseloads, agencies and the overall system. Cumulative numbers were shared at monthly lead agency meetings so agencies could see how they measured up against their peers. The Red Green Chart, a point-in-time measurement, became famous among us and worked for several years. It was the single most important document that we had to demonstrate that we were doing what we promised. It allowed us to know what was or was not working and where there was room for improvement. And it emphasized our commitment to transparency.

The broad release decision was an excellent one and grounded in what most serious efforts have found: Provider agencies learned from each other; healthy competition was engendered; and collaborative learning became a core process for us. When we moved to the more sophisticated, systematic, and ultimately more effective Institute for Healthcare Improvement (IHI) system, we knew that it was better, but many of us still valued the clarity and simplicity of the Red Green Chart.

We migrated to be compatible with Cincinnati Children's child-data platform, reluctantly at first. For years, the Red Green Chart was how we measured quality and how we answered the "what" questions. Our data and efforts would help us with the "why"—finding the answers.

The IHI Model for Improvement allowed us to build upon the Red Green Chart by not only noting where targets were not being met but also offering a way to improve performance. Even though our unit might have initially been an "n of one," or a small test of change, we knew that by moving slowly and carefully, we were constructing a firm foundation for modification. In the P&G vernacular, this was described as "make a little, sell a little, learn a lot."

And the IHI model prevented big mistakes. Better to make limited errors than to launch a community-wide change without being aware of the potential hazards. The IHI model for improvement asks three questions:

1. *What are you trying to accomplish? (Set smart aim)* We identified specific, measurable, and time-bound projects that would help us solve a problem or identify an innovative approach that could be spread across other home visitors and agencies.

2. *How will we know that the change is an improvement? (Measure)* We used small samples to provide quick results and minimize disruption to current work, and we collected data to track performance. The data helped us identify agencies with best-practice approaches and those that could be improved. Understanding the variation across the system helped guide project development and monitor small-scale testing.

3. *What changes can we make that will result in improvement? (Test)* Typically, we tested ideas with one family at a time using the IHI plan-do-study-act (PDSA) cycles to learn what could reliably be replicated. Our initial cycles were on the smallest scale possible. And we followed the IHI guideline to try ideas with one family to help us know which ideas could be adapted, adopted, or abandoned.

For ECS, I added a fourth question: *Is our QI work expanding our ability to apply actionable findings?* To move from what we know to what we do?

For the QI work at ECS, we focused on one-to-two projects at a time, keeping in mind that the projects needed to be meaningful to the participants and amenable to changes that the home visitor could make. Further, we needed to have baseline data available to track pre- and post-QI results. The focus was always on outcomes, but initially we examined process measures to ensure that the infrastructure was sound for changes we might want to make. Along with Massie as our quality improvement consultant from

Cincinnati Children's and project lead, both research director Ammerman and I also were trained in quality improvement strategies by Cincinnati Children's. This enabled us to assist and guide the work at ECS.

Results of QI efforts were reported on a specified schedule to the ECS board and the program committee using a dashboard structure for easy review. The report included the range of performance measures among agencies and descriptions of interventions tied to each of the results. The report and dashboard were part of our efforts to be transparent, show results, and learn from failures.

Population-Level Performance Monitoring

Measuring success for the whole population served is a critical facet of measurement for any child-and-family-service organization. At a minimum, these measures are typically used to show results, and in many cases, performance is tied to financial incentives or penalties. This is true for home visiting, particularly in Ohio.

Every nonprofit has its own set of metrics to judge performance along with its requirements for accountability and transparency. The point here is that whatever the measures, they must accurately reflect the organization's activity and outcomes, and leadership must be willing to be candid so that funders and stakeholders know whether the organization is meeting its commitment. If not, how do they plan to improve? The importance of the quality of the organization's data cannot be minimized or ignored.

Initially, our outcomes for performance were focused on birth outcomes for mothers and babies, child health, developmental progress, positive parent-child interaction, and achievement of life goals. For process we used referrals, engagement, retention, and operation. We continued to update the metrics quarterly and to share the results among all agencies. We were able to begin to add in our experience with our QI projects, turning trend numbers into implementation opportunities. Performance monitoring for the population served was an equally important aspect

Leadership must be willing to be candid so that funders and stakeholders know whether the organization is meeting its commitment.

of measurement. The data collected for QI and population-level performance monitoring were the same, yet they were applied in different ways.

Here is a real-life example. In January 2015, we found that only 72% of children actively enrolled in ECS were fully immunized by age two. We aimed to improve that rate to 85% by June 2016. Past performance for the last three quarters had been below 70%, and monthly numbers ranged from 57% to 74%. At that time, roughly 30 ECS children turned two each month. Using QI small tests of change, we engaged in several activities to improve the immunization rate, including partnering with medical providers, improving access to and timely utilization of statewide databases, educating home visitors to be more aware of when children were due to be vaccinated, and reporting progress on the monthly ECS performance reports. This enabled us to meet our goal.

Over time, in line with federal and state-required performance measures and our own priorities for success, we monitored a broader set of measures. This enabled ECS to show impact on an array of important aspects of health and well-being for mothers, infants, and young children. This includes positive results in the following areas.

- **Child health and development:** Compared to their peers, children in ECS had the advantage of better child health, including lower rates of infant mortality and prematurity, higher rates of on-time immunizations, fewer developmental delays, and more nurturing and learning with their parents.

- **Improved maternal well-being and life course:** Mothers in ECS had the advantage of getting more timely prenatal care, support for smoking cessation, and maternal depression treatment. In line with their life plans, they were more likely than their peers to delay subsequent pregnancies, to complete high school, to be employed, and to have greater earnings.

Showing results on multiple measures across the ECS population served reflects the purpose and essence of performance monitoring.

What Results Were Achieved?

These results from 2017 were typical of what was achieved among the families who participated in ECS. The families served by home visiting fared better than comparison populations in terms of education, employment, maternal and infant health, mental health, early relationships, child development, and more.

More Education and Employment

Mothers in ECS were more likely to:

- *Complete high school*: 80% of mothers had a high school degree by the time their child was 24 months.
- *Return to work or education following the birth of their baby*: More than 70% of ECS mothers returned to school or work.
- *Be employed*: 38% of ECS mothers reported employment at time of enrollment, increasing to 77% by the time children reached 15 months.
- *Have increased income*: 25% of employed mothers in ECS reported an annual household income of less than $3,000 at enrollment; this rate of extreme poverty decreased to 15% by the time children are 15 months.

Improved Maternal Well-Being and Life Course

Mothers in ECS had the advantage of:

- *Being reached and served in communities with high levels of poverty and disinvestment*: Using an intensive engagement strategy in a high-risk Cincinnati neighborhood, ECS increased retention in the program by 30%.
- *Getting depression treatment*: Among mothers with major depressive disorder who received Moving Beyond Depression services in ECS, 70% were successfully treated.
- *Delayed subsequent pregnancies*: Mothers with robust participation in ECS had a 33% lower risk for rapid, repeat pregnancy than mothers who had lower participation.

Better Child Health and Development

Compared to their peers, children in ECS had the advantage of:

- *Less infant mortality*: Babies in families enrolled in ECS were 60% less likely to die as infants, in the first year of life.
- *Being born on time*: More than 90% of ECS children were born on time, not prematurely.
- *Healthy infant development*: Over 95% of ECS babies were developing normally on their first birthday, compared to 82% in similar populations. More completed home visits were linked to higher rates of optimal development.
- *Opportunities to learn at home*: 95% of parents were actively involved in their child's learning.
- *Being nurtured*: By 15 months of age, 72% of children lived in homes with a high level of emotional support and nurturing early relationships.
- *Getting ready for school*: 86% of families who graduated from ECS had a plan to send their children to preschool.

Source: Analysis of eECS internal data.

Publicly funded programs delivered by nonprofit organizations in communities across the country, including home visiting programs, are expected to show results. Moving the needle for the ECS population served is a primary goal, and in some cases, such as in Ohio Help Me Grow, payments or incentives are tied to performance. At the same time, as discussed previously, with programs reaching only 20% of need, it is difficult to move the needle on outcomes for the community population overall. Since performance monitoring relies so heavily on collecting the right data of the highest possible quality, it is worth discussing how we got data to do our measurement.

Some Data Challenges

Finding Baseline Data

As a part of our business-oriented thinking, we knew that we needed to be able to quantify our work. We needed baseline data to assess where we were on day one and then, going forward, we needed a system to house and analyze the information we would collect to gauge our progress.

One story focuses on our search for data to shape the Task Force phase-one recommendations. David R. Walker, smart and senior at P&G, was helping us identify and collect information to construct recommendations for the report. He was stunned when he realized what data did not exist. He let us know that there is no way P&G could conduct its business given such sparse information, and he was sure that we had to look harder and be more aggressive. Finally, Walker decided to send a few P&G people to Washington, DC, to find what we were unable to produce. Sadly, they came back empty-handed. The data problem was not just a local one but rather it was—and continues to be, although it is improved—a national issue. Too often decisions are made without adequate information.

What the Washington, DC trip did was to underscore the need to require that the new ECS program at Cincinnati Children's

Hospital would have adequate funding to conduct QI, evaluation, and research to improve and guide decision-making for program operation, outcome monitoring, and return on investment.

Help came from Cincinnati Children's, which insisted on good measurement, research, and evaluation as requirements for its participation. We were able, with the hospital's support, to secure funding sufficient to develop a sound research focus, high-quality staff, and leadership from two invaluable, nationally known researchers focused on children and families—Ammerman, a PhD clinical psychologist, and Putnam, a physician, psychiatrist, and international expert in child abuse.

As time passed, what we as an organization encountered was not unique. Too often, even when we know what to do, we cannot do it, perhaps because of not enough funding, perhaps public attention is focused in a different direction, perhaps the need is not obvious.

Our response was just to keep learning, doing what we knew was right and making the case publicly as effectively as we could.

When P&G's then-CEO Pepper provided testimony to the United States Senate in April 2014 to support The Strong Start for America's Children Act (a piece of legislation designed to bolster Head Start, child care, pre-K, and home visiting programs), he said, "In business we rarely have the luxury of making an investment decision with as much evidence as we have to support the economic value of investing in early childhood development and education." So, the case for the value of early childhood investment in children and families for economic development and family well-being was clear.

In 2014, while the new federal home visiting program, MIECHV, had been launched and would collect data and information on QI, performance monitoring, and evaluation for the thousands of home visiting programs now supported by grants to states, the data were not yet in. Many studies of home visiting models pointed to the effectiveness of the services under research conditions (Duggan et al. 2022; Supplee et al. 2021; Green et al. 2020; Greenwood et al. 2018; American Academy of Pediatrics 2017; Minkovitz et al.

2016; Avellar and Supplee 2013; Duggan et al. 2013; Goyal et al. 2013; Olds et al. 1997; Olds et al. 1988). At the same time, Walker found as he looked for data about the effectiveness of specific programs operating in communities that the data/information on their effectiveness were lacking.

Yet, we succeeded in collecting data to an extent we could not have initially envisioned. Since our inception in 1999, ECS had accumulated extensive data for over 700,000 home visits. Carefully collected and validated for accuracy, this data file, we believed, would be a treasure for scientists. We moved the file to Cincinnati Children's where it became part of a Maternal and Child Health Data Hub at the Children's Research Foundation and over time to researchers outside of our institution. The file is expected to continue to grow, including not only the initial 700,000 visits but additional data for the approximately 30,000 visits that are made annually to families in ECS. The hope is that it will in time become the kind of data file that Walker searched for over 20 years ago. Such data could serve as groundwork for early childhood system efforts.

The Need for Good Data

Having clean, reliable data for decision-making is fundamental. Yet, many nonprofit agencies have little or no history of collecting, collating, and analyzing data. Nor do they have staff people trained in those disciplines to help. There are two reasons: First, historically many nonprofits were not asked for data to show results. Second, in general, nonprofits simply did not have the funds to pay for data collection and management. Many nonprofits were faced with the need to document their effectiveness but lacked the personnel or the resources to do so.

Increasingly, government entities and philanthropists want to see results from their investments and, without an ability to use data to document what is happening, not only are agencies unable to answer the key questions, they also cannot compete well for funds. Gone are the days when an agency can point to happy clients as evidence of success. Funders and policy makers legitimately want to know what happened, who was served, and what were the outcomes? Was it cost effective? Were improved outcomes sustained? At ECS, we were fortunate because, under the guidance of Cincinnati Children's and with funding from the United Way, we were able to build and sustain a vigorous evaluation and research component for our program.

The data issue had two components: Do you have the data? And is it reliable? Data integrity was frequently subject to being compromised, because as data were entered into multiple data-collection systems, entry errors were possible. As a recipient of both public and private dollars, there were multiple opportunities for error by ECS. Each transaction had the potential for a mistake. Further, the data collection systems had varying levels of compatibility, and the person entering the data was often dependent on someone else, in our case home visitors and agencies, for information. Repeated checks and balances were required, and staff was needed to do the work.

We needed reliable data for analysis, and therein lies a challenge. Within ECS, we could enlist our provider agencies individually and collectively to check and check again before they submitted data to us. And then we could go over it again. However, not all organizations are able to engage in this labor-intensive process. So, when it comes time to compare or combine data from one organization to that of another, the data may not reflect the same rigor. As data are entered into various systems, the opportunity for error increases, and we were submitting data to federal and state governments, home visiting program models, funders, grant allocators, and program partners.

To offer some idea of what this looks like, in addition to reports required for grants and fundraising, annually we collected and analyzed data for, at a minimum, 52 reports, many of them mandatory. We maintained a report activity timeline with the following information:

1. Activity/core evaluation
2. Description
3. Purpose
4. Key tasks
5. Stakeholders
6. Why important
7. Impact if ECS doesn't do it
8. Priority
9. Estimated effort
10. Other resources needed
11. Timeline
12. What/how could ECS improve how this activity is done

For ECS, data and information from these reports were used to monitor agency compliance and performance, to support research grants and evaluation projects, to meet program requirements, and to comply with local, state, and federal regulations. I remember a conversation from early in my tenure when we were just beginning to receive a sizable amount of data, and our agencies/home visitors were finally comfortable with the data collection processes. Every Monday morning, we had an evaluation team meeting. We presented reports from information that had been compiled by the agencies during the previous week. In this case, the focus was on the number of children who had died while in our program and how we had recorded those deaths. The report was a part of our careful monitoring of our infant mortality experience. Our scientific director and our evaluation director asked—as they always did—dozens of questions about the data: How were they collected? What was missing? Were the numbers duplicated or unduplicated? Who recorded them? Have they been verified? It was a barrage of questions, yet typical of how we analyzed all of our findings so that we could issue complete and accurate reports based on careful review of our forms and inventories.

In the case of the infant death data, the information became a central part of our infant mortality study, ultimately published as an article in the journal *Pediatrics* (Donovan et al. 2007). It also reinforced the realization that evidence-based home visiting properly implemented can be an important element in reducing the unacceptably high rates of infant mortality in our community. (This was not a finding in other home visiting research published at the time.) As we examined our findings more closely, we realized that not only were our mortality rates low, but there was no racial disparity, bringing to mind a crucial question—why, when we have carefully validated a finding, and know how to deliver the program that leads to that finding, isn't the program expanded to allow more mothers and more infants to benefit? The answer continues to elude me. It's clear the science is not being followed, or worse.

A Web-Based System—eECS

Another important facet of the ECS data story is about the creation—and possible dissemination—of a web-based platform that would house our data, create the data files, and allow analysis of the information we would collect. This was essential to managing the volume of data we collected and wanted to use for QI, performance measurement, and research and evaluation.

We were able to secure support—using United Way funds—to contract with the University of Cincinnati to build a web-based data-collection system to meet our data collection and analysis needs. Having looked all over the country for a system compatible with our program, we realized that what we wanted did not exist. Although ECS now works with multiple systems from different states, programs, and research holdings, the locally created eECS seems to be the gold standard.

Jonathan Kopke, a technology genius—he would object to my use of the word—worked with our multiple stakeholders to create a system that he defined as "user-friendly." Countless hours of testing were needed before even the smallest change was made to eECS. The exhaustive process was replicated over and over again, which is why it worked so well. Often the recommended changes came from the home visitors themselves as they offered new solutions to old problems, confirming the system was absolutely user-friendly. eECS has been the place we visited when we have really needed to understand what was happening with our families (Kopke et al. 2003).

Well after we started using eECS, Kopke admitted something that I hadn't known. When he started on the project in February 2000, he had never created a web-based system. Parts of the ECS system had to be written in five different computer languages: Cold Fusion, CSS, T-SQL, HTML, and JavaScript, and he didn't know any of them. Remarkably, he learned them all and gave us a system that was perfect for our work, user-friendly, and the envy of other home visiting programs. He calls the years with us the best years of his career. Twenty-one years after its creation, he was still supporting the ECS software. A replacement system being developed by the Biomedical Informatics people at Cincinnati Children's was in the works as of this writing.

Kopke recently told me:

> When we launched eECS, many of the home visitors were uncomfortable about having to use the computer for the first time, so, to ease their minds, I always insisted that if the ECS software crashed, it was my fault and not theirs. And, if any home visitor experienced a crash, I would send them a note saying "thank you for helping us perfect our software. To me, you are worth a hundred grand," and I would enclose a 100 Grand candy bar. The postage cost more than the candy, but I always imagined the recipient going around to her friends at her agency and saying, "Look at this!" Then they all knew that it was okay to be relaxed about using the software, even if that led to a crash.

Over time, the home visitors came to appreciate eECS as a resource. One of our home visitors commented that her peers across the country did not have access to an eECS-type resource, and in many cases were still using spreadsheets or their state database. Kopke reflected on his time with ECS by saying, "Over all of my years with ECS, there may have been a few bad computer days, but there's never been a single bad person day." This is another example of infusing new thinking and professionalism into the role of the home visitor.

In terms of missed opportunities, we believed that eECS had the potential to be replicated for home visitation programs across the country. We tried to sell it, but there were many obstacles that prevented the sale and subsequent development of a source of income for ECS. It was clear that for us to monetize and sell eECS, we needed upfront money without any guarantee that there was a market. Organizations like ours don't have access to monies that are not specifically allocated to service delivery or program operation. And, of course, we were not a tech company and discovered that we would need other people/organizations to do most of the work. The role and rewards for ECS likely would be small.

Further, an essential question that we asked ourselves was whether we would be trying to sell a product to entities that didn't have the money to buy it, and did we have the financial and personnel resources to support growth and continued maintenance of the product? eECS needed a bigger play with an organization able to fully develop it, take it to market, and promote it. It was our idea and we not only created it but also effectively used it for two decades. But the opportunity to make it available to others, to build upon a tested/tried/validated resource was not available to us. This underscored one of the primary reasons that nonprofits are so limited in their ability to create independent revenue streams and therefore have to rely on funding from government entities or private donors.

Late in my tenure, ECS continued to record data from visits into eECS, but far less than in earlier years. State systems have improved, and if we were to continue to use both systems, their protocol would require our home visitors to enter data twice— once into the state system and again into eECS.

Our eECS provided a flexible independent system for our QI, performance, and evaluation work. The eECS system was scheduled to be replaced with the more state-centric approach, which is not ideal, but necessary. This may be a good example of being careful about what you wish for: For many years we exhorted the states to do a better job of data collection and offered eECS—a tried-and-tested option that worked. However, over time, the states accessed other resources and slowly built their own systems. They operate effectively, and ECS will be required to use them as a condition of accepting state funds. The situation was, as Ammerman aptly described it, "a dog-eat-dog world and we were a teacup Chihuahua."

Actionable Research

A basic tenet of our three-pronged approach to measurement using QI, performance measurement, research and evaluation efforts also came from the private sector—most notably P&G—who let us know that research was not done to sit upon a shelf but to be acted upon. With our roots in an academic medical institution, we knew about the science, but to support our mission to ensure that all children had an optimal start, we also had to move from the "bench to the bedside," which in our case was the community. We needed to incorporate what we learned into improved service delivery and/or improved family outcomes. Because we are serving families, this is fundamentally different than the type of research and development that might go into a product such as new pharmaceuticals or vaccines.

> Research is not done to sit upon a shelf but to be acted upon.

Although it may seem elementary, it was essential to us that measurement in the context of ECS concentrate on actionable information and new knowledge. With limited resources, prioritizing investigative work that can actually lead to program changes is imperative (Goyal et al. 2016). Spector, our quality improvement consultant, cautioned us to ask ourselves whether what we planned to study had the potential to be usable and whether the findings would be helpful for home visitors and families.

Once our original quality improvement questions were answered, and we could define for ourselves and other stakeholders that we were on the right path, something discouraging but not unexpected occurred. In several cases, we identified an actionable finding that would have improved services for families, but scale-up and/or replication did not occur because we didn't have the funds for implementation. It is axiomatic to repeat: What we wanted to do and what we were able to do was proportional to the resources that were available to us and whether we complied with federal, state, and model requirements.

Three Faces of Measurement in Action

The three faces of measurement have been used and have been important to the success of ECS from the beginning. They are complementary yet different. QI helped us focus on whether we were doing the right things and how to improve day-to-day operations. Performance monitoring let us know if we were improving outcomes for the group of families served. Evaluation and research constitute a broader inquiry that is not always directed to specific program impact questions. However, the new knowledge generated through research can and should inform improvement.

Data collection and data analyses are further complicated by the near impossibility of using gold-standard, randomized clinical trial research designs because the time frame is too long (children grow up), the expense is high, and most important, clinical trials by definition mean that some children would receive no help at all. So, absent the gold standard but focused and committed to answering questions in a reliable way, we applied all our measurement tools in search of increased understanding.

We kept the three types of measurement in mind—quality improvement, performance and results accountability, and evaluation and research. And to that we added: seeking measurement that leads to an opportunity to use our findings in actionable ways. The challenge for a program like ECS was to use measurement work to guide program operation and deliver better outcomes for families. The RAND Corporation said it best in its 2017 research brief, noting, "The research creates a path for policy makers and a road for researchers (Karoly et al. 2017)." Focusing on actionable research and quality improvement methods showed us how to do it.

While ECS had much learning with relevance to other home visiting programs, most opportunities to scale those findings within our community and with other cities and states were unrealized. Some key actionable findings include those on the following list, but it should be noted that although we found areas ripe for change, we were not always able to move forward to apply them for lasting change to our program or the field of home visiting.

ECS Actionable Results from Outcome Data

1. Moms who join ECS at less than 26 weeks gestation and receive at least eight prenatal home visits have a 60% reduced risk of preterm birth.

    Our Response: Work more systematically to identify and enroll moms earlier in pregnancy. Using data from our eECS database, we found that in calendar year 2018, 75% of the moms enrolled by 28 weeks received an average of 11 prenatal home visits. This is a good example of an actionable finding that should have been adopted by programs state- and nationwide because what we had demonstrated presented an opportunity to improve the outcomes for moms and babies by reducing preterm birth. Although we disseminated the finding widely, nothing changed at either the governmental or program level.

2. Moms who became aware of the ECS program as a result of our concentrated work in the Avondale community joined ECS earlier and stayed longer, but we also found that earlier enrollment was not associated with improved parenting.

Our Response: Restore and expand the community initiative, and develop more-focused parenting interventions. We were able to concentrate more intentionally on parenting, but we were not able to locate public or private funds to grow the community intervention.

3. Moms with even a moderate adherence to the recommended home visiting schedule display a 30% reduction in repeat pregnancy prior to 18 months.

   Our Response: Use QI strategies to increase the number of moms who accept more home visits. Using small tests of change to test and modify how home visitors delivered services and engaged families might have helped to increase the number of participants receiving the recommended number of visits.

4. Children in ECS often struggle with literacy and language skills as identified through scores on the standardized tests and measures.

   Our Response: Adopt a more systematic approach into the curriculum to boost vocabulary acquisition and literacy. This problem offers insight into a different aspect of an inability to move on known findings because funds were not available to follow up. Research tells us that words and conversation matter even at the earliest ages. We found grant money to contract with the LENA organization to engage families in the important back-and-forth vocalization with infants (one part of what is sometimes called "serve and return" interactions) to shape the developing brain. We were able to conduct the grant work but once again, there was no money to spread the strategies within ECS or to other programs within Ohio or Kentucky.

5. On-track development for children is associated with lower levels of parenting stress. Parenting stress, trauma, and family violence occur at high rates and are significant issues within ECS.

Our Response: Elevate addressing trauma as a priority within the delivery of home visiting services, both locally and with home visiting as a discipline. Work to reduce stress more systematically for the mom, especially during the first year of life, by providing trauma-informed training for all ECS home visitors. In this case, the state of Ohio also instituted statewide training for home visitors who were encountering magnified stress levels among parents as a result of the COVID-19 pandemic.

6.   Moms who have experienced trauma are more likely to exhibit depressive symptoms and have low levels of social support. Mom's depression frequently affects the child as her ability to parent is diminished.

Our Response: In addition to providing Moving Beyond Depression services through a trained therapist, ECS now offers trauma-informed training for home visitors. Remember, however, that the Moving Beyond Depression set of services is only available where there are funds to pay for it. Even though the efficacy of this new model has been established through random trials and experiential evidence, public funds are often not available to pay for the treatment.

7.   Moms are highly responsive to affirmation of their parenting skills and grateful for time spent addressing their needs and desire more help as they return to school or work.

Our Response: Incorporate a more positive approach to the interaction of the home visitor and the mom, concentrating on a plan and hope for the future. ECS continues to do this and one visible manifestation could be developing a clever charting system to highlight achievement of goals and mark progress. Brentley did this with vigor during the Avondale mom's group meetings. Each meeting began with a celebration and that celebration could be for such things as a new tooth or a full-term pregnancy. It was less important what was being celebrated; the point was to highlight the positive experiences of the families and the successes of these incredible moms.

8. Attrition rates in home visiting remain high and stable over time. Motivational interviewing and qualitative projects have not improved retention: Although moms say that they do not want reduced interaction, only 25% of moms remain engaged until the end of the program when the child is three years old. This finding is endemic to the entire field of home visiting.

   Our Response: Conduct additional focus groups and interviews with individual moms for further learning. We found that moms leaving the program early might actually be a positive response, with moms reporting that they felt strong enough and capable enough to "fly" on their own. In addition, more extensive research was needed to determine "what works best for whom" to link program offerings more effectively with the needs of the individual family. One national program, the Nurse-Family Partnership, has begun offering families an opportunity to work with home visitors to make a plan for frequency and length of visits with that specific family.

9. Moms who are enrolled in ECS are more likely to access early intervention services for developmental risks and delays than comparable families who did not participate in the program.

   Our Response: Continue to encourage families to work with their home visitors and to act when developmental delays are suspected. The relationship between home visiting and early intervention is a good example of coordination that is effective.

10. Bringing fathers into the program intentionally led to more effective co-parenting.

    Our Response: Funding to continue sought but not secured. This is another instance of having new and important information about a better way to deliver home visiting that we were unable to incorporate into the program because funding was not available.

Actionable Results from ECS Quality Improvement

The following examples show greater detail about the interaction of different measurement tools and approaches in a process of improving ECS services. Having a wider array of skills, staff capacity, and data available enhanced our ability to respond to challenges within our service delivery system and were meaningful for the field at large.

Greater Use of Trauma-Informed Care

We became aware of the prevalence (about 70%) of experienced or perceived interpersonal trauma affecting our families, and we knew that there was a high likelihood that the trauma would subsequently affect the foundational early relationships and social/emotional development of the child (website for SAMHSA, "Understanding Child Trauma"). Hence, we obtained a grant to train our home visitors so that they could more effectively respond to the trauma they were seeing. We provided a six-month professionally led course in trauma-informed care for all home visitors. Our anticipated benefits for families included more responsive parenting, improved safety of home environments, and enhanced child development. And importantly, our home visitors themselves expressed great personal interest in this course, too, as it responded to similar needs in their own lives.

Our QI tools helped us understand whether the training had the desired impact on home-visitor service delivery. Over time, performance monitoring would tell us if family context and early relationships were improved. Our evaluation instruments helped us document success, while our research offered depth and explanation. And, because multiple facets of measurement were hallmarks of ECS, we had such breadth of approaches ready to respond to this important insight and need for program improvement.

The work of ECS also provided some new insights related to complex outcomes, such as infant-mortality reduction, literacy and language development, and social/emotional development. These important learnings for the field were made public through the ECS annual report; frequent data briefs; local, state, and national presentations; peer-reviewed articles; board, staff, and agency reports; and media notices, as warranted.

Yet challenges remained for the ECS program and the field in general for empiric knowledge around which outcomes were clearly and substantively improved by enrolling in home visiting.

This research agenda has now been defined as: What works best for whom, and how many visits (what dosage) of what content are needed to achieve specific outcomes? Supports to answer those and similar questions are typically funded through research grants and/or private funders. They are important to confirm the role of home visiting in the important continuum of services for children.

Expanding Outreach and Enrollment

Outreach and enrollment of moms was always a challenge. There were those families who sought us out and joined because they recognized the benefits. Others who might benefit faced barriers to enrollment. We had to ask ourselves: Were they aware of the program? How could we reach the moms who might be the ones who could benefit yet were not enrolled? Did some women find the program threatening or objectionable? Did they perceive it to be culturally sensitive and responsive? Did we ask them for an unrealistic time commitment? Were they afraid or cautious about having someone come into their homes? Were they skeptical about the strategy itself or perceive it as unlikely to be helpful to them? Were there implicit bias factors that were real but not obvious to ECS?

We did some exploration through qualitative research, convening numerous focus groups, individual interviews, and ethnographic studies to attempt to answer two seemingly simple questions: Why don't women who could benefit from the program join? And why do families who join typically only stay 18 months? These were basic questions on the surface but far more complicated and worthy of sincere and honest study. Various investigations conducted by

Neera Goyal, MD, a pediatrician with a special interest in perinatal outcomes, clearly understood "bench to bedside." She led us to greater understanding of the timing of enrollment and duration of participation (Goyal et al. 2018; Goyal et al. 2017; Goyal et al. 2016; Goyal et al. 2014; Goyal et al. 2013).

Unexpectedly, as mentioned previously, we gained one valuable insight into the questions about length of program enrollment: we began to understand that moms who were leaving the program at 18 months were not leaving because we had failed, but rather, because we and they had succeeded. Moms told us that they had developed confidence in themselves and were ready to go forth on their own. They had become better positioned to take action for themselves and their children, they were going back to school and back to work, and they were doing what we encouraged and aimed to support—being independent and using self-agency to achieve their goals.

Work Left Undone

Other topics have appeared that additionally needed strong, actionable measurement and research. These include: the potential for improving the relationship between home visiting and pediatric primary care; the opportunity to support tiered community teams that would include home visitors along with community health workers and other outreach workers; and the focus on creating a two-generational and community-building approach that would lead to better coordinated systems of services for families.

Importantly, what underlies the possibility of success for any of these services and initiatives is both understanding and taking action to reduce the role of racism in families' lived experiences with home visiting services, health care, trauma, depression, and other factors that affect daily life. We saw the importance of changing structural racism to maximize the opportunity for success among the families and children served. Measurement has been identified as a key part of state and national efforts to reduce racism and bias in child and family services (Wien et al. 2023; Dyer et al. 2022; Hardeman et al. 2022; Condon et al. 2021; Zephryin 2021; Bruner 2017; Ellis and Dietz 2017; Johnson and Theberge 2007).

ECS Measurement Contributions to the Field of Home Visiting

The ECS measurement strategies and research agenda brought many new insights to the field of home visiting, including topics related to impact on birth outcomes, why mothers engage or continue participation in home visiting, the attributes of effective home visitors, and the value of community engagement and enhancements. As previously discussed, one research project, led by Putnam and Ammerman, resulted in the development of a new evidence-based in-home cognitive behavioral therapy program called Moving Beyond Depression, which works in tandem with home visiting to effectively treat maternal depression.

Here, guidance came to us from Kay Johnson, a national expert in maternal and child health, who consulted with ECS for nearly 20 years. Using her decades of national experience, Johnson urged us to ask penetrating and often uncomfortable questions about what we were doing and why. With her nearly encyclopedic knowledge of home visiting policies and procedures, Johnson helped us place our concerns and issues within the context of agendas larger than our own. We wanted to place this line of thinking on the national stage, to offer a format for scientists, program and business leaders, funders, and policy makers working in the home visiting space to consider new ideas and new findings together.

It was Johnson who worked with us and the Pew Charitable Trusts Home Visiting Campaign in 2011 to implement our idea to establish the first National Summit on Quality in Home Visiting. We called it a "marketplace of ideas," and what we envisioned was a meeting where our colleagues could gather to learn about what we were learning, how legislation might affect our work, and how public and private funders were supporting home visiting as a prevention strategy for children birth-to-three years of age. After the first five years of annual Home Visiting Summits, the distinguished Ounce of Prevention Fund (and now renamed Start Early) assumed leadership for the summit, and in 2021 the summit celebrated its 10th year with over 1,200 attendees. What began in 2011 with 400 people grew to become an important national forum, maintaining the original concepts of learning from each other, supporting the crucial role of science and policy in home visiting, and determining how home visiting fit within the larger context of early childhood programming.

We envisioned that a national summit could be held to address the seminal questions that the RAND Corporation first asked in its 1997 report, *Investing in Our Children*. RAND analysts expressed concern that "it is unclear what will happen to these programs (home visiting) once the media spotlight moves on and budgets tighten." The report highlighted the difficulty in understanding why successful programs work—what are optimal program designs? How can prevention and early intervention programs best target those who would benefit most? Can scaled programs produce the same results? What is the full range of benefits? How will the programs be affected by the changing social safety net? In short, RAND advocated for increased research to determine why programs work, for building and expanding the evidence base, not just resting upon it.

ECS as an Innovation Lab

The experience of ECS in its efforts to become a laboratory for innovation further illuminates why nonprofits are so often stymied in their quest to improve and grow. When our for-profit colleagues identify a product or a service with potential, they can finance their proof-of-concept activities, sometimes by using internal research and development funds, or support from outside investors or seed money. They typically have research and development components within their business structure, specifically focused on finding new products or upgrading existing products. The lifeblood of the company is maintaining market share, and that is done by continuing to produce something a consumer would want to buy or needs to use. Typically, money within for-profit organizations is allocated for growth and expansion. As examples, the toothpaste that seemed fine this year is improved next year with additional whitening properties or ingredients to maintain gum health. The dog food is upgraded to be more balanced and healthier. These are improvements that not only add value to the consumer but also bring market value to the company.

What happens in the nonprofit world is that funds are rarely available for such improvements, or sufficiently resourced for growth and development. Rather, budgets are built with minimal overhead and organizations are lauded for spending the lowest amount possible even for basic service, in our case the home visit. What might help an organization like ours to improve family outcomes or to disseminate a new strategy to other home visiting programs is not supported. The concept of entrepreneurial thinking and the excitement of innovation are thus often lost. With them goes the opportunity to improve our intervention, to bring new dollars to the enterprise and simply to be stronger. The growth equation does require initial money for development and testing, subsequent funding to bring the idea to market, and finally support for sustainability. Grants can work at steps one and two, but the long-term sustainability issue largely falls to public-sector funders, which is usually harder to move.

For example: we used public and private grant money to create the Moving Beyond Depression intervention and minimally create public awareness. What we never had was the public-sector money that would have allowed us to scale Moving Beyond Depression more broadly to states and large home visiting programs and to sustain the effort, even though we had demonstrated that mothers improved dramatically with the intervention. And that although there was an initial cost, reduced expenditures may be possible as the mother's depression was treated and she was able to be a better parent, less dependent over the years on the health care system.

The idea for taking ECS from a local/regional program to an innovation lab with national impact came up in 2018 and 2019. To begin to understand where we might fit in the landscape, we did some brand comparisons of other think tank or innovation lab type organizations working on early childhood and/or home visiting issues. The scope and scale of our innovations in program delivery and research were unique. We had lessons to share, tools that could add value for others, and evidence-based practices to disseminate. This direction fit with what we had been doing. Yet how could we make the leap, given limited resources that were primarily dedicated to direct services in our community? How could we be both a highly successful home visiting program and an innovation lab without substantial new resources?

So, here is where we aimed with the ECS innovation lab. Our ECS staff, working with our board and the scientific advisory committee in 2020–2021, recognized the need for improved focus and specificity for our initiatives. Further, we wanted to capitalize on what we saw as our role in the home visiting field. We were a laboratory for innovation in home visiting and used three evidence-based home visiting models, three types of measurement (QI, performance, and evaluation and research), and innovative augmentations while supporting strong parenting and child development annually for nearly 2,000 families.

We knew that over the years, we had become much more sophisticated and that there were an estimated 4,000 to 5,000 local home visiting programs operating in agencies across the country. In essence, we had a self-imposed "identity crisis" as we analyzed who we were now and what ECS could/should become in the next 20 years, building on our strengths and learning from our failures.

ECS was at a crossroads. For more than 20 years, we had a robust service-delivery program, with measurement and research efforts that contributed to improving services for the local program and programs nationally. Yet we did not think that we had achieved our full potential. Moreover, the home visiting field itself had changed considerably, especially since 2014 when the federal MIECHV home visiting program had been fully implemented. Funding options shifted, more questions emerged about how home visiting fit into early childhood systems, a clearer picture emerged of the limits of existing knowledge about home visiting, and new questions and approaches to guide research were being considered. As a result, we saw an opportunity for ECS to reconceptualize its efforts and to assume a position of innovation and leadership by taking the opportunity to answer important questions in the field, leading to substantive program improvements.

But to be seen as a leader in generating ideas for improving home visitation, we required national recognition for our work and the branding to provide awareness. We saw the designation of ECS as an innovation lab as a path to establish our role on the national stage, leveraging our expertise and that of Cincinnati Children's and building upon our learnings and our accomplishments.

To make that happen three things were needed: funding to support an innovation lab infrastructure, concurrence for the initiative among our stakeholders, and a commitment to focused work.

We knew that we would initially be unable to compete with the large and well-funded initiatives at the Harvard Center on the Developing Child, the federally funded Home Visiting Applied Research Collaborative (HARC) at Johns Hopkins Bloomberg School of Public Health, the Children's Hospital of Philadelphia (CHOP), and the University of Chicago's Chapin Hall. Yet with our own data infrastructure, service capacity, and the expertise at Cincinnati Children's, we knew the right pieces were in place for what we wanted to do.

The locus of our strength was our broad vision not just for what might appeal to a funder but also what we could do to uncover what makes home visiting effective and what makes it relevant. We knew that ECS was impactful, but it could be better. We were in a perfect place to begin to answer these questions because we were one of the few places in the country where home visiting was grounded in an outstanding children's medical center, where multiple models of service were used, and where the focus on

> For an organization to assume a position of innovation and leadership, it needs national recognition for the work it is doing and branding to provide awareness.

innovation for improved outcomes had been a tradition. Moreover, we had used the three types of measurement and had a large database and set of skills from which to build.

We agreed that both the strength and weakness of most evidence-based home visiting work was the breadth of what the program hoped to accomplish with families, but we acknowledged that we could not do it all. We knew that we must accept the role of home visiting as part of a solution, part of a continuum of services for families and young children. We acknowledged continued success for all of us was dependent upon collaboration and cooperation with the community—how well we worked together to solve problems and improve our intervention.

Without discarding the work we were doing, we believed that if we could concentrate on one clearly defined, measurable outcome that was important to families in home visiting programs, we could "move the needle" for that outcome. We chose Ready for Pre-K as the focus. The aim was to ensure that all children leaving ECS would be on track on all areas of development, ready to thrive in the preschool setting, and with the start that they needed to succeed in school and in life.

If we were able to make definitive and verifiable statements about how home visiting contributes to achieving that outcome, we could substantially add to the reasons for supporting home visiting at all funding levels.

The innovation lab, we argued, was the right structure to engage in that kind of focused, deliberate work. Yet we knew that the lab could not operate without a budget for infrastructure, including content experts and staff. Becoming an innovation lab would position us as a trusted organization that could be relied upon to advance an innovative, focused mission, as well as providing high-quality services for families.

We wanted the innovation lab to be chaired by a business executive or someone who would have a realistic view of the entire system. We stressed the importance of a clear, concise mission and focused meetings.

> Becoming an innovation lab would position us as a trusted organization that could be relied upon to advance an innovative, focused mission, as well as providing high-quality services for families.

As I retired from my role as president of ECS, the innovation lab concept was still being considered by the staff and the board. The idea had not been implemented, even though support for the idea remained strong and the possibilities were recognized. Without funding for the infrastructure, a vibrant innovation lab cannot exist.

The Need for Evidence

There is an important discussion occurring at a national level that has the potential to change the way in which nonprofits define evidence to support the effectiveness of their programming. Think tanks and foundations, including the Brookings Institute, Pew Charitable Trust, American Enterprise Institute, Harvard Center on the Developing Child, Urban Institute, and several government entities (e.g., Government Accountability Office) are addressing the essential question: What really constitutes evidence to guide public investments?

The word *evidence* has different meanings for different people. Definitions have become facile, and the word itself has been so overused that when we say that a home visiting program, for example, is evidence-based, it is not altogether clear what that means. This is a particularly important question, since federal law requires that MIECHV funds be used primarily to fund evidence-based home visiting.

Katharine B. Stevens, PhD, then a scholar at the American Enterprise Institute, wrote in her unpublished manuscript titled "Why We Need New Evidence Standards for Publicly Funded Social Programs" that "A distinct set of standards, uniquely relevant to research to guide policy decision making, is badly needed. The central question those standards must answer is: What effect size on which outcomes must be demonstrated to provide policymakers with a high degree of confidence that people's lives will be positively impacted in a substantial and meaningful way?" She calls for increased focus on significant impact, outcomes, study quality, and numbers of studies (Personal communication, unpublished manuscript).

At ECS, the challenge to define those terms has been central to our work because, without knowing what was working—and, importantly, why—the value of our work could not be ascertained. We began with a focused effort to determine how we could obtain accurate and timely data for decision-making. With our strong foundation in measurement, we were able to create the mechanisms to collect, verify, and analyze our data. We hired staff to work on those assignments, we became well-positioned to operate in a data-informed world. We were fortunate to have the resources for these activities, but many nonprofits do not have the staff or the systems to manage the data needs for an evidence-based program. We have done a thorough job identifying the "what" part of the data equation. Answering the "why" questions has been more elusive, as is often the case.

We have needed data for multiple reasons: Our home visiting program models have data requirements which may or may not be concurrent with what we are being asked to provide to the state and federal governments. Some states have a central repository for data while others do not. Some funded programs are required to provide data while others aren't. And beyond just having the data itself, a way to ensure that the organization's data are accurate is sorely needed. Further, sometimes, decisions are made using the data, but sometimes decisions are made politically rather than based on verified data that supports effectiveness. The accountability that has been given a voice is not heard, and consequently we don't build upon what is working.

And there is still so much that we don't know at ECS and in the field of home visiting. Our studies don't yet tell us all we want to know about what works for whom. Systematic reviews and national evaluations have not found highly significant impact on all the promised outcomes of home visiting. Does the data give us the evidence to answer such questions as: Are we starting early enough? Does what we do to encourage people to continue for the first two years do that? Could we effectively provide a few visits to all new mothers with more intensive services for those who want

> Nonprofits
> must have the
> opportunity to do
> more research and
> better use the data
> they collect as they
> try to solve big,
> complex problems,
> not only for
> themselves but for
> the communities
> they serve.

and need more support? Are we meaningfully engaging families as partners? Can we achieve the impact we want without strong early childhood systems, including transitions to quality early care and education at age three?

Nonprofits must have the opportunity to do more research and better use the data they collect as they try to solve big, complex problems, not only for themselves but for the communities they serve.

The basic questions are: 1) What is sound and reliable evidence for a finding? 2) Under what conditions will policy and funding decisions be based on documented outcomes and the ability to implement the finding? These are not new concerns. The relevant literature is replete with examples of evidence being minimized and programs that are working not growing or not being disseminated to reach their potential. Rather, new programs often then come along with new promises and new leadership and public enthusiasm—and they do not always work out, either.

We need an investment vision to effectively triage and support programs that have been proven to work and to eliminate or improve those that don't. We need investments for a system of coordinated community-wide services based upon transparency, accountability, and documented evidence of effectiveness, and the learning agenda to demonstrate clear progress.

Stevens characterizes it by asking what standards should be applied to research to guide public funding of interventions for early childhood home visiting programs that aim to improve the well-being of children and adults. Specifically, what are the appropriate criteria for the design and quality of studies used to inform policy decisions about home visiting, and what constitutes a sufficiently large effect on key outcomes to warrant public spending?

In 2018, the Early Childhood Data Collaborative, convened by the national organization Child Trends, reported that for investments in early childhood, policymakers and other stakeholders need "access to data about the use and quality of early childhood services (Jordan et al. 2018). Yet early childhood data are often disconnected and housed within multiple state agencies. As a consequence, decision makers frequently lack the comprehensive information they need." And obtaining that information rests upon finding a commonly accepted definition of evidence and a willingness within policy and philanthropic organizations to really use that information to make public policy and funding decisions.

The consideration of evidence and data responds to an early and continued query from our business colleagues: What will be the most compelling measures that we will have in the next few years that will document that this program is making a major difference? And are those findings actionable? These two questions are, to me, the animating factor for our entire research and evaluation work. We have made forward strides, and found many encouraging answers, but more definitive and next-stage evidence is needed. That requires funding to continue building on what we have in place.

> Find a commonly accepted definition of evidence and a willingness within policy and philanthropic organizations to really use that information.

Lessons

1. **Align and co-design measurement efforts with input from key stakeholders**. Engage the board, staff, and families when designing strategies for measurement, data collection, and defining success. The work must be respectful and not put undue burden on families, communities, or the workforce and should not conflict with organizational values and mission.

2. **Use the three faces of measurement**: quality improvement (QI using small tests of change), population-level performance monitoring (impact on population-level outcomes), and research and evaluation (to study what works and innovate). Using all three will help the nonprofit understand and improve program operation and program outcomes. The combination of these three approaches uses your data in different ways and creates a comprehensive approach to measurement.

3. **Clearly define what is meant** by the term *evidence* in the context of your work. Differentiate among the terms evidence,

Research and development functions in the nonprofit world are typically funded by grants and/or contracts, leaving little time or support for innovation and iterative learning.

evidence-based, and evidence-informed. Don't forget that innovation generates new evidence that allows programs to grow and adapt as families, communities, and policies change.

4. **Ensure that your measurement and research is actionable,** that you can apply what you learn. Use the data you collect for making decisions, solving problems, and improving outcomes. Strive always to not only report what happened, but also why it happened so that appropriate changes can be made.

5. **Secure dedicated funding for the administration of the measurement and research and development (R&D) infrastructure** so that these efforts can be productive and on a firm foundation. Remember that grants and/or contracts rarely cover the total cost of data, QI, and evaluation.

Remember, research and development functions in the nonprofit world are typically funded by grants and/or contracts, leaving little time or support for innovation and iterative learning.

Chapter 8

Funding for Nonprofits Is Complex and Challenging

The area causing the most consternation among nonprofits is almost always funding. Anyone who has any relationship with a nonprofit is aware not only of the problems but also some of the remedies employed to attempt to improve the situation. In the case of ECS we have been able to leverage our private-sector contributions, drawing down additional public dollars by using private money as a match. We have also had success independently raising private dollars even though our local founding partners are outstanding fundraisers themselves.

I have often described funding for nonprofits as ephemeral because most funding decisions are not under the control of the nonprofit itself. Rather, politics, policies (new or existing), and administrative or program requirements determine how money will be allocated. Admittedly, sometimes advocacy can be used to influence decisions, but the entire funding process is fraught with vagaries, which means that the revenue streams are neither dependable nor consistent. Improved attention to program accountability and funding programs that either have demonstrated success and/ or have the potential to be effective could level the process and result in better outcomes. Creating nonprofit budgets from one year to the next requires informed guesswork and flexibility. And because budgets are policy—whether it is the funder's budget or the budget of the organization itself—revenue, public or private, determines what behaviors and what outcomes are incentivized.

> Most funding decisions are not under the control of the nonprofit itself. Rather, politics, policies (new or existing), and administrative or program requirements determine how money will be allocated.

The nonprofit organization makes its best assumptions for its budget based on experience and an eye on the future, keeping costs down and performance high. It must work diligently with administrative and elected officials to explain the work and provide the reason to fund—the reason to believe. Statistics, outcomes, personal experiences, evidence of effectiveness, and descriptions of need are used to buttress the story.

There are many good and worthy causes vying for attention. Competition is strong, and often a true zero-sum game. Hope is high. But even though ECS ably executed our mission to the best of our ability, there was always an implicit understanding that how far we could go was largely determined by public and private-sector emergent strategic agendas and subsequent funding decisions, and we had precious little opportunity to influence internal planning and decisions.

For ECS, our funding challenges arose from the realities of the impact of the philanthropic sector that were not unique to us: 1) the tendency in communities to fund something new rather than something that is demonstrating that it works; 2) the hesitancy of nonprofit organizations to operate collaboratively for fear of losing their identity or their funding; 3) the pressure upon nonprofits to keep operating costs too low and thus stymie innovation and growth; 4) the imperative from some elected and appointed officials who live in election cycles to want outcomes too quickly—especially problematic for early childhood programs when the child needs to grow to exhibit the outcomes that we seek. Finally, and ironically, for most nonprofits: 5) the total cost of the service is not fully covered and thus each service delivered results in a loss—the more services the organization delivers, the more money it loses.

The funding conundrum is compounded by the persistent problem described so accurately by Dan Pallotta in his 2008 book *Uncharitable*. He generally discusses the dilemma of non-profits that are asked to solve the most intractable problems with the lowest budgets. Often, overhead costs higher than 10% are

> The nonprofit organization makes its best assumptions for its budget based on experience and an eye on the future, keeping costs down and performance high.

typically not acceptable. Public-sector money is allocated for services with little designated for administration, professional development, innovation, research, evaluation, program enhancement, or program growth—paradoxically the very activities that could lead to improved program operation and implementation of new strategies or the development of new products that could produce new revenue.

Funding for ECS

Public Monies

Public-sector funding requires active lobbying at all levels—local, state, and federal. Our work at ECS concentrated on the local and state levels, with supportive advocacy from early childhood organizations at the federal level. While ECS never received support from the City of Cincinnati, in the early days we received more than $1 million annually in funds from the federal Temporary Assistance to Needy Families (TANF) program designated by the State of Ohio to the Hamilton County Job & Family Services Agency (JFS). Support also came from the Ohio Department of Health (MIECHV/Help Me Grow), and the Kentucky Health Cabinet (HANDS). Kentucky made the decision to use Medicaid funds and proceeds from its tobacco settlement to pay for the home visiting services. All these funding sources required frequent reauthorization and were subject to budget pressure and political decision-making.

For example, in 2001, the Hamilton County Job & Family Services agency had a large budget shortfall. Our million dollars in TANF Hamilton County funding was eliminated, even though we were able to rally strong advocacy from business leadership. It was an enormous setback and we had to adjust. The impact was twofold: Fewer families could be enrolled, and less Ohio money could be brought to the county to pay for services for residents.

For many years, the Commonwealth of Kentucky was able to pay nearly 80% of the cost of the visits, while in Ohio the fraction was closer to 70%. In both cases, we subsidized with private dollars to cover the actual cost to deliver the service, and achieve the outcomes we promised to our families.

Moreover, in both states, the public investment in early intervention programs was insufficient to really make a "step change" in enrolling and addressing the level of need and risk. We were never able to move beyond serving approximately 20% of those families who qualified for our service, and at 20%, the community needle moves insignificantly. The *National Home Visiting Yearbook* documents similar gaps between the size of the population that might benefit from home visiting and the number of actual participants documented for the United States overall and for each state.

A contributing factor to the funding instability is that, as new people occupy public and private leadership positions, the focus or the interest in one program or another changes, and the process of educating, cajoling, and convincing begins anew. In any event, ECS did not grow.

The reality was obvious to many: Without an improved funding formula, ECS would be unable to move beyond meeting 20% of the need for its services. Doing more with less was not an option, as we operated with only an 11% administrative cost and we were committed to a high quality, comprehensive program with verifiable results, not a program watered down to accommodate the funding source.

During our many meetings with administrators and legislators to secure public funds for ECS and Help Me Grow in Ohio and HANDS in Kentucky, the leaders almost uniformly acknowledged the importance of our service and our ability to deliver. However, when it came time to vote—to create the budget—competition for dollars was fierce, decisions were not always made with evidence, prevention programs had difficulty documenting bad outcomes they had prevented, and children had no vote.

Moreover, the government-funding model for educating children is upside down, with the least amount of funding available for the earliest and most critical learning period. When I wrote to the mayor of Cincinnati in 2002 asking that ECS be considered as part of the Cincinnati Empowerment Zone and/or the Anthem Neighborhood Development program, I ended my letter with these words: "Each one of our families represents a success story—each family has an improved chance for themselves, for their children, and for our community. Isn't that, after all, what community means, what empowerment zones and neighborhood development are all about?" We received no funding.

But the outcomes were not all bad. Beginning in 2019, Ohio adopted a more-favorable funding formula, and Governor DeWine demonstrated interest and support for the kind of evidence-based home visiting provided by ECS and Help Me Grow. Soon after DeWine was sworn in as governor—within hours—he appointed LeeAnne Cornyn to the senior position of State Director of Children's Initiatives, a new position for the state of Ohio. Her job was to coordinate children's services and programs both from the service and the state agency perspective. I was asked to be the vice chair for what became the Governor's Advisory Committee on Home Visitation. With broad representation from various interest groups in the field, by March 2019, in only three months, we had produced a set of recommendations that are still being used to guide program development and implementation.

As the pandemic shadow covered us all in 2020, having the DeWine administration recommendations, coupled with fine work from the Ohio Department of Health and Medicaid program, gave high-risk families a lifeline, even when they stopped receiving the in-home visits that anchored our work.

In his introductory letter for the 2019 report *Recommendations of the Governor's Advisory Committee on Home Visitation*, DeWine explained why he supported this work:

> When I was a young man, I would often plant maple seeds with my grandfather. In fact, he continued to

> plant seeds every year up to his death, knowing fully that he may never live to see them grow. Today, my son John taps those very same maple trees to produce syrup for our family to enjoy. Much like my grandfather planted those maple seeds many years ago, we must plant the seeds to ensure that our families and children are strong and healthy for years to come. I believe that evidence-based home visiting is that seed. (DeWine, 2019)

At ECS, we have advocated for policy choices that focus on issues rather than organizations. We wanted to put the money where the need was greatest and where evidence of success was visible. Further, we have stressed that money should follow programs that can measure positive outcomes for families. Our belief from day one has been that you get what you measure. We provided well-documented service for over 28,000 families (56,000 people) over our 20-year history. Those numbers are far from perfect but much better than zero.

Additionally, as we followed the trends in public financing, our work was underway to create a strategy for paying for services based on outcomes rather than fee for service. Certainly, there is strong and credible recognition that programming for infants in the early years matters and agreement that the better investment is in prevention rather than later remediation.

Private Monies

When ECS was being created in the late 1990s, one of the key players was the United Way. Our program emanated from the study commissioned by the United Way board and participation by our other two founding partners, Cincinnati Children's and the Community Action Agency. Private dollars were made available for the planning and the initial launch of the program. United Way was the largest financial supporter, but funds were also donated by other organizations and individuals who recognized that the ECS mission was founded on good science and a definable, unmet need.

The public monies from Ohio and Kentucky were augmented by private dollars—approximately 30% of the service cost in Ohio and 20% of the cost in Kentucky—to deliver the high-quality program that led to positive outcomes.

We have been aware and have articulated frequently that programs like ECS cannot be carried on the shoulders of philanthropy alone. However, the private-sector contributions are important for success. In addition to subsidizing the cost of the home visits, we depended upon private money to pay for what the public sector didn't, including but not limited to program administration, evaluation and research, training and staff development, community outreach, marketing, program enhancements such as treatment for maternal depression, early literacy, and books. Cincinnati Children's provided sizable in-kind support. We were fortunate.

The funding picture has become even more complicated, as philanthropic-fundraising paradigms are shifting nationwide, especially for donations that have historically been made by employees through their employers. First, many employers have moved away from involvement in an employee's philanthropic choices. Rather, they ask only that the employee be charitable, but they do not suggest to whom the money should be donated. Some employers are using philanthropic giving platforms that include snapshot descriptions of many worthy organizations and the potential donor chooses from among them. Organization profiles are displayed online so the organization itself must have a strong, concise case statement delivered in a compelling manner to win donations in a highly competitive and totally remote marketplace.

Moreover, as people retire earlier and often with funds to invest, they may want to have a role in the nonprofit they are supporting. They can offer the kind of guidance from experienced, smart volunteers that we have been able to benefit from for more than 20 years. Further, these donors want to be assured that their charitable investment is producing results, a reasonable request.

A big looming "moose on the table" is this: Under what conditions will funders, public or private, be willing to make difficult and
often unpopular decisions that result in decreasing and/or elim-
inating funding for organizations that are not producing results?
Secondarily, but certainly contributory, is whether the organization itself actually has enough funding to produce what they have
promised to deliver and to validate that the strategy is working.

The Founding Partners' Essential Role in Sustainability

The United Way has been steadfast in its ongoing support for
ECS, since the idea of ECS became a reality in 1999. For that first
United Way Campaign that included ECS in its fundraising story,
there were two important voices speaking to the community. First,
George Schaefer, then president of Fifth Third Bank and chair of
the 1999 United Way campaign, specifically cited ECS as a primary
reason for contributing to the campaign. He also initiated and suc-
cessfully raised additional funds through his $250,000 Fifth Third
Bank Challenge Match. That same year, Cincinnati Children's
CEO Michael Fisher was the Campaign Major Gift Chair, and
through his efforts the number of United Way $10,000 Alexis de
Tocqueville donors doubled from 100 to 200.

Representing the business community and contributing close to
$1.8 million annually in recent years, the United Way has been
ECS's largest private-sector donor. We were careful over the years
to respect the interwoven relationship between ECS and our
partners who had their own fundraising activities. We kept what
we were doing relatively small and did not interfere with how
they were raising money. Several times we mounted campaigns
for something specific—the Avondale community engagement,
books for our families, or matching a grant from an especially gen-
erous donor. Each time we openly discussed the campaigns with
our partners. But typically, over the years, we deferred to their
decisions and always were deeply appreciative of their generos-
ity. There were no legal regulations that committed support from

any one of the partners to ECS, yet we delivered on our promise, and they delivered on theirs. The collaborative relationship among the three organizations is an excellent example of the new kind of organizational structure required to produce the best outcomes and use resources most effectively.

As the managing partner, Cincinnati Children's provided in-kind services that our auditors valued at approximately $300,000 per year. We were housed at Cincinnati Children's, and were able to use their accounting, budgeting, financial planning, office support, human resources, and research infrastructure, rather than purchasing those separately ourselves.

Philanthropy and Fundraising Efforts

Over the years, as Bill Shore explains in his beautiful and mesmerizing book *The Imaginations of Unreasonable Men*, funders have begun moving from just investing in programs to investing in operations that are able to address complex social problems—the social determinants of health versus simply immunization for measles, for instance, or the implication of one's birth ZIP code as opposed to a kindergarten readiness score. Shore emphasizes that investments need to be made in operations, capacity, and leadership, prioritizing sustainability and scale—what he calls a horizontal, not a vertical, strategy—one that enables nonprofits to get to scale and sustain themselves instead of depending on philanthropic subsidies. That is exactly what ECS endeavored to do (Shore 2012). Shore's book is built around six lessons which should be embraced by every nonprofit:

1. Invest in bringing existing solutions to scale rather than discovering new ones. Make existing solutions affordable, scalable, and sustainable.
2. Most failures in life are failures of imagination.
3. It's the economics. Have an organization that is sustainable.
4. Create new markets and generate wider public support to solve big problems.

5.   Solve not salve. Do not just ameliorate problems.
6.   Have the soul of a competitor. Collaboration has merits but it
      is in the soul of competition that we get better.

Shore urges nonprofits to believe in the superiority of our vision
even when no one else does, and he ends with a statement that
could be the descriptor for ECS, "There is no such thing as unreasonable when it comes to a mother doing what is necessary for
her child."

As ECS worked toward sustainability, understanding that
our philanthropy needed to be diversified, out of necessity we
embarked upon three distinct private fundraising efforts. These
new campaigns focused on what we already did and on dollars that
could help ECS scale, or so we thought. We focused on new dollars
and new donors.

The first, entitled Let One More Child Succeed, was initiated
by Walker and launched in 2005, asking donors to pay for ECS
services for one high-risk, ECS-eligible family for one year. The
idea was to raise incremental funds to "sponsor" a child for one
to three years, and although we were operating with a waiting list,
open up a space for a Let One More Child Succeed child, thereby
making a direct connection between the donor's gift and a new
family receiving the service.

We explained to United Way that this campaign would likely
bring new dollars and new donors to ECS as we targeted churches,
civic associations, small businesses, the ECS board, board associates, and foundations. We maintained this would bring new
groups and individuals into the United Way sphere of influence.
The United Way would, by extension, be offering a new branded
charitable "product" to a broader audience.

In the second campaign, we set out to raise money for the special
program for the Avondale community. At that time, we had a
waiting list for program enrollment and were hesitant to encourage
new moms to join the program, when we knew we couldn't serve
them in a timely way. With the infusion of funding for Avondale,

however, we were able to make a different decision for Avondale moms in the community where both our offices and Cincinnati Children's were located. We knew that the community needed help. Through philanthropy and leadership from two ECS board members, Carter and Walker, and one senior corporate executive from Federated, Thomas Cody, we were able to raise just over $1 million to serve any program-eligible family living in Avondale. The results were exciting, as 85% of eligible moms joined us and were able to record positive outcomes (Every Child Succeeds 2016).

Another philanthropic fundraising campaign, Every Child Is Me, was initiated in 2018, when the Walker family made a $1 million grant to ECS. The couple suggested that this donation be used as a challenge match to raise funds to serve more families and take advantage of the opportunity to leverage state money with private money. The Walkers saw this strategy as a way "to multiply the impact of their gift and to help to ensure that every child in our community has an optimal start." They were clear in their intention to see this money put to work in the community in the next few years after the funds were received. They were not interested in creating an endowment fund and wisely let us know that they understood that "grant" money like this is always welcome but also presents management issues because it is one-time money rather than an ongoing source of funding.

We used an external-fundraising consultant, Ignite Philanthropy, whose mission was to work with private donors and nonprofits to leverage their resources and ideas to leverage their impact. Our senior ECS staff and board team were able to launch the Every Child Is Me campaign in late 2019. We raised a total of $4 million, ending just weeks before the pandemic hit.

Finally, and most importantly, we created Bringing Books to Babes to ensure that every single child in our program would have a library of age-appropriate books. Led by two longtime ECS board members and early literacy advocates, Mary Ellen Cody and Digi Schueler, we were able to raise over $400,000 in 10 years, allowing us to purchase books for our children, books that were delivered by the home visitors. This expanded our early literacy initiative with books that every family received every month, books that often were the only books in the home.

We had other smaller fundraising initiatives and in-kind contributions over the years for specific projects or programs. Through all of these fundraising activities we discovered one important reality. Typically, funders like to provide support for specific, mostly visible activities. They do not, nor I believe should not, provide operating capital for the organization. We received extensive media attention from Time Warner, large contributions of products for our warehouse and parent aid bags from a variety of large Cincinnati-area corporations. We received help to buy books and provide limited services for families from Cincinnati Bell, Fifth Third Bank, and Cincinnati's Underground Railroad Freedom Center. We were able to generate seed money for new ideas, all the money coming from the private sector.

> Public sources of funds must support ongoing basic operation for programs that have been shown to be effective.

But it is the public sources of funds that must support ongoing basic operation for programs that have been shown to be effective, and the programs must buttress that support with a reporting structure that is transparent and verifies effectiveness. It is important to try to build upon what is working rather than duplicating efforts or not taking advantage of what has been learned.

It is true that whether the money is coming from a public or a private source, the funders make decisions, because as they support one initiative or another, they provide room for that initiative to grow. They make choices. It is hard work because funders must be aware of not only the immediate outcomes of what they support but also the possible unintended consequences for community expansion and/or coordination. Further, they need to be brave, because so often it is easier to say yes than no, and too often holding organizations accountable comes with significant challenges.

The unstable nature of funding itself is compounded by communities that, over time, select or launch new programs rather than building on those that are operational and have been shown to work.

Beginning early in our development, and with guidance from our private-sector board chair, we prepared a simple piece for our ECS board and for the community to explain how we were making a difference and to demonstrate that the investment in ECS produced results and delivered on its promise as a good, strong prevention program. Our reports, as case statements too, listed those results and then explained how ECS was different from other good programs:

1. It was a unique collaboration of public and private resources, securing more than $1 in private money for every $3 the government was investing.
2. It used a business approach and applied accountability to the delivery of a social service, which meant measuring everything, continuous quality improvement, and process management.
3. It had the support of Cincinnati Children's for evaluation and research management, scientific rigor, and community credibility.
4. It used clearly defined measures and dashboarding to let investors and the community see and know that this program was working.

We typically continued by listing our special initiatives (e.g., Avondale community partnership, maternal-depression treatment, connecting to pediatric care, and emerging literacy). But many of these innovations and successful pilot projects ended due to lack of continuing funds. We explained that in how we addressed several key issues facing Cincinnati, including poverty, benefits were needed for two (and maybe three) generations. Measured outcomes were needed, and collaboration with our provider agencies and with our community was necessary for the use of private money to draw down public dollars for greater Cincinnati.

We offered not only the reason to believe but also the facts to support it. However, even with outstanding results and documentation, low overhead, and addressing a recognized need, ECS was not able to grow to serve more families who are eligible for the ECS free and voluntary service.

The "Going to Scale" Jeffrey Bradach piece published in the *Stanford Social Innovation Review* (2003) described an issue that ECS has faced almost since its inception: "The failure to replicate social programs is usually attributed to problems of strategy and management. Much of the time it is simply a problem of money. The fact that dollars seldom follow success is one of the most vexing problems nonprofit leaders face."

New ideas are advanced; someone wants to try a new program and dollars are reallocated, siphoned off to another program or another idea. The opportunity to grow what is working is lost.

Several years after we were launched as a program and we were demonstrating that we were delivering on our promise to the community, another early childhood program was brought to greater Cincinnati as part of a national initiative. We saw opportunities for our program and the new program, also sponsored by the United Way, to collaborate. Our focus was the prenatal period and services for children from birth to age three; theirs was childcare, school readiness, and continued child development. Over time, however, they did not seem to be endorsing home visiting as a key strategy, and we couldn't understand why—it felt divisive and competitive. Conversations with leadership helped to ameliorate the differences, but we should not have needed to have those conversations at all. What was going on? Was it turf issues, control issues, lack of awareness, absence of confidence?

As complementary and competing programs popped up, the funders and the public became confused. We needed to make it easier for funders to focus and cooperate, not harder. At one point, a local public official who was vying for "share of voice" diluted our opportunity to make our case, strengthen public endorsement, and secure additional funding. As we had seen in the past, needs are infinite while resources are finite. It is imperative that programs producing quantifiable results are funded and that nonprofits are held accountable for promises made and outcomes delivered.

Sustainability, consistency, and predictability are key, keeping in mind that point-in-time interventions need continuity for long-term effects.

Blended and Braided Funding

It is obvious that a primary challenge for any nonprofit is to keep itself funded, and in the case of ECS, we had our public dollars—local, state, and federal in Ohio and Kentucky—and our private philanthropic dollars from a variety of sources, including the United Way. In addition, we sought additional outside funding that included research and other program support.

Using calendar year 2006 as an example, in addition to public monies from the states of Ohio and Kentucky for direct service delivery, we were able to generate funds from various public and private funders for special projects and enhance our administrative skills for blending and braiding funding.

- Retention study grant: federal Maternal and Child Health Bureau research funds, $1 million over four years
- Maternal-depression pilot: Cincinnati Health Foundation, $270,000 over four years
- Maternal-depression treatment program: National Institute of Mental Health, $450,000 over three years
- Assuring a smoke-free home (ASH): Tobacco Use Prevention and Control Foundation, $1.45 million over four years
- Infant mortality study: Cincinnati Children's, $30,000
- Let One More Child Succeed/Avondale expansion: individual donors, $620,000

Other support came from the RAND Corporation for a cost-benefit analysis to investigate how their services for young mothers could be improved with the inclusion of a home visiting component, from Ethicon Endo Surgery for our University of Michigan intern and from the National Center for Family Literacy in Louisville, Kentucky, to help us create a model for emerging/early literacy beginning in the prenatal period.

Funding Beyond the Home Visit Itself

Identifying funds to support our evaluation and research activity was not easy because we, like many organizations, required financial support to be able to hire people skilled in measurement, development, marketing, and government relations. With an emphasis on low overhead for nonprofits, funders who supported us were willing to pay for our home visiting service but rarely to include salaries for other parts of the infrastructure. Our affiliation with Cincinnati Children's has allowed us to buy time from faculty at the Research Foundation and to supplement staff time using private dollars. Successful grant budgets allow portions of salaries to be funded through the grant. But it is a constant and unfortunate balancing act, which ultimately caused us to miss many good opportunities for learning because we could not afford to hire people to do the work.

The problem has a second angle. As we uncovered compelling findings that we wanted to incorporate into our work with families, we found ourselves knowing what to do but unable to identify funds to actually do it. There were many such situations over the last two decades: deploying the early literacy LENA strategies; continuing the focus on executive function highlighted during our pilot work with Ellen Galinsky, then chief science officer at the Bezos Foundation, and founder and director of Mind in the Making (Galinsky 2010); continuing our effective community engagement opportunities based on our Avondale experience; integrating the successful shortened perinatal engagement identified through StartStrong.

Our continual quest for funds had two broad objectives: first, the quality delivery of home visits and second, anything beyond basic service that was important to helping families achieve the best possible start for their children. Sometimes I described the situation by saying disparagingly that Diogenes looked for an honest man while I just looked for money. It was a sentiment not unique to me. Here are two examples of what typically happened:

Example One

ECS was able to obtain grants for the research that allowed us to develop an in-home treatment for the maternal depression that affects roughly half of all moms enrolled in ECS. Maternal depression was a problem that we were eager to address on two levels—to help the mom herself and to help the child. Research let us know that if the mother suffers from depression, she has little left to give to the child—care, attention, stimulation, and bonding are all reduced. Developmental opportunities for the child are truncated, as are the foundational relationships. This is at least a two-generational concern. Following the research and development work, we sought and received a large philanthropic grant to make Moving Beyond Depression available, but only for ECS mothers and within certain time and dollar limits. We made numerous presentations to legislators and policymakers asking for public monies to offer Moving Beyond Depression statewide through their home visiting programs, Help Me Grow (MIECHV) in Ohio and HANDS in Kentucky. We were not successful. As the philanthropic grant was ending, Ohio Medicaid agreed to pay for the service under certain conditions but at a rate that we could not afford. Fortunately, one of our Ohio provider agencies was willing to take over program administration and could accommodate the reduced payment using its own funds to bridge the reimbursement shortfall. ECS agreed to continue to train the therapists and assist with data collection and analysis. We were not able to identify a similar situation for Kentucky, and moms in Kentucky do not have access to Moving Beyond Depression.

Example Two

We knew that what home visitors were being asked to do on a daily basis was complex and stressful. We hired good people for these professional positions and trained them using our own resources along with training opportunities provided by Ohio and Kentucky.

Yet we also knew that there were few guidelines to define the important role of home visitor. There was not a certification process or even a set of specified skills that a home visitor would need or could work to achieve. The term *home visitor* was nearly generic, so someone called a home visitor could be a nurse, a social worker, a home health aide, a community health worker, a health navigator, a child-development specialist, a teacher, or an interested person without any of those designations who wants to work with perinatal women and young children in their homes. There is not a single, uniform description of what a home visitor, with a certain set of specialized skills, delivering an identified curriculum, needs to be able to do—what is expected of them? We believed that home visitors deserved an opportunity to have their skills recognized and certified, adding to their professional designation. We talked of career ladders, time for classes and curriculum development, internships and strategies for transferability of experience if a home visitor relocates to a new community. However, other than what states provide to fund their own training opportunities, there is not a source of money to pay for career development for home visitors, although several states are working on plans: most notably, Virginia, with its Institute for the Advancement of Family Support Professionals.

If we require a well-trained, professional workforce for home visiting, then we need to recognize that we must have funds available so that learning and certification may occur. The hairdresser needs a license. Doesn't the person working with our highest-risk families and their children deserve the same consideration? As of this writing, no funds exist for this initiative.

Money needs to be allocated where it will have the largest impact, where efficacy can be validated. Funders need to be diligent about requiring clear evidence of success as well as the behaviors they incentivize through funding support.

Lessons

1. Work to achieve a public-private funding mix augmented with entrepreneurial revenue when possible. Understand that long-term sustainable programs cannot be built on the shoulders of either government or philanthropy alone; rather, multiple funding resources are required.

2. Keep budget and mission aligned. The budget is the policy of your organization. Funding choices often require bravery while remaining focused on the core mission activities.

3. Accept that for both public and private-sector funders, the nonprofit organization must provide information about fiscal management, program operations, and outcomes. Be accountable and transparent with fiscal data and budget realities. Work with funders to establish which outcomes will be used to validate success. Report progress on a regular basis and consider creating a dashboard.

4. Keep in mind operational money may be the most difficult to secure. Philanthropic investments are generally attracted to innovation or a specific project rather than ongoing operations.

5. Aim to generate income. Without income, nonprofits continue to be reliant on government and philanthropic dollars alone and rarely become self-sustaining. Income from products or services can fund operations which are rarely funded by public or private dollars.

6. Recognize that despite long-term commitments, the priorities of funders shift over time. New ideas or concepts can be compelling and attractive to funders. Be prepared to tell your story well, to make your work relevant in the current context.

Chapter 9

Supporting Nonprofits to Address Social Challenges

I initially began writing this book to recount the evolution of ECS, a regional nonprofit organization with programs delivering enhanced evidence-based home visiting models through multiple community-based agencies. We had built a sophisticated organization on the strength of what the model developers and other researchers had identified about how to support mothers and their young children. Our approach from the start was designed to take advantage of what science told us about brain development in young children and to give our children the best possible start in life. ECS was launched and guided by outstanding community leaders, broad-based community engagement, continuous learning and improvement, and an imperative to link science with strong program implementation.

For over 20 years, my accumulated files, articles, and correspondence documented our challenges and our successes. The story, I believed, was one worth telling because although we began with strong support and we delivered the program with vigor, we were highly successful in some areas but less so in others. What, I asked myself, could we have done better? Where did we miss opportunities? What were the barriers to success? What are the lessons for other nonprofit organizations trying to address large social changes or effectively replicate program models?

If you are a leader of a nonprofit organization, what I hope you will draw from this book is a new and perhaps different way of thinking about how one might initiate, manage, and fund a nonprofit. When you consider your nonprofit, how do you address problems? Are you getting outcomes that you didn't expect? Are you getting sound information to document what is happening in the organization and how you are—or are not—succeeding? Is your funding incentivizing the right behaviors to lead to the outcomes you seek, remembering that budgets are policies? Have you considered the unanticipated consequences of funding and policy initiatives, policymaker changes, and competition? Are you brave when you are called upon to make unpopular decisions, looking squarely at the truth and responding appropriately? Are you taking small steps at first and breaking down the organization into what will attract funding based on need and merit and not what is currently philanthropically popular? Do you lean on accountability for guidance and transparency?

If you are a community leader—from private business, the faith community, a community action agency, other endeavors—what I hope you will take away are ideas about how to promote social good in your community. Are you volunteering your time and talents to help nonprofits succeed? What does your enterprise know that could be shared? Are you learning about the context of the community, the families that live there and the challenges they face? Are you part of the leadership that holds organizations accountable and will guide community change?

If you are a leader in philanthropy, what I hope you will reflect upon is how the narrow funding for demonstration projects does not add up to sustainable change and how to consider investments in longer-term growth and success of nonprofits aligned with your mission. So many foundations ask for a proposal that includes ideas about how efforts will be sustained, yet these are well beyond the control of most local nonprofit entities. And, when demonstration projects show successful results, what role can you play in taking things to the next level of scale and spread, rather than just chalking it up as a strong evaluation? Do you have responsibility to sustain what you have built for the benefit of the community?

If you are in government—in the legislative or executive branch—I hope you will see ways that programmatic and funding silos create limits on the potential for large-scale results in supporting families' success and in creating optimal conditions for the next generation to grow. How can you use your role to increase opportunities for the service recipient? How can you remove barriers to community development and coordinated action? What I hope all readers will draw from this work is a new and perhaps expanded way of thinking about how our collective efforts can improve conditions for nonprofits and our communities.

Questions One Must Ask Upon Reflection

As I began to assess and reflect upon our work from my new vantage point as the retired program president, I could see the work and our evolution in a different way. I've been able to view the larger landscape and consider where we fit. I can be more realistic about expectations, more cognizant of the challenges facing all nonprofits, not just ours. This new perspective was illuminating. When days were filled morning to night with daily operations—budgets, staffing, reports, big and small emergencies—there was little time for reflection or more broad-based thinking. I realized that the ECS story was one worth telling, not to recount in detail how our days unfolded but rather the *what*, *how*, and *why* we were able to have some success but not always be able to achieve everything we set out to do. Rather, ECS was emblematic of a highly successful, well-supported nonprofit existing within a large community landscape where improved program coordination was needed and nonprofits continued to encounter barriers to success. As with many nonprofits, we were limited by various factors beyond ourselves, by structures and strategies embedded deeper in the funding, policy, and community mindsets.

ECS created a new respected institution in greater Cincinnati, identifying partners and stakeholders, creating linkages and

> As with many nonprofits, we were limited by various factors beyond ourselves, by structures and strategies embedded deeper in the funding, policy, and community mindsets.

systems for service delivery, gaining credibility and trust, and, not insignificantly, maintaining funding for over 20 years.

We were able to exist as a strong program, but we were never able to significantly impact population health, serving only a fraction of those families eligible for our service. A fundamental question is this: Why, when we had most of the tools, community support, and a clear definition of need, couldn't we serve more families? The answers are embedded in the reasons why most nonprofits can advance only so far—but no farther. The reasons likely include siloed programs, political decision making, policy and funding challenges, family perceptions and misunderstandings about the services, and perhaps deeper root causes that are just coming to light. These are barriers both subtle and overt. Creating a community forum to consider problems collaboratively, not just for ECS but for early childhood programming writ large, was not a priority. The explanations harken back to the early admonition from P&G's John Pepper to business and community leadership when he asked for support for children ages birth to three, to give them the best possible start in life. "What is it about this that you don't understand?" he pleaded.

Community-based nonprofits need individuals at the forefront focused on better coordination of services, reduced fragmentation, support for validated outcomes of success, more-accessible resources linked to an overarching emphasis on creating the continuum of service within the community. We need more authentic engagement in the co-design of services and systems, to overcome longstanding systemic barriers. We need a strong, well-respected community forum that includes home visiting as one part of that broader continuum. Collaboration is vital, and that was my second important lesson.

Need to elevate the co-design and systemic barriers issues

For those who think that a cooperative program delivery to enhance lives is impossible, look at what some other countries can do for their pregnant women and young children. Or, as Pepper once told us, "Our situation (in the US) is morally and ethically wrong. It is unfair for children's futures to be so influenced by their family income, or by the ZIP code into which they are born."

This continuum needs to be based not only on "what works best for whom" but also what works best for the community, rather than highlighting one program or another. It means devising a strategy that leads to making hard and brave choices regarding what stays and what goes. It also means that available resources are deployed most effectively so that a maximum impact can be achieved and receive help.

It seems obvious to me now—as a more objective observer—that a central place for making decisions for funding allocations, determining geographic service areas, clarifying program focus, and validating efficacy and equity is required if there is to be community-level change. And finally, what was illuminated was this: How do nonprofits ultimately operate most effectively when, as you have now read repeatedly, they are called upon to solve the most intractable problems with inadequate budgets, low overhead, and often limited information for decision-making? How can entrepreneurship by nonprofits be supported by funders on a more sustainable basis?

What was clear was that even as nonprofits like ECS approach their work with a business mindset and an entrepreneurial spirit, the ability to generate revenue and to help themselves become more independent is limited, because rarely are funds available to support even the most basic exploration of new ideas and new ways of delivering service.

Public monies and private monies are episodic and too-often based on political considerations. Time and again at ECS as we advanced innovative ideas to help families and grow our program, we encountered a wall, an impenetrable wall, and we could not go forward. Rather than having an environment where innovation and growth were valued, we found ourselves in a place where we had to move ahead slowly, if at all, not cause too much confusion and not be seen as too demanding. Most of our initiatives have been detailed in the previous chapters but basically, the wall, the largest impediment, is the inability to garner funds for the infrastructure and structural changes needed to take innovation to market and to scale effective strategies. Some changes are financial, others could address structural racism and poverty and improve opportunity for families.

Guidelines for Health and Human Services Nonprofits

Using ECS as a case example, what follows are essential guidelines that we have followed and that could apply to most any mission-driven nonprofit delivering health and human services:

1. You are first and foremost a service organization with a vision; meaning research or other activities are important but secondary.
2. Do not overpromise. Be aware of the complexity of what you set out to do and temper expectations for what is possible, recognizing what the barriers are.
3. Work toward organizational autonomy with a balanced budget by identifying ways to generate new revenue that are not dependent on public monies or philanthropic donations alone. Understand that success may be small at first, but finding seed money for a good idea could produce benefits.
4. Ensure that when you measure your outcomes and/or monitor your program operation, you secure information that is actionable for your organization. In many ways you begin at the end by identifying what you need to know and then figuring out how to find the answer.
5. Work within your community as collaboratively as possible. Acknowledging that scarce funds and program designs inevitably push toward competition, engaging in collaboration to build a more effective system is critical to achieving population-level results. Be willing to make concessions to find a more unified approach to delivering services to families who need what you bring.
6. Partnering with families is key to effective service design and delivery. Nonprofit organizations must listen to and be responsive to the concerns of those they serve.
7. Join with others for larger social change. Even the most effective, efficient, well-led and supported nonprofit may not be able to achieve what it knows is possible, due to powerful forces working against disruptive cultural change.

Missed Opportunities

Nearly all nonprofits are charged with helping to solve big, important problems, frequently seemingly intractable problems. They are called upon to address these problems with inadequate budgets, low overhead, and too often limited information for decision-making. Opportunities to generate entrepreneurial income are stymied because even when they create a product or a strategy with income potential, they don't have the funds for implementation.

Within these constraints, what could ECS, as a successful program, have done better? Where were the opportunities to create alliances, investigate program operational issues, educate the public, use our resources more effectively? Not knowing if the outcome could be different, with 20 years of knowledge and data, and what might we have done differently? With additional resources, determination, and partnerships we might have:

1. Mined the data file from home visits—nearly 700,000 records—with research to help us better understand the effectiveness of ECS, not only the *what* but the *why*. How many home visits does it take to achieve good outcomes? What works best for whom?

2. Developed a stronger and more sustainable funding approach, permitting us to serve more than 20% of the eligible population, to reach more families who would enroll and use our services.

3. Become a learning and innovation lab for the state or region, helping to affect the adoption of tested innovations.

4. Better understood how to deliver quality programming at scale and effect improved implementation—fidelity plus adaptation leads to improvement.

5. More thoroughly disseminated program innovation and enhancements—such as Moving Beyond Depression, Mom's Groups and community engagement, family success criteria, early literacy, and Let's Talk Baby—for the benefit of ECS families and the field of home visiting.

6. Secured resources to ensure that ECS's community engagement efforts were as robust and effective as possible, continuing what we started in Avondale.

7. Built on our pilot project to adopt and sustain tiered teams with clarified roles for home visitors and community health workers, as well as better career ladders for those in both roles in the workforce.

8. Improved linkages with pediatric primary care and other programs sharing common interest and focus, building on our relationship with Cincinnati Children's.

9. Fostered a stronger early childhood system with a continuum of care through better alliances with related maternal and early childhood programs—beginning prenatally.

10. Placed a stronger focus on a two-generational approach, giving more attention to maternal health, self-agency, and opportunities.

Lessons

The case of ECS is exemplary in many ways, as an example of positive gains and missed opportunities by a community-based, mission-driven nonprofit organization. The primary issue here is not whether the focus is early childhood or housing or nutrition, but rather how we can come together to effectively deploy available resources to really solve societal problems—not to turn our eyes, to present facile solutions, not to despair and be daunted by the scope of the need. How do we work cooperatively in our communities? How do we ensure accountability for effective service delivery, system change, and improved outcomes? How do we structure our partnerships, operations, and financing to ensure maximum success? In essence, how do we collectively adopt innovative ways of thinking about the challenges and effective ways to take them on that are both cooperative and competitive?

There is no foolproof strategy for creating and managing a successful nonprofit; I am unable to offer a panacea for community services fragmentation. Rather, I am presenting what I have found to be the key components of our successful venture, learnings from more than two decades leading ECS and outlining some of the societal factors that make this work so difficult and the challenges so daunting.

This case study documents learnings that have relevance far beyond one small program in Cincinnati, Ohio. And there is value in codifying those learnings for those who guide mission-driven nonprofits, work within them, fund them, and use their services.

1. Focus on investments to solve problems, not just fund programs. Nonprofits are called upon to solve the world's most intractable problems with constrained budgets and pressures to succeed in short time frames. This is a huge challenge because if investments are not made that are commensurate with the size of the problem, only temporary or partial solutions are possible. The responsibility for funders is to hold organizations accountable and to make decisions based on evidence rather than social or political preferences. Changes in funding approaches that are focused on equity and structural changes to support family and community wellbeing are needed.

2. Understand that the system may not need more money but rather money spent more wisely. Systems and financing structures need to be improved to incentivize improved administration and deployment of services and dollars. At the same time, simply coordinating existing services better when there are big gaps in service systems cannot be the solution. Sometimes, more dollars and services are needed.

3. Remember that transparency, accountability, and outcome measurement are keys to success for mission-driven nonprofit organizations. We should all agree that the three measurement approaches can drive learning and improvements. These should be a priority and not be an afterthought or compromised.

4. Engage community. Strong, brave leadership along with community consensus and authentic partnerships are foundational to long-term success. A sustainable and scalable community-level response is based upon trust, effective cooperation, and collaboration among like-minded individuals and organizations that can together demonstrate value and results. Engaging the people who use services in the co-design and improvement of services and systems is essential.

5. Advance equity. Community-level, mission-driven nonprofit organizations have great potential for changing services and systems in ways that can reduce disparities (e.g., by race/ethnicity, income, geography, health status, gender, and other factors). Assessing the role of the organization in advancing equity in partnership with others is a place to start. Assuring that services are provided equitably, without discrimination or bias, is fundamental. It all begins with listening and learning together.

6. Use good business sense. Ensure nonprofits have: the latitude and resources to generate multiple sources of revenue—private, public, and entrepreneurial; sound business plans to be both sustainable and scalable; opportunities to follow science as well as community priorities, and leadership that is at least two steps ahead of current thinking.

A Closing Reflection on Perseverance

In 2011, John Pepper presented the keynote at the National Summit on Quality in Home Visiting that ECS hosted in Washington, DC with the Pew Charitable Trusts. Several years later, Pepper and I had breakfast with Shannon Jones, the former Ohio state representative and Ohio senator, who had initiated several important pieces of legislation and was widely recognized as a champion for issues that supported children and women. Pepper sent her a copy of his "Acting on What We Know to Be True" speech to illustrate the long-term nature of the journey we are on. Jones followed up with an email, and wrote:

> Thank you for sharing the speech. Honestly it was a little depressing in that 7 years later we still must fight for this! While my head understands the political process necessary for change, my heart is broken in the knowledge of the sheer volume of children who are failing to meet their potential while we corral the political will to do that which the evidence tells us we should. I am also haunted by the racial inequities that persist while we try to "figure it all out." But I know that much progress has been made in the last 7 years—we certainly know more anyway—so I will try to be inspired by your decades-long commitment

In his speech, Pepper described the moral imperative and called upon all of us to continue our life-changing work. He told us:

> Helping every child grow up to be all he or she can be and helping every mother help her child do just that: I cannot imagine a more noble undertaking. A calling that demands that, no matter how hard it is, we act on what we know to be true.

Pepper ended his talk with a favorite text from Rabbi Tarfon (known as one of the first fathers of Judaism quoted in the *Mishnah*, *Perkei Avot 2.16*): "You are not obligated to complete the work, but neither are you free to desist from it."

Appendix A: General References

Acevedo-Garcia, Dolores, McArdle, Nancy, Hardy, Erin F., Crisan, Unda I., Romano, Bethany, Norris, David, Baek, Mikyung, Reece, Jason. "The Child Opportunity Index: Improving Collaboration Between Community Development and Public Health." *Health Affairs* 33, no. 11(2014): 1948–57. doi: 10.1377/hlthaff.2014.0679.

Acevedo-Garcia, Dolores, Noelke, Clemens, McArdle, Nancy, Sofer, Nomi, Hardy, Erin F., Weiner, Michelle, Baek, Mikyung, Huntington, Nick, Huber, Rebecca, Reece, Jason. "Racial and Ethnic Inequities in Children's Neighborhoods: Evidence From the New Child Opportunity Index 2.0." *Health Affairs* 39, no. 10 (2020):1693–1701. doi: 10.1377/hlthaff.2020.00735.

Adonis. "Celebrating Childhood." From *Selected Poems*, trans. Khaled Mattawa. New Haven, CT: Yale University Press, 2010. Originally published in *The New Yorker*. May 22, 2006. https://www.newyorker.com/magazine/2006/05/22/for-celebrating-childhood-by-adonis.

American Academy of Pediatrics, Garner, Andrew S., Yogman, Michael, et al., Committee on Psychosocial Aspects of Child and Family Health, Section on Developmental and Behavioral Pediatrics, Council on Early Childhood. "Preventing Childhood Toxic Stress: Partnering With Families and Communities to Promote Relational Health." *Pediatrics* 148, no. 2 (2021): e2021052582.

American Academy of Pediatrics, Duffee, James H., Mendelsohn, Alan L., Kuo, Alice A., Legano, Lori A., Earls, Marian F., et al., Council on Community Pediatrics; Council on Early Childhood; Committee on Child Abuse and Neglect. "Early Childhood Home Visiting." *Pediatrics* 140, no. 3 (2017): e20172150. doi: 10.1542/peds.2017-2150.

American Academy of Pediatrics. "Early Brain Development." Updated July 15, 2022. https://www.aap.org/en/patient-care/early-childhood/early-childhood-health-and-development/early-brain-development/.

American Academy of Pediatrics, Garner, Andrew S., Shonkoff, Jack P. et al., Committee on Psychosocial Aspects of Child and Family Health; Committee on Early Childhood, Adoption, and Dependent Care; Section on

Developmental and Behavioral Pediatrics. "Early Childhood Adversity, Toxic Stress, and the Role of the Pediatrician: Translating Development Science into Life Health." *Pediatrics* 129, no. 1 (2012): e224-31. doi: 10.1542/peds.2011-2662.

American Psychological Association and American Academy of Pediatrics Policy Statement: Toomey, Sara L., Cheng, Tina L.; APA-AAP Workgroup on the Family-Centered Medical Home. "Home Visiting and the Family-Centered Medical Home: Synergistic Services to Promote Child Health." *Academic Pediatrics* 13, no. 1 (2013): 3–5. doi: 10.1016/j.acap.2012.11.001.

Avellar, Sarah A., Supplee, Lauren H. "Effectiveness of Home Visiting in Improving Child Health and Reducing Child Maltreatment." *Pediatrics* 132, Suppl. 2 (2013): S90-9. doi: 10.1542/peds.2013-1021G.

Badger, Earladeen, Sutherland, James. "Mother Training as a Means of Accelerating Childhood Development in a High Risk Population." *Pediatric Research* 8 (1974): 342. doi: 10.1203/00006450-197404000-00011.

Bai, Ge, Zare, Hossein, Eisenberg, Matthew D., Polsky, Daniel, Anderson, Gerard F. "Analysis Suggests Government and Nonprofit Hospitals' Charity Care Is Not Aligned With Their Favorable Tax Treatment." *Health Affairs* 40, no. 4 (2021): 629–636. doi: 10.1377/hlthaff.2020.01627.

Barton, Jared, Jimenez, Pegah Naemi, Biggs, Jacklyn, Garstka, Teri A., Ball, Thomas C. "Strengthening Family Retention and Relationships in Home Visiting Programs through Early Screening and Assessment Practices." *Children and Youth Services Review* 118 (2020): 105495. doi: 10.1016/j.childyouth.2020.105495.

Bethell, Christina, Jones, Jennifer, Gombojav, Narangerela, Linkenbach, Jeffrey, Sege, Robert. "Positive Childhood Experiences and Adult Mental and Relational Health in a Statewide Sample: Associations Across Adverse Childhood Experiences Levels." *JAMA Pediatrics* 173, no.11 (2019): e193007. doi: 10.1001/jamapediatrics.2019.3007.

Bradach, Jeffrey L. "Going to Scale: The challenge of replicating social programs." *Stanford Social Innovation Review,* Spring (2003): 19–25.

Bruner, Charles. "ACE, Place, Race, and Poverty: Building Hope for Children." *Academic Pediatrics* 17, no. 7S (2017): S123–S129. doi: 10.1016/j.acap.2017.05.009.

Bruner, Charles, et al. *Young Child Health Transformation: What Practice Tells Us* (Working Paper, InCK Marks Child Health Care Transformation Series, April 2020). http://www.inckmarks.org/webinars/InCKMarksPracticeTransformationComponentfinalpdf.pdf.

Bruner, Charles, Hayes, Maxine. "For an effective overhaul of US health, prioritize the youngest and most vulnerable." Opinion. *The Hill.* August 30, 2021.

Burlingham, Bo. *Small Giants: Companies That Choose to Be Great Instead of Big.* Portfolio, 2005.

Burrell, Lori, Crowne, Sarah K.S., Ojo, Kristen D., et al. "Mother and Home Visitor Emotional Well-Being and Alignment on Goals for Home Visiting as Factors for Program Engagement." *Maternal and Child Health Journal* 22 no. 1 Suppl (2018): 43–51. [Published correction appears in Aug. 22, 2018.] doi: 10.1007/s10995-018-2535-9.

Burstein, Dina, Yang, Chloe, Johnson, Kay, Linkenbach, Jeff, Sege, Robert. "Transforming Practice with HOPE (Healthy Outcomes from Positive Experiences)." *Maternal and Child Health Journal* 255, no. 7 (2021): 1019–1024. doi: 10.1007/s10995-021-03173-9.

Campbell, Frances, Conti, Gabriella, Heckman, James J., Moon, Seong H., Pinto, Rodrigo, Pungello, Elizabeth, Pan,Yi. "Early Childhood Investments Substantially Boost Adult Health." *Science* 343, no. 6178 (2014): 1478–1485. doi: 10.1126/science.1248429.

Cannon, Jill S., Kilburn, M. Rebecca, Karoly, Lynn A., Mattox, Teryn, Muchow, Ashley N., Buenaventura, Maya. "Investing Early: Taking Stock of Outcomes and Economic Returns from Early Childhood Programs." *RAND Health Quarterly* 7, no. 4 (2018).

Carnegie Corporation of New York. *Starting Points: Meeting the Needs of Our Youngest Children*. New York, 1994. https://www.carnegie.org/publications/starting-points-meeting-the-needs-of-our-youngest-children/.

Center for the Developing Child at Harvard University. *From Best Practices to Breakthrough Impacts: A Science-Based Approach to Building a More Promising Future for Young Children and Families*. Cambridge, MA: Harvard University, 2016. https://developingchild.harvard.edu/resources/from-best-practices-to-breakthrough-impacts/.

Center for the Developing Child at Harvard University. *In Brief: The Science of Early Childhood Development*. Cambridge, MA: Harvard University, 2007. https://developingchild.harvard.edu/resources/inbrief-science-of-ecd/.

Center for the Developing Child at Harvard University. "Brain Architecture." https://developingchild.harvard.edu/science/key-concepts/brain-architecture/.

Center for the Developing Child at Harvard University. *Connecting the Brain to the Rest of the Body: Early Childhood Development and Lifelong Health Are Deeply Intertwined*. Working Paper No. 15. Cambridge, MA: Harvard University, 2020. https://developingchild.harvard.edu/resources/connecting-the-brain-to-the-rest-of-the-body-early-childhood-development-and-lifelong-health-are-deeply-intertwined/.

Center for the Developing Child at Harvard University. *Three Principles to Improve Outcomes for Children and Families: 2021 Update*. Cambridge, MA: Harvard University, 2021. https://developingchild.harvard.edu/resources/three-early-childhood-development-principles-improve-child-family-outcomes/.

Center for the Developing Child at Harvard University. "Five Facts About Health That Are Often Misunderstood." https://developingchild.harvard.edu/resources/5-facts-about-health-that-are-often-misunderstood/.

Centers for Disease Control and Prevention. *Essentials for Childhood: Creating Safe, Stable, Nurturing Relationships and Environments for All Children.* Atlanta GA: National Center for Injury Prevention and Control, Division of Violence Prevention, CDC, 2018.

Chazan-Cohen, R., Raikes, H.H., Vogel, C. "V. Program Subgroups: Patterns of Impacts for Home Based, Center Based, and Mixed-Approach Programs." Monographs of the Society for Research in Child Development, 78, no. 2 (2013): 93–109. doi: 10.1111/j.1540-5834.2012.00704.x.

Chen, Wei-Bing, Spiker, Donna, Wei, Xin, Gaylor, Erika, Schachner, Abby, Hudson, Laura. "Who Gets What? Describing the Non-Supervisory Training and Supports Received by Home Visiting Staff Members and Its Relationship with Turnover." *American Journal of Community Psychology* 63, nos. 3–4 (2019): 298–311. doi: 10.1002/ajcp.12331.

Condon, Eileen M. "Maternal, Infant, and Early Childhood Home Visiting: A Call for a Paradigm Shift in States' Approaches To Funding." *Policy and Politics in Nursing Practice* 20, no. 1 (2019): 28–40. doi: 10.1177/1527154419829439.

Condon, Eileen M., Londono, Tobon A., Jackson, B., Holland, Margaret L., Slade, Arietta, Mayes, Linda, Sadler, Lois. "Maternal Experiences of Racial Discrimination, Child Indicators of Toxic Stress, and the Minding the Baby Early Home Visiting Intervention." *Nursing Research* 70, no. 5S, Suppl 1 (2021): S43–S52. doi: 10.1097/NNR.0000000000000529.

Corona, Anna, Leahy, Maura, Taft, Kate. *A Roadmap for Collaboration among Title V, Home Visiting, and Early Childhood Systems Programs.* Washington, DC: Association of Maternal and Child Health Programs, 2020. https://amchp.org/wp-content/uploads/2021/11/UPDATED_AMCHP_Roadmap-for-Improved-EC-Collaboration_Sept-2021.pdf.

"Despite Efforts, Children's Plight Virtually Unchanged," *Cincinnati Enquirer* (Cincinnati, OH), February 1, 1998 (1).

DeWine, Mike. *Recommendations of the Governor's Advisory Committee on Home Visitation.* Office of the Governor of Ohio. March 2019. https://content.govdelivery.com/attachments/OHOOD/2019/03/08/file_attachments/1169434/Visitation%20Report%20Final.pdf.

diversitydatakids.org. 2023. Waltham, MA: Institute for Child, Youth and Family Policy, Heller School for Social Policy and Management, Brandeis University.

Drotar, D., Robinson, J., Jeavons, L., Lester Kirchner, H. "A Randomized, Controlled Evaluation of Early Intervention: The Born to Learn Curriculum." *Child: Care, Health and Development,* 35, no. 5 (2009): 643–649. doi: 10.1111/j.1365-2214.2008.00915.x.

Duggan, Anne K., Bower, Kelly. M., Spinosa, Ciara. Z., O'Neill, Kay, Daro, Debra, Harding, Kathryn, Ingalls, Allison, Kemner, Allison, Marchesseault, Christa, Thorland, William. "Changing the Home Visiting Research Paradigm: Models' Perspectives on Behavioral Pathways and Intervention Techniques to Promote Good Birth Outcomes." *BMC Public Health* 22, no. 1 (2022): 1024. doi: 10.1186/s12889-022-13010-5.

Duggan, Anne K., Minkovitz, Cynthia. S., Chaffin, M., Korfmacher, Jon., Brooks-Gunn, Jeanne, Crowne, Sarah, Filene, Jill, Gonsalves, Kay, Landsverk, John, Harwood, Robin. "Creating a National Home Visiting Research Network." *Pediatrics* 132, Supplement 2 (2013): S82–S89. doi: 10.1542/peds.2013-1021F.

Duggan, Anne, Caldera, Debra, Rodriguez, Kira, Burrell, Lori, Rohde, Charles, Crowne, Sarah S. "Impact of a Statewide Home Visiting Program to Prevent Child Abuse." *Child Abuse & Neglect* 31, no. 8 (2007): 801–27. doi: 10.1016/j.chiabu.2006.06.011.

Duggan, Anne, McFarlane, Elizabeth, Fuddy, Loretta, Burrell, Lori, Higman, Susan M., Windham, Amy, Sia, Calvin. "Randomized Trial of a Statewide Home Visiting Program: Impact in Preventing Child Abuse and Neglect." *Child Abuse & Neglect* 28, no. 6 (2004): 597–622. doi: 10.1016/j.chiabu.2003.08.007.

Dyer, Lauren, Bell, Caryn, Perez, Susan, Crear-Perry, Joia, Theall, Katherine, Wallace, Maeve. "US County-Level Prevalence and Spatial Distribution of Optimal Birth Outcomes 2018–2019." *Scientific Reports*, 12, no. 1 (2022): 16535. doi: 10.1038/s41598-022-20517-9.

Ellis Wendy R., Dietz, William H. "A New Framework for Addressing Adverse Childhood and Community Experiences: The Building Community Resilience Model." *Academic Pediatrics* 17, no. 7S (2017): S86–S93. doi: 10.1016/j.acap.2016.12.011.

Every Child Succeeds. "About Every Child Succeeds." https://www.everychild succeeds.org/about.

Every Child Succeeds. *Home Visiting = Engaged Communities + Family Success* (Cincinnati, OH: Every Child Succeeds, 2016). 36–39.

Finello, Karen M., Terteryan, Araksi, Riewerts, Robert J. "Home Visiting Programs: What the Primary Care Clinician Should Know." *Current Problems in Pediatric and Adolescent Health Care* 46, no. 4 (2016): 101–125. doi: 10.1016/j.cppeds.2015.12.011.

First5 California. "What We Do." https://www.ccfc.ca.gov/whatwedo/index .html#where/.

Folger, Alonzo T., Brentley, Anita L., Goyal, Neera K., Hall, Eric S., Sa, Ting, Peugh, James L., Teeters, Angelique R., Van Ginkel, Judith B., Ammerman, Robert T. "Evaluation of a Community-Based Approach to Strengthen Retention in Early Childhood Home Visiting." *Prevention Science*, 17, no. 1 (2016): 52–61. doi: 10.1007/s11121-015-0600-9.

"Futurist Laurel Cutler." *Inc.*, November 1, 1987. https://www.inc.com/maga zine/19871101/3986.html.

Galinsky, Ellen. *Mind in the Making: The Seven Essential Life Skills Every Child Needs*. New York: HarperCollins, 2010.

Galinsky, Ellen. *The Six Stages of Parenthood*. Addison-Wesley, 1987.

Garner, Andrew S. "Home Visiting and the Biology of Toxic Stress: Opportunities to Address Early Childhood Adversity." *Pediatrics* 132, Supplement 2 (2013): S65–S73. doi: 10.1542/peds.2013-1021D.

Garner, Andrew S., Storfer-Isser, Amy, Szilagyi, Moira, Stein, Ruth E.K., Green, Cori M., Kerker, Bonnie D., O'Connor, Karen G., Hoagwood, Kimberly E., McCue Horwitz, Sarah. "Promoting Early Brain and Child Development: Perceived Barriers and the Utilization of Resources to Address Them." *Academic Pediatrics*, 17, no. 7 (2017): 697–705. doi: 10.1016/j.acap.2016 .11.013.

Garner, Andrew S., Shonkoff, Jack P., Siegel, Benjamin S., Dobbins, Mary, Earls, Marian F., McGuinn, Laura, Pascoe, John, Wood, David; Committee on Psychosocial Aspects of Child and Family Health. "Early Childhood Adversity, Toxic Stress, and the Role of the Pediatrician: Translating Developmental Science Into Lifelong Health." *Pediatrics.* 129, no 1. (2012): e224–231. doi: 10.1542/peds.2011-2662.

Ghandour, Reem M., Hirai, Kristin A., Moore, Lara R., Robinson, Jennifer W., Kaminski, Kelly Murphy, Lu, Michael C., Kogan, Michael D. "Healthy and Ready to Learn: Prevalence and Correlates of School Readiness among United States Preschoolers." *Academic Pediatrics* 21, no. 5 (2021): 818–829. doi: 10.1016/j.acap.2021.02.019.

Goyal, Neera K., Rome, Martha G., Massie, Julie A., Mangeot, Colleen, Ammerman, Robert T., Breckenridge, Jye, Lannon, Carole M. "Piloting a Statewide Home Visiting Quality Improvement Learning Collaborative." *Maternal and Child Health Journal* 21, no. 2 (2017): 275–282. doi: 10.1007/ s10995-016-2206-7.

Goyal, Neera K., Teeters, Angelique, Ammerman, Robert T. "Home Visiting and Outcomes of Preterm Infants: A Systematic Review." *Pediatrics* 132, no. 3 (2013): 502–16. doi: 10.1542/peds.2013-0077.

Green, Beth, Sanders, Mary Beth, Tarte, Jerod M. "Effects of Home Visiting Program Implementation on Preventive Health Care Access And Utilization: Results from a Randomized Trial of Healthy Families Oregon." *Prevention Science* 21, no. 1 (2020): 15–24. doi: 10.1007/s11121-018-0964-8.

Greenwood, Peter W., Karoly, Lynn A., Everingham, Susan S., Houbé, J., Kilburn, M. Rebecca, Rydell, C. Peter, Sanders Matthew, Chiesa, James. "Estimating the Costs and Benefits of Early Childhood Interventions: Nurse Home Visits and the Perry Preschool." In *Costs and Benefits of Preventing Crime*: pp. 123–148. London: Routledge, 2018. doi: 10.4324/9780429501 265-5.

Gruendel, Janice, Logan, Allison. "The Bridgeport Baby Bundle: A Unified Approach to Supporting All Families with Very Young Children." Yale School of Medicine News. February 28, 2020. https://medicine.yale.edu/news-article/the-bridgeport-baby-bundle-a-unified-approach-to-supporting-all-families-with-very-young-children/.

Halfon, Neal. "Socioeconomic Influences on Child Health: Building New Ladders of Social Opportunity." *JAMA* 311, no. 9 (2014): 915–919. doi: 10.1001/jama.2014.608.

Halfon, Neal. "The Networks We Need For Early Childhood." *Governing.* February 7, 2015. https://www.governing.com/gov-institute/voices/col-early-childhood-community-partners-collaboration.html.

Halfon, Neal, Uyeda, Kimberly, Inkelas, Moira, Rice, Thomas. *Building Bridges: A Comprehensive System for Healthy Development and School Readiness.* Building State Early Childhood Comprehensive Systems Series, Number 1. Los Angeles, CA: UCLA Center for Healthier Children, Families and Communities, 2004.

Hardeman, Rachel R., Kheyfets, Anna, Mantha, Allison B., Cornell, Andria, Crear-Perry, Joia, Graves, Cornelia, Grobman, William, James-Conterelli, Sascha, Jones, Camara, Lipscomb, Breana, Ortique, Carla, Stuebe, Alison, Welsh, Kaprice, Howell, Elizabeth A. "Developing Tools to Report Racism in Maternal Health for the CDC Maternal Mortality Review Information Application (MMRIA): Findings from the MMRIA Racism & Discrimination Working Group." *Maternal and Child Health Journal.* 26, no. 4 (April 2022): 661–669. doi: 10.1007/s10995-021-03284-3. Epub (January 2022). Erratum in *Maternal and Child Health Journal* (February 2022): PMID: 34982327.

Harlem Children's Zone. https://hcz.org/.

Haroz, Emily E., Ingalls, Allison, Kee, Crystal, Goklish, Novaline, Neault, Nicole, Begay, Marissa, Barlow, Allison. "Informing Precision Home Visiting: Identifying Meaningful Subgroups of Families Who Benefit Most from Family Spirit." *Prevention Science: Journal of the Society for Prevention Research* 20, no. 8 (2019): 1244–1254. doi: 10.1007/s11121-019-01039-9.

Health Share of Oregon. "All:Ready." https://www.healthshareoregon.org/health-equity/allready.

Heckman, James J. *Giving Kids a Fair Chance.* Cambridge, MA: MIT Press, 2013.

Heckman, James J. *Nurse-Family Partnership: Parental Education and Early Health Results in Better Child Outcomes.* The Heckman Equation, 2017. https://heckmanequation.org/www/assets/2017/07/F_HECKMAN_NurseFamilyPartnership_071317.pdf.

Institute for the Advancement of Family Support Professionals. https://institutefsp.org/.

Institute for Healthcare Improvement. https://www.ihi.org.

James, Julia. "Health Policy Brief: Nonprofit Hospitals' Community Benefit Requirements." *Health Affairs*, February 25, 2016. doi: 10.1377/hpb2016 0225.954803.

Johnson, Kay, Applegate, Mary, Gee, Rebekah E. "Improving Medicaid: Three Decades of Change to Better Serve Women of Childbearing Age." *Clinical Obstetrics and Gynecology* 58, no. 2 (2015): 336–354. doi: 10.1097/GRF.000 000000000115.

Johnson, Kay, Bruner, Charles. *A Sourcebook on Medicaid's Role in Early Childhood: Advancing High Performing Medical Homes and Improving Lifelong Health*. Des Moines, IA: Child and Family Policy Center, 2018. https://www.inckmarks.org/docs/pdfs_for_Medicaid_and_EPSDT_page/ SourcebookMEDICAIDYOUNGCHILDRENALL.pdf.

Johnson, Kay, Knitzer, Jane. *Early Childhood Comprehensive Systems that Spend Smarter: Maximizing Resources to Serve Vulnerable Children*. Project THRIVE Issue Brief No. 1. New York: National Center for Children in Poverty, Columbia University Mailman School of Public Health, 2006.

Johnson, Kay, Theberge, Suzanne. *Reducing Disparities Beginning in Early Childhood*. Project THRIVE Issue Brief Short Take No. 4. New York: National Center for Children in Poverty, 2007.

Johnson, Kay. *No Place Like Home: State Home Visiting Policies and Programs*. New York, NY: The Commonwealth Fund, 2001. Available at: https://www. commonwealthfund.org/publications/fund-reports/2001/may/no-place -home-state-home-visiting-policies-and-programs.

Jones Harden, B., Chazan-Cohen, R., Raikes, H., Vogel, C. "Early Head Start Home Visitation: The Role of Implementation in Bolstering Program Benefits." *Journal of Community Psychology*, 40, no 4 (2012): 438–455. doi: 10.1002/jcop.20525.

Jordan, Elizabeth, King, Carlise, Banghart, Patti, Nugent, Courtney. *Improving the Lives of Young Children through Data*. The Early Childhood Data Collaborative. Child Trends, November 8, 2018. https://www.childtrends .org/publications/improving-the-lives-of-young-children-through-data.

Karoly, Lynn A., Greenwood, Peter W., Sohler Everingham, Susan S., Hoube, Jill, Kilburn, M. Rebecca, Rydell, C. Peter, Sanders, Matthew, Chiesa, James, Cannon, Jill S. *Decades of Evidence Demonstrate That Early Childhood Programs Can Benefit Children and Provide Economic Returns*. Santa Monica, CA: RAND Corporation, 2017. https://www.rand.org/pubs/ research_briefs/RB9993.html.

Karoly, Lynn A., Greenwood, Peter W., Sohler Everingham, Susan M., Hoube, Jill, Kilburn, M. Rebecca, Rydell, C. Peter, Sanders, Matthew, Chiesa, James. *Investing in Our Children: What We Know and Don't Know About the Costs and Benefits of Early Childhood Interventions*. Santa Monica, CA: RAND Corporation, 1998. https://www.rand.org/pubs/monograph_reports/ MR898.html.

Karoly, Lynn A., Kilburn, M. Rebecca, Cannon, Jill S. *Early Childhood Interventions: Proven Results, Future Promise*. Santa Monica, CA: RAND Corporation, 2005. https://www.rand.org/pubs/monographs/MG341.html.

Karoly, Lynn A., Kilburn, M. Rebecca, Cannon, Jill S. *Proven Benefits of Early Childhood Interventions*. Santa Monica, CA: RAND Corporation, 2005. https://www.rand.org/pubs/research_briefs/RB9145.html.

Karr-Morse, Robin, Wiley, Meredith S. *Ghosts in the Nursery: Tracing the Roots of Violence*. New York: Atlantic Monthly Press, 2013.

Kilburn, M. Rebecca, Karoly, Lynn A. *The Economics of Early Childhood Policy: What the Dismal Science Has to Say about Investing in Children*. Santa Monica, CA: RAND Corporation, 2008. https://www.rand.org/pubs/occasional_papers/OP227.html.

King, Carlise, Perkins, Victoria. *How Policymakers Can Support Early Childhood Data Governance*. Early Childhood Data Collaborative. Bethesda, MD: Child Trends, 2019. https://www.childtrends.org/publications/how-policymakers-can-support-early-childhood-data-governance.

Kotulak, Ronald. *Inside the Brain—Revolutionary Discoveries of How the Mind Works*. Kansas City, KS: Andrews McMeel Publishing, 1996.

Kotulak, Ronald. "Inside the Brain: Revolutionary Discoveries of How the Mind Works." *Preventive Medicine* 27 no. 2 (1998): 246–247. doi: 10.1006/pmed.1998.0281.

Lawrence, David. American Association of Newspaper Editors. April 14, 2000.

Lewy, Daniela, Casau, Armelle. *Addressing Racial and Ethnic Disparities in Maternal and Child Health Through Home Visiting Programs*. Issue Brief. Hamilton, NJ: Center for Health Care Strategies, 2021. https://www.chcs.org/resource/addressing-racial-and-ethnic-disparities-in-maternal-and-child-health-through-home-visiting-programs/.

Lippincott, J. Getting to the Goal Line: An Independent Report. Success by 6. May 2006.

Love, John M., Kisker, Ellen E., Ross, Christine, Schochet, Peter, Brooks-Gunn, Jeanne, Paulsell, Diane, et al. *Making a Difference in the Lives of Infants and Toddlers and Their Families: The Impacts of Early Head Start. Volumes I-III: Final Technical Report [and] Appendixes [and] Local Contributions To Understanding The Programs And Their Impacts*. Washington, DC: U.S. Department of Health and Human Services, Head Start Bureau, 2002.

Luby, Joan L. "Poverty's Most Insidious Damage: The Developing Brain." *JAMA Pediatrics* 169, no. 9 (2015): 810–811. doi: 10.1001/jamapediatrics.2015.1682.

McLeod Grant, Heather, Crutchfield, Lesley R. "Measuring Social Impact: Creating High-Impact Nonprofits." *Stanford Social Innovation Review* 5, no. 4 (2007): 32–41. doi: 10.48558/chqo-fz58.

McFarlane, Elizabeth, Dodge, Rachel A., Burrell, Lori, Crowne, Sarah, Cheng, Tina L., Duggan, Anne K. "The importance of early parenting in at-risk families and children's social-emotional adaptation to school." *Academic Pediatrics* 10, no. 5 (2010): 330–337. doi: 10.1016/j.acap.2010.06.011.

Mead, Margaret. "The Study of Contemporary Western Culture." In *The World Ahead: An Anthropologist Anticipates the Future*, ed. Robert B. Textor. Vol. 6 of *Margaret Mead: The Study of Contemporary Western* Culture. New York: Berghahn Books, 2005.

Minkovitz, Cynthia S., O'Neill, Kay M.G., Duggan, Anne K. "Home Visiting: A Service Strategy to Reduce Poverty and Mitigate Its Consequences." *Academic Pediatrics* 16, no. 3, Supplement (2016): S105-S111. doi: 10.1016/j.acap.2016.01.005.

Mistry, Kamila B., Minkovitz, Cynthia S, Riley, Anne W., Johnson, Sara B., Grason, Holly A., Dubay, Lisa C., Guyer, Bernard. "A New Framework for Childhood Health Promotion: The Role of Policies and Programs in Building Capacity and Foundations of Early Childhood Health." *American Journal of Public Health* 102, no. 9 (2012): 1688–96. doi: 10.2105/AJPH.2012.300687.

Morris, Amanda S., Hays-Grudo, Jennifer, Kerr, Kara L., Beasley, Lana O. "The Heart of the Matter: Developing the Whole Child through Community Resources and Caregiver Relationships." *Developmental Psychopathology* 33, no. 2 (2021): 533–544. doi: 10.1017/S0954579420001595.

Naik, Gautam. "Baby Steps: Cincinnati Applies a Corporate Model to Saving Infants." *The Wall Street Journal*. June 20, 2006.

National Academies of Sciences, Engineering, and Medicine; Health and Medicine Division; Board on Population Health and Public Health Practice; Committee on Applying Neurobiological and Socio-Behavioral Sciences from Prenatal Through Early Childhood Development: A Health Equity Approach, ed. Negussie, Yamrot, Geller, Amy, DeVoe, Jennifer E. *Vibrant and Healthy Kids: Aligning Science, Practice, and Policy to Advance Health Equity*. Washington, DC: National Academies Press, 2019. doi: 10.17226/25466.

National Academies of Sciences, Engineering, and Medicine; Division of Behavioral and Social Sciences and Education; Board on Children, Youth, and Families, ed. Breiner, Heather, Ford, Morgan, Gadsden, Vivian L. *Parenting Matters: Supporting Parents of Children Ages 0–8*. Washington DC: National Academies Press, 2016.

National Home Visiting Resource Center. *2021 Home Visiting Yearbook*. Arlington, VA: James Bell Associates and the Urban Institute, 2021. https://nhvrc.org/yearbook/2021-yearbook/

National Institute for Children's Health Quality (NICHQ). "Early Childhood Comprehensive Systems Collaborative Improvement and Innovation Network (ECCS CoIIN)." https://www.nichq.org/project/early-childhood-comprehensive-systems-collaborative-improvement-and-innovation-network-eccs.

National Research Council, Institute of Medicine. *From Neurons to Neighborhoods: The Science of Early Childhood Development*, ed. Jack P. Shonkoff and Deborah A. Phillips. Washington, DC: The National Academies Press, 2000. doi: 10.17226/9824.

Nygren, Peggy, Green, Beth, Winters, Katie, Rockhill, Anna. "What's Happening During Home Visits? Exploring the Relationship of Home Visiting Content and Dosage to Parenting Outcomes." *Maternal and Child Health Journal* 22, Supplement 1 (2018): 52–61. doi: 10.1007/s10995-018-2547-5. Erratum in: 2018 Aug 22.

Ohio Business Roundtable. *What Difference Are We Making? An Assessment of the State of Early Learning In Ohio.* 2017. https://indd.adobe.com/view/2586dc3f-7fb1-486a-929d-74dcae650066.

Olds, David L., Kitzman, Harriet, Anson, Elizabeth, Smith, Joyce A., Knudtson, Michael D., Miller, Ted, Cole, Robert, Hopfer, Christian, Conti, Gabriella. "Prenatal and Infancy Nurse Home Visiting Effects on Mothers: 18-Year Follow-up of a Randomized Trial." *Pediatrics* 144, no. 6 (2019): e20183889. doi: 10.1542/peds.2018-3889.

Olds, David L., Eckenrode, John, Henderson, Charles R. Jr, et al. "Long-Term Effects of Home Visitation on Maternal Life Course and Child Abuse and Neglect: Fifteen-Year Follow-up of a Randomized Trial." *JAMA* 278, no. 8 (1997): 637–643. doi: 10.1001/jama.1997.03550080047038.

Olds, David L., Kitzman, Harriet. "Can Home Visitation Improve the Health of Women and Children at Environmental Risk?" *Pediatrics* 86, no. 1 (1990): 108–16. doi: 10.1542/peds.86.1.108.

Olds, David L., Henderson, Charles R. Jr, Tatelbaum, Robert, Chamberlin, Robert. "Improving the Life-Course Development of Socially Disadvantaged Mothers: A Randomized Trial of Nurse Home Visitation." *American Journal of Public Health* 78, no. 11 (1988): 1436–1445. doi: 10.2105/AJPH.78.11.1436.

Pallotta, Daniel. *Uncharitable: How Restraints on Nonprofits Undermine their Potential.* Lebanon, NH: University Press of New England, 2008.

Paradis, Heather A., Sandler, Mardy, Manly, Jody T., Valentine, Laurie. "Building Healthy Children: Evidence-Based Home Visitation Integrated With Pediatric Medical Homes." *Pediatrics* 132, Supplement 2 (2013): S174–S179. doi: 10.1542/peds.2013-1021R.

Perrin, James M., Lu, Michael C., Geller, Amy, DeVoe, Jennifer E. "Vibrant and Healthy Kids: Aligning Science, Practice, and Policy to Advance Health Equity." *Academic Pediatrics* 20, no. 2 (2020): 160–162. doi: 10.1016/j.acap.2019.11.019.

Rashid, Yasir, Ammar, Rashid, Akib Warraich, Muhammad, Sabir, Sana Sameen, Waseem, Ansar. "Case Study Method: A Step-By-Step Guide for Business Researchers." *International Journal of Qualitative Methods* 18 (2019). doi: 10.1177/1609406919862424.

Reed, Lillian, Oxenden, McKenna. "A Look Back at U.S. Rep. Elijah Cummings' Most Powerful Speeches." *Baltimore Sun*. October 17, 2019.

Roby, Erin, Shaw, Daniel S., Morris, Pamela, et al. "Pediatric Primary Care and Partnerships Across Sectors to Promote Early Child Development." *Academic Pediatrics* 21, no. 2 (2021): 228–235. doi: 10.1016/j.acap.2020.12.002.

Sabo, Samantha, Wightman, Patrick, McCue, Kelly, Butler, Matthew, Pilling, Vern, Jimenez, Dulce J., Martin, Celaya, Rumann, Sara. "Addressing Maternal and Child Health Equity through a Community Health Worker Home Visiting Intervention to Reduce Low Birth Weight: Retrospective Quasi-Experimental Study." *BMJ Open* 11, no. 6 (2021): e045014. doi: 10.1136/bmjopen-2020-045014.

Sandel, Megan, Faugno, Elena, Mingo, Angela, Cannon, Jessie, Byrd, Kymberly, Acevedo-Garcia, Dolores, Collier, Sheena, McClure, Elizabeth, Boynton-Jarrett, Renee. "Neighborhood-Level Interventions to Improve Childhood Opportunity and Lift Children Out of Poverty." *Academic Pediatrics* 16, no. 3 Supplement (2016): S128–35. doi: 10.1016/j.acap.2016.01.013. Erratum in: 2017 Jan–Feb;17, no 1: 104.

Schorr, Lisbeth B., Schorr, Daniel. *Within Our Reach: Breaking the Cycle of Disadvantage*. New York: Anchor Books, Penguin Random House, 1988.

Schorr, Lisbeth B. *Common Purpose: Strengthening Families and Neighborhoods to Rebuild America*. New York: Anchor Books, Doubleday, 1997.

Schorr, Lisbeth B. "Ending Child Poverty in America: An Impossible Dream?" Medium. June, 2022. https://lbschorr89.medium.com/ending-child-poverty-in-america-an-impossible-dream-c32cad8ffbca.

Scott, Karen A., Britton, Laura, McLemore, Monica R. "The Ethics of Perinatal Care for Black Women: Dismantling the Structural Racism In 'Mother Blame' Narratives." *Journal of Perinatal and Neonatal Nursing* 33, no. 2 (2019): 108–115. doi: 10.1097/JPN.0000000000000394.

Sege, Robert D., Harper Browne, Charlyn. "Responding to ACES with HOPE: Health Outcomes From Positive Experiences." *Academic Pediatrics* 17, no. 7 Supplement (2017): S79–S85. doi: 10.1016/j.acap.2017.03.007.

Shaw, Daniel S., Mendelsohn, Alan L., Morris, Pamela A. "Reducing Poverty-Related Disparities in Child Development and School Readiness: The Smart Beginnings Tiered Prevention Strategy that Combines Pediatric Primary Care with Home Visiting." *Clinical Child and Family Psychology Review* 24, no. 4 (2021): 669–683. doi: 10.1007/s10567-021-00366-0.

Shonkoff, Jack P., Garner, Andrew S.; Committee on Psychosocial Aspects of Child and Family Health; Committee on Early Childhood, Adoption, and Dependent Care; Section on Developmental and Behavioral Pediatrics. "The Lifelong Effects of Early Childhood Adversity and Toxic Stress." *Pediatrics* 129, no. 1 (2012): e232–e246. doi: 10.1542/peds.2011-2663.

Shonkoff, Jack P., Boyce, W. Thomas, McEwen, Bruce S. "Neuroscience, Molecular Biology, and the Childhood Roots of Health Disparities: Building a New Framework for Health Promotion and Disease Prevention." *JAMA* 301, no. 21 (2009): 2252–2259. doi: 10.1001/jama.2009.754.

Shore, Bill. *The Cathedral Within: Transforming Your Life by Giving Something Back*. New York: Random House, 1999.

Shore, Bill. *The Imaginations of Unreasonable Men: Inspirations, Vision, and Purpose in the Quest to End Malaria*. New York: Public Affairs, 2012.

Silovsky, Jane, Bard, David, Owora, Arthur H., Milojevich, Helen, Jorgenson, Ashley. "Risk and Protective Factors Associated with Adverse Childhood Experiences in Vulnerable Families: Results of a Randomized Clinical Trial of SafeCare®." *Child Maltreatment* 28(2), 384–395. doi: 10.1177/107755 95221100723

Sjoberg, Gideon, Orum, Anthony M., and Feagin, Joe R. *A Case for the Case Study*. Chapel Hill, NC: University of North Carolina Press, 2016.

Solberg, Leif I., Mosser, Gordon, McDonald, Sharon. "The Three Faces of Performance Improvement: Improvement, Accountability and Research." *Joint Commission Journal on Quality Improvement* 23, no. 3 (1997): 135–147.

Spurlino, Jim. *Business Bullseye: Take Dead Aim and Achieve Great Success*. Hearndon, VA: Amplify Publishing, 2021.

Substance Abuse and Mental Health Services Administration. "Understanding Child Trauma." https://www.samhsa.gov/child-trauma/understanding-child -trauma.

Supplee, Lauren H., Ammerman, Robert T., Duggan, Anne K., List, John A., Suskind, Dana. "The Role of Open Science Practices in Scaling Evidence-Based Prevention Programs." *Prevention Science*. Epub ahead of print, 2021 Nov 15. doi: 10.1007/s11121-021-01322-8.

Supplee, Lauren H., Duggan, Anne. "Innovative Research Methods to Advance Precision in Home Visiting for More Efficient and Effective Programs." *Child Development Perspectives* 13, no. 3 (2019): 173–179. doi: 10.1111/ cdep.12334.

Tandon, Darius, Parillo, Kathleen, Jenkins, Carrie, Jenkins, Jenine, Duggan, Anne. "Promotion of Service Integration among Home Visiting Programs and Community Coalitions Working with Low-Income, Pregnant, and Parenting Women." *Health Promotion Practice* 8, no. 1 (2007): 79–87. doi: 10.1177/1524839905278851.

Tout, Kathryn, Schaefer, Catherine, Boddicker-Young, Porsche, et al. *Addressing Early Childhood Health Equity in Communities and States: Overview and Key Findings from the ECHE Landscape Project*. Joint Issue Brief: National Institute for Children's Health Quality and Child Trends, 2021. https://cms. childtrends.org/wp-content/uploads/2021/03/ECHEExecutiveSummary _ChildTrends_April2021.pdf.

Toomey, Sara L., Cheng, Tina L. APA-AAP Workgroup on the Family-Centered Medical Home. "Home Visiting and the Family-Centered Medical Home: Synergistic Services to Promote Child Health." *Academic Pediatrics* 13, no. 1 (2013):3–5. doi: 10.1016/j.acap.2012.11.001.

Tschudy, Megan M., Toomey, Sara L., Cheng, Tina L. "Merging Systems: Integrating Home Visitation and the Family-Centered Medical Home." *Pediatrics* 132, Supplement 2 (2013): S74-S81. doi: 10.1542/peds.2013 -1021E.

United Way of Greater Cincinnati. *2020 UWGC Annual Report—Final 5-2-22.* https://www.uwgc.org/sites/default/files/2022-05/UWGC_AnnualReport _2020.pdf.

United Way of Greater Cincinnati. https://www.uwgc.org.

United Way of Greater Cincinnati. "Welcome to Our Nonprofit Portal." https:// www.uwgc.org/for-nonprofits.

US Department of Health and Human Services. Administration for Children and Families. "Home Visiting Evidence of Effectiveness: What Is Home Visiting Evidence of Effectiveness?" https://homvee.acf.hhs.gov/.

US Department of Health and Human Services. Office of Disease Prevention and Health Promotion. "Social Determinants of Health." https://health.gov/ healthypeople/priority-areas/social-determinants-health.

US Department of Health and Human Resources. Health Resources and Services Administration Maternal and Child Health. "Early Childhood Systems Programming." https://mchb.hrsa.gov/earlychildhoodcomprehen sivesystems.

Wagner, Mary, Spiker, Donna. *Multisite Parents as Teachers Evaluation: Experiences and Outcomes for Children and Families.* Menlo Park, CA: SRI International, 2001. https://web.archive.org/web/20101213070439/http:// policyweb.sri.com/cehs/publications/patfinal.pdf.

Wasik, Barbara Hanna, Bryant, Donna M. *Home Visiting: Procedures for Helping Families.* Thousand Oaks, CA: Sage Publications, 2001.

West, Allison, Duggan, Anne K., Gruss, Kelsey, Minkovitz, Cynthia S. "The Role of State Context in Promoting Service Coordination in Maternal, Infant, and Early Childhood Home Visiting Programs." *Journal of Public Health Management and Practice* 26, no. 1 (2020): E9-E18. doi: 10.1097/PHH.0000 00000000907.

West, Allison, Duggan, Anne, Gruss, Kelsey, Minkovitz, Cynthia S. "Service Coordination to Address Maternal Mental Health, Partner Violence, and Substance Use: Findings from a National Survey of Home Visiting Programs." *Prevention Science* 22, no. 5 (2021): 633–644. doi: 10.1007/s11 121-021-01232-9.

West, Allison, Duggan, Anne, Gruss, Kelsey, Minkovitz, Cynthia S. "The Role of State Context in Promoting Service Coordination in Maternal, Infant, and Early Childhood Home Visiting Programs." *Journal of Public Health*

Management and Practice 26, no. 1 (2020): E9-E18. doi: 10.1097/PHH.00 0000000000907.

Wien, Simone, Miller, Andres L., Kramer, Michael R. "Structural Racism Theory, Measurement, and Methods: A Scoping Review." *Front Public Health*, 11 (2023):1069476. doi: 10.3389/fpubh.2023.1069476.

Williams, Corrine M., Cprek, Sarah, Asaolu, Ibiola, English, Brenda, Jewell, Tracey, Smith, Kylen, Robl, Joyce. "Kentucky Health Access Nurturing Development Services Home Visiting Program Improves Maternal and Child Health." *Maternal and Child Health Journal* 21, no. 5 (2017): 1166–1174. doi: 10.1007/s10995-016-2215-6.

Williams, Venice Ng, McManus, Beth M., Brooks-Russell, Ashley, Yost, Elly, Allison, Mandy A., Olds, David L., Tung, Gregory J. "A Qualitative Study of Effective Collaboration among Nurse Home Visitors, Healthcare Providers and Community Support Services in the United States." *Health & Social Care in the Community* 30, no. 5 (2022): 1881-1893. doi: 10.1111/hsc.13567.

Williams, Venice, Ng, Lopez, Connie, Cignetti, Tung, Gregory J., Olds, David L., Allison, Mandy Atlee. "A Case Study of Care Co-ordination between Primary Care Providers and Nurse Home Visitors to Serve Young Families Experiencing Adversity in the Northwestern United States." *Health and Social Care in the Community* Jul 30, no. 4 (2021):1400–1411 doi: 10.1111/hsc.13470.

Willis, David W., Chavez, Selena, Lee, Jang, Hampton, Patsy, Fine, Amy. *Early Relational Health National Survey: What We're Learning from the Field*. Washington, DC: Center for the Study of Social Policy, 2020. https://cssp.org/resource/early-relational-health-survey.

Willis, David W., Paradis, Nichole, Johnson, Kay. "The Paradigm Shift to Early Relational Health: A Network Movement." *ZERO TO THREE Journal*, 42, no. 4 (2022): 22–30.

Willis, David, FrameWorks Institute. *Building Relationships: Framing Early Relational Health*. Washington, DC: FrameWorks Institute and Center for the Study of Social Policy, 2020. https://cssp.org/resource/building-rela tionships-framing-early-relational-health/

Willis, David W., Johnson, Kay. *The Collaboration and Alignment of MCHB's Early Childhood Investments through Title V, MIECHV, and ECCS Impact Programs: A Qualitative Analysis*. Prepared for the Association of Maternal and Child Health Programs by the Center for the Study of Social Policy and Johnson Group Consulting, Inc., 2020.

Willis, David, Sege, Robert, Johnson, Kay. "Changing the Mindset: Foundational Relationships Counter Adversity with HOPE." Washington, DC: Center for the Study of Social Policy. May 21, 2020. https://cssp.org/2020/05/changing -the-mindset-foundational-relationships-counter-adversity-with-hope/.

Yin, Robert K. *Case Study Research: Design and Methods (Applied Social Research Methods)*. Thousand Oaks, CA: Sage Publications, 1984; 1989; 1994; 2003; 2009; 2013; 2014; and 2017.

Yin, Robert K. *Case Study Research and Applications: Design and Methods, 6th Edition*. Thousand Oaks, CA: Sage Publications, 2017.

Zephyrin, Laurie C. "Changing the Narrative and Accelerating Action to Reduce Racial Inequities in Maternal Mortality." *American Journal of Public Health* 111, no. 9 (2021): 1575–1577. doi: 10.2105/AJPH.2021.306462.

Appendix B:
Every Child Succeeds References

Ammerman, Robert T. "Opportunities and Challenges in Addressing Maternal Depression in Community Settings." *JAMA Psychiatry* 74, no. 8 (2017): 775–776. doi: 10.1001/jamapsychiatry.2017.1173.

Ammerman, Robert T., Altaye, Mekibib, Putnam, Frank W., Teeters, Angelique R., Zou, Yuanshu, Van Ginkel, Judith B. "Depression Improvement and Parenting in Low-Income Mothers in Home Visiting." *Archives of Women's Mental Health* 18, no. 3 (2015): 555–563. doi: 10.1007/s00737-014-0479-7.

Ammerman, Robert T., Chen, Jie, Mallow, Peter J., Rizzo, John A., Folger, Alonzo T., Van Ginkel, Judith B. "Annual Direct Health Care Expenditures and Employee Absenteeism Costs in High-Risk, Low-Icome Mothers with Major Depression." *Journal of Affective Disorders* 190, Jan (2016): 386–394. doi: 10.1016/j.jad.2015.10.025.

Ammerman, Robert T., Mallow, Peter J., Rizzo, John A., Putnam, Frank W., Van Ginkel, Judith B. "Cost-Effectiveness of In-Home Cognitive Behavioral Therapy for Low-Income Depressed Mothers Participating in Early Childhood Prevention Programs." *Journal of Affective Disorders* 208, Jan (2017): 475–482. doi: 10.1016/j.jad.2016.10.041.

Ammerman, Robert T., Peugh, James L., Putnam, Frank W., Van Ginkel, Judith B. "Predictors of Treatment Response in Depressed Mothers Receiving In-Home Cognitive Behavioral Therapy and Concurrent Home Visiting." *Behavior Modification.* 36, no. 4 (2012): 462–481. doi: 10.1177/0145445512447120.

Ammerman, Robert T., Peugh, James L., Teeters, Angelique R., Putnam, Frank W., Van Ginkel, Judith B. "Child Maltreatment History and Response to CBT Treatment in Depressed Mothers Participating in Home Visiting." *Journal of Interpersonal Violence* 31, no. 5 (2016): 774–791. doi: 10.1177/0886260514556769.

Ammerman, Robert T., Peugh, James L., Teeters, Angelique R., Sakuma, Kari-Lyn K., Jones, Damon E., Hostetler, Michelle L., Van Ginkel, Judith B., Feinberg, Mark E. "Promoting Parenting in Home Visiting:

A CACE analysis of Family Foundations." *Journal of Family Psychology* 36, no. 2 (2022): 225–235. doi: 10.1037/fam0000888.

Ammerman, Robert T., Putnam, Frank W., Altaye, Mekibib, Chen, Liang, Holleb, Lauren J., Stevens, Jack, Short, Jodie A., Van Ginkel, Judith B. "Changes in Depressive Symptoms in First Time Mothers in Home Visitation." *Child Abuse and Neglect* 33, no. 3. (2009): 127–138. doi: 10.1016/j.chiabu.2008.09.005.

Ammerman, Robert T., Putnam, Frank W., Altaye, Mekibib, Stevens, Jack, Teeters, Angelique R., Van Ginkel, Judith B. "A Clinical Trial of In-Home CBT for Depressed Mothers in Home Visitation." *Behavioral Therapy* 44, no. 3 (2013): 359–372. doi: 10.1016/j.beth.2013.01.002.

Ammerman, Robert T., Putnam, Frank W., Altaye, Mekibib, Teeters, Angelique R., Stevens, Jack, Van Ginkel, Judith B. "Treatment of Depressed Mothers in Home Visiting: Impact on Psychological Distress and Social Functioning." *Child Abuse and Neglect* 37, no. 8 (2013): 544–554. doi: 10.1016/j.chiabu.2013.03.003.

Ammerman, Robert T., Putnam, Frank W., Bosse, Nicole R., Teeters, Angelique R., Van Ginkel, Judith B. "Maternal Depression in Home Visitation: A Systematic Review." *Aggressive and Violent Behavior* 15, no. 3 (2010): 191–200. doi: 10.1016/j.avb.2009.12.002.

Ammerman, Robert T., Putnam, Frank W., Chard, Kathleen M., Stevens, Jack, Van Ginkel, Judith B. "PTSD in Depressed Mothers in Home Visitation." *Psychological Trauma* 4, no. 2 (2012). doi: 10.1037/a0023062.

Ammerman, Robert T., Putnam, Frank W., Kopke, Jonathan E., Gannon, Thomas A., Short, Jodie A., Van Ginkel, Judith B., Clark, Margaret J., Carrozza, Mark A., Spector, Alan R. "Development and Implementation of a Quality Assurance Infrastructure in a Multisite Home Visitation Program in Ohio and Kentucky." *Journal of Prevention & Intervention in the Community* 34, no. 1–2. (2007): 89–107. doi: 10.1300/J005v34n01_05.

Ammerman, Robert T., Putnam, Frank W., Stevens, Jack, Bosse, Nicole R., Short, Jodie A., Bodley, Amy L., Van Ginkel, Judith B. "An Open Trial of In-Home CBT for Depressed Mothers in Home Visitation." *Maternal and Child Health Journal* 15, no. 8 (2011): 1333–1341. doi: 10.1007/s10995-010-0691-7.

Ammerman, Robert T., Scheiber, Francesca A., Peugh, James L., Messer, Erica P., Van Ginkel, Judith B., Putnam, Frank W. "Interpersonal Trauma and Suicide Attempts in Low-Income Depressed Mothers in Home Visiting." *Child Abuse and Neglect* 97 (2019): 104126. doi: 10.1016/j.chiabu.2019.104126.

Ammerman, Robert T., Shenk, Chad E., Teeters, Angelique R., Noll, Jennie G., Putnam, Frank W., Van Ginkel, Judith B. "Impact of Depression and Childhood Trauma in Mothers Receiving Home Visitation." *Journal of Children and Family Studies* 21, no. 4 (2012): 612–625. doi: 10.1007/s10826-011-9513-9.

Baggett, Kathleen M., Davis, Sheeber, Lisa B., Ammerman, Robert T., Mosley, Elizabeth A., Miller, Katy, Feil, Edward G. "Minding the Gatekeepers: Referral and Recruitment of Postpartum Mothers with Depression into a Randomized Controlled Trial of a Mobile Internet Parenting Intervention to Improve Mood and Optimize Infant Social Communication Outcomes." *International Journal of Environmental Research and Public Health* 17, no. 23 (2020): 8978. doi: 10.3390/ijerph17238978

Bowers, Katherine, Ding, Lili, Gregory, Samantha, Yolton, Kimberly, Ji, Hong, Meyer, Jerrold, Ammerman, Robert T., Van Ginkel, Judith B., Folger, Alonzo. "Maternal Distress and Hair Cortisol in Pregnancy Among Women with Elevated Adverse Childhood Experiences." *Psychoneuroendocrinology* 95 (2018): 145–148. doi: 10.1016/j.psyneuen.2018.05.024.

Bowers, Katherine, Ding, Lili, Yolton, Kimberly, Ji, Hong, Nidey, Nichole, Meyer, Jerrold, Ammerman, Robert T., Van Ginkel, Judith B., Folger, Alonzo. "Pregnancy and Infant Development (PRIDE)—A Preliminary Observational Study of Maternal Adversity and Infant Development." *BMC Pediatrics* 21, no. 1. (2021): 452. doi: 10.1186/s12887-021-02801-1.

Bowers, Katherine, Folger, Alonzo T., Zhang, Nanhua, Sa, Ting, Ehrhardt, Jennifer, Meinzen-Derr, J., Goyal, Neera K., Van Ginkel, Judith B., Ammerman, Robert T. "Participation in Home Visitation Is Associated with Higher Utilization of Early Intervention." *Maternal and Child Health Journal* 22, no. 4 (2018): 494–500. doi: 10.1007/s10995-017-2415-8.

DeLano, Kelly, Folger, Alonzo T., Ding, Lili, Ji, Hong, Yolton, Kimberly, Ammerman, Robert T., Van Ginkel, Judith B., Bowers, Katherine A. "Associations between Maternal Community Deprivation and Infant DNA Methylation of the SLC6A4 Gene." *Front Public Health* 27, no. 8 (2020): 557195. doi: 10.3389/fpubh.2020.557195.

Donovan, Edward F., Ammerman, Robert T., Besl, John, Atherton, Harry, Khoury, Jane C., Altaye, Mekibib, Putnam, Frank W., Van Ginkel, Judith B. "Intensive Home Visiting Is Associated with Decreased Risk of Infant Death." *Pediatrics* 119, no. 6. (2007): 1145–1151. doi: 10.1542/peds.2006-2411.

Folger, Alonzo T., Ammerman, Robert T. "Development of a Trauma-Informed Approach in Home Visiting." Home Visiting Applied Research Collaborative (HARC) Research Brief. 2022. https://www.ecsresearch.org/new-page-1.

Folger, Alonzo T., Bowers, Katherine A., Dexheimer, Judith W., Sa, Ting, Hall, Eric S., Van Ginkel, Judith B., Ammerman, Robert T. "Evaluation of Early Childhood Home Visiting to Prevent Medically Attended Unintentional Injury." *Annals of Emergency Medicine* 70, no. 3 (2017): 302–310. doi: 10.1016/j.annemergmed.2017.01.029.

Folger, Alonzo T., Brentley, Anita L., Goyal, Neera K., Hall, Eric S., Sa, Ting, Peugh, James L., Teeters, Angelique R., Van Ginkel, Judith B., Ammerman, Robert T. "Evaluation of a Community-Based Approach to Strengthen

Retention in Early Childhood Home Visiting." *Prevention Science* 17, no. 1 (2016): 52–61. doi: 10.1007/s11121-015-0600-9.

Folger, Alonzo T., Ding, Lili, Ji, Hong, Yolton, Kimberly, Ammerman, Robert T., Van Ginkel, Judith B., Bowers, Katherine. "Neonatal NR3C1 Methylation and Social-Emotional Development at 6 and 18 Months of Age." *Frontiers in Behavioral Neuroscience* 5, no. 13 (2019): 14. doi: 10.3389/fnbeh.2019.00014.

Folger, Alonzo T., Putnam, Karen T., Putnam, Frank W., Peugh, James L., Eismann, Emily A., Sa, Ting, Shapiro, Robert A., Van Ginkel, Judith B., Ammerman, Robert T. "Maternal Interpersonal Trauma and Child Social-Emotional Development: An Intergenerational Effect." *Paediatric Perinatal Epidemiology* 31, no. 2 (2017): 99–107. doi: 10.1111/ppe.12341.

Goyal, Neera K., Ammerman, Robert T., Massie, Julie A., Clark, Margaret, Van Ginkel, Judith B. "Using Quality Improvement to Promote Implementation and Increase Well Child Visits in Home Visiting." *Child Abuse and Neglect* 53 (2016): 108–117. doi: 10.1016/j.chiabu.2015.11.014.

Goyal, Neera K., Brown, Courtney M., Folger, Alonzo T., Hall, Eric S., Van Ginkel, Judith B., Ammerman, Robert T. "Adherence to Well-Child Care and Home Visiting Enrollment Associated with Increased Emergency Department Utilization." *Maternal and Child Health Journal* 24, no. 1 (2020): 73–81. doi: 10.1007/s10995-019-02821-5.

Goyal, Neera K., Folger, Alonzo T., Hall, Eric S., Teeters, Angelique, Van Ginkel, Judith B., Ammerman, Robert T. "Multilevel Assessment of Prenatal Engagement in Home Visiting." *Journal of Epidemiology and Community Health* 70, no. 9 (2016): 888–894. doi: 10.1136/jech-2014-205196.

Goyal, Neera K., Folger, Alonzo T., Sucharew, Heidi J., Brown, Courtney M., Hall, Eric S., Van Ginkel, Judith B., Ammerman, Robert T. "Primary Care and Home Visiting Utilization Patterns among At-Risk Infants." *The Journal of Pediatrics* 198 (2018): 240–246.e2. doi: 10.1016/j.jpeds.2018.03.012.

Goyal, Neera K., Hall, Eric S., Jones, David E., Meinzen-Derr, Jareen K., Short, Jodie A., Ammerman, Robert T., Van Ginkel, Judith B. "Association of Maternal and Community Factors with Enrollment in Home Visiting among At-Risk, First-Time Mothers." *American Journal of Public Health* 104, Supplement 1 (2014): S144–151. doi: 10.2105/AJPH.2013.301488.

Goyal, Neera K., Hall, Eric S., Meinzen-Derr, Jareen K., Kahn, Robert S., Short, Jodie A., Van Ginkel, Judith B., Ammerman, Robert T. "Dosage Effect of Prenatal Home Visiting on Pregnancy Outcomes in At-Risk, First-Time Mothers." *Pediatrics* 132, Supplement 2 (2013): S118–S125. doi: 10.1542/peds.2013-1021J.

Hall, Eric S., Goyal, Neera K., Ammerman, Robert T., Miller, Megan M., Jones, David E., Short, Jodie A., Van Ginkel, Judith B. "Development of a Linked Perinatal Data Resource from State Administrative and Community-Based Program Data." *Maternal and Child Health Journal* 18, no. 1 (2014): 316–325. doi: 10.1007/s10995-013-1236-7.

Herbst, Rachel B., McClure, Jessica M., Ammerman, Robert T., Stark, Lori J., Kahn, Robert S., Mansour, Mona E., Burkhardt, Mary C. "Four Innovations: A Robust Integrated Behavioral Health Program in Pediatric Primary Care." *Family Systems Health* 38, no. 4 (2020): 450–463. doi: 10.1037/fsh0000537.

Hutton, John S., Gupta, Resi, Gruber, Rachel, Berndsen, Jennifer, DeWitt, Thomas, Ollberding, Nicholas J., Van Ginkel, Judith B., Ammerman, Robert T. "Randomized Trial of a Children's Book Versus Brochures for Safe Sleep Knowledge and Adherence in a High-Risk Population." *Academic Pediatrics* 17, no. 8 (2017): 879–886. doi: 10.1016/j.acap.2017.04.018.

Hutton, John S., Lin, Li, Gruber, Rachel, Berendsen, Jennifer, DeWitt, Thomas, Van Ginkel, Judith B., Ammerman, Robert T. "Shared Reading and Television Across the Perinatal Period in Low-SES Households." *Clinical Pediatrics* 57, no. 8 (2018): 904–912. doi: 10.1177/0009922817737077.

Jones, David E., Tang, Mei, Folger, Alonzo, Ammerman, Robert T., Hossain, Md M., Short, Jodie, Van Ginkel, Judith B. "Neighborhood Effects on PND Symptom Severity for Women Enrolled in a Home Visiting Program." *Community Mental Health Journal* 54, no. 4 (2018): 420–428. doi: 10.1007/s10597-017-0175-y.

Kopke, Jonathan E., Carrozza, Mark, Witherow, Beth Ann, Van Ginkel, Judith B., Putnam, Frank, Ammerman, Robert T. "Every User Succeeds." *AMIA Annual Symposium Proceedings.* 2003;2003: 898.

Lee, Alex. *Are Mothers Establishing Medical Home Visiting During the First Weeks of Life?* Internal report prepared for Every Child Succeeds, 2010.

Mahabee-Gittens, E. Melinda, Ammerman, Robert T., Khoury, Jane C., Stone, Lara, Meyers, Gabe T., Witry, John K., Merianos, Ashley L., Mancuso, Tierney F., Stackpole, Kristin M.W., Bennett, Berkeley L., Akers, Laura, Gordon, Judith S. "Healthy Families: Study Protocol for a Randomized Controlled Trial of a Screening, Brief Intervention, and Referral to Treatment Intervention for Caregivers to Reduce Secondhand Smoke Exposure among Pediatric Emergency Patients." *BMC Public Health* 17, no. 1 (2017): 374. doi: 10.1186/s12889-017-4278-8.

Messer, Erica P., Ammerman, Robert T., Teeters, Angelique R., Bodley, Amy L., Howard, Jessica, Van Ginkel, Judith B., Putnam, Frank W. "Treatment of Maternal Depression with In-Home Cognitive Behavioral Therapy Augmented by a Parenting Enhancement: A Case Report." *Cognitive Behavioral Practice* 25, no. 3 (2018): 402–415. doi: 10.1016/j.cbpra.2017.10.002.

Nidey, Nichole, Bowers, Katherine, Ammerman, Robert T., Shah, Anita N., Phelan, Kieran J., Clark, Margaret J., Van Ginkel, Judith B., Folger, Alonzo T. "Combinations of Adverse Childhood Events and Risk of Postpartum Depression among Mothers Enrolled in a Home Visiting Program." *Annals of Epidemiology* 52 (2020): 26–34. doi: 10.1016/j.annepidem.2020.09.015.

Shenk, Chad E., Ammerman, Robert T., Teeters, Angelique R., Bensman, Heather E., Allen, Elizabeth K., Putnam, Frank W., Van Ginkel, Judith B. "History of Maltreatment in Childhood and Subsequent Parenting Stress in At-Risk, First-Time Mothers: Identifying Points of Intervention During Home Visiting." *Prevention Science* 18, no. 3 (2017): 361–370. Erratum in: *Prevention Science* 18, no. 3 (2017): 371. doi: 10.1007/s11121-017-0758-4.

Teeters, Angelique R., Ammerman, Robert T., Shenk, Chad E., Goyal, Neera K., Folger, Alonzo T., Putnam, Frank W., Van Ginkel, Judith B. "Predictors of Maternal Depressive Symptom Trajectories Over the First 18 Months in Home Visiting." *American Journal of Orthopsychiatry* 86, no. 4 (2016): 415–424. doi: 10.1037/ort0000159.

About the Author

Considered an innovative strategist and leader, Judith Van Ginkel's career has been distinguished by 40 years of strong and effective nonprofit leadership including encouraging public-private partnerships, supporting program initiatives with sound research, emphasizing the importance of working cooperatively, thinking entrepreneurially, urging funders both public and private to provide the resources for organizations to validate the effectiveness of their work and listening to those who will be served as well as those who deliver the service.